St. Louis Community College

Library

5801 Wilson Avenue
St. Louis, Missouri 63110

The Complete Garden

Arnold Leggett
Pat Falge

FINDER'S GUIDE NUMBER EIGHT

The Complete Garden

Arnold Leggett
Pat Falge

OLIVER PRESS
WILLITS, CALIFORNIA
CHARLES SCRIBNER'S SONS
NEW YORK

12-22-76

Library of Congress Card Number   75-7451
ISBN   0-914400-11-8

Drawings by Linda Falge
Cover by Chuck Hathaway

First Printing April 1975

OLIVER PRESS
1400 Ryan Creek Road
Willits, California 95490

CHARLES SCRIBNER'S SONS
New York

CONTENTS

INTRODUCTION

In the last few years, interest in gardening has increased dramatically. More and more people are raising their own food due to the spiraling prices in supermarkets as well as for the satisfaction that comes in working with the land. People in the cities and suburbs are beginning to make use of what space they have available for gardening. People in the country are intensifying their efforts to produce better gardens with greater yields.

One of the first steps in setting up a garden is to decide what to plant. It is the purpose of this book to provide sources for those seeds and tools which the homesteader or suburban gardener may wish to use in bringing food from the earth. Here are listed not only the basic corn and potatoes, but also many new and exotic varieties of roots, herbs, fruit trees and other seeds and plants. Both the experienced gardener and the novice can use this book. It eliminates the hassle of running from store to store, only to find that they are sold out of Zucchini seeds or Jerusalem Artichokes. It is much simpler to look in the Master Index for whatever variety you had planned for the space between the strawberries and turnips, find which companies sell it, and write for the catalogs. Then, while waiting for the seeds to arrive, you can spade the garden and look forward to a summer of gardening and a good harvest.

The Complete Garden consists of two main indexes: a **MASTER INDEX** and a **COMPANY INDEX**. The **MASTER INDEX** is a list of products alphabetically arranged. If you are looking for a particular product, first check for it in the **MASTER INDEX**. The **MASTER INDEX** will tell you which company or companies offer that product. Next, check the **COMPANY INDEX** to find out more about each company listed. The **COMPANY INDEX** offers information about each company, the range of its products and services, as well as giving details about its catalog. If the description of a company sounds interesting, by all means write to the company directly. Only the company itself can provide final, authoritative information about its products and prices. Don't hesitate to write to more than one company, if more than one company provides the product in which you are interested. In this way you can compare before you buy.

MASTER INDEX

DYSSODIA
   Clyde Robin Seed Co., Inc.
EARTHWORM books
   Shield's Publications
EARTHWORMS
   Bronwood Worm Farms
   Ferndale Gardens
   Lakeland Nurseries Sales
   Connie Mahan's Annelid Acres
ECCREMOCARPUS
   W. J. Unwin, Ltd.
ECHEVERIA
   DeGiorgi Company, Inc.
   Geo. W. Park Seed Co., Inc.

Now that you are ready to use *The Complete Garden,* a word about service, shortages and prices. Rapidly rising prices are a painful fact of modern life. Suppliers of garden supplies are suffering from this malady like everyone else. Since it takes time to prepare, print and distribute catalogs, prices are often outdated by the time they are received. Only the companies themselves can give you a firm price at any given time. Then there is the matter of critical shortages of various supplies. The manufacturers or distributors of garden supplies are affected by shortages as are other businesses, and this sometimes results in delayed deliveries. Finally, as most everyone must have noted by now, the United States Postal Service is, to put it mildly, not what it used to be. For these reasons, patience and understanding may be necessary in dealing with the suppliers of garden supplies during these trying

COMPANY INDEX

BRONWOOD WORM FARMS
P.O. Box 28
Bronwood, GA 31726

PRODUCTS:

earthworms

Bronwood Worm Farms sell large hybrid redworm breeders, standard size redworm breeders, medium size hybrid redworms, bed-run redworms, African nightcrawler fishworms and gray nightcrawlers in lots of up to 100,000 worms. They enclose complete instructions with each order and the instructions were completely revised in 1971. The revised instructions show that it is easier and cheaper to raise earthworms than was once thought, and that the beds are prepared differently than they once were.

Instructions free.

WORMS

COMPANY INDEX

ALEXANDER'S BLUEBERRY NURSERIES
1224 Wareham Street   Dept. A
Middleboro, MA 02346

PRODUCTS:

blueberry plants	peonies
daylilies	raspberry plants
lilacs	

This company offers many
plants. They have blueberries,
lilacs, raspberries, other edible
plants and rare and unusual
perennials. They also have daylilies and peonies. They have
an unusual feature for those of
you lucky enough to live in
and around Middleboro. It is a
"pick-your-own blueberry

BLUE-
BERRIES

field" during the season! They use no chemical sprays or fertilizers on any of their soil or fruit. People are invited to visit
their farms in season to see the plants in bloom or taste the
various varieties of blueberries and raspberries before they
make their selections. Complete cultural directions are sent
with each order for blueberries, lilacs, etc. Everything is
guaranteed.

Catalog: 2 stamps or self-addressed envelope with 2 stamps.

ALUMINUM GREENHOUSES, INC.
14615 Lorain Ave.
Cleveland, OH 44111

PRODUCTS:

greenhouse heaters
greenhouse heating cable
greenhouses
greenhouse vents
greenhouse watering systems

Aluminum Greenhouses, Inc., manufactures prefabricated, standardized, aluminum greenhouses and related accessories.

GREENHOUSE

Everlite aluminum greenhouses claim to be the first standard prefabricated aluminum greenhouses manufactured in the United States. For years, Aluminum Greenouses, Inc., has maintained the reputation as a supplier of Everlite home greenhouses of the finest quality. Among these are hundreds of installations that have been specified by architects throughout the country. Modifications of their standard models are available. Please consult with them. A few of the educational and institutional installations include University of Arizona Poultry Farm, Tucson, Arizona; Institute of Nuclear Energy, Belgrade, Yugoslavia; Lake Erie Junior Nature & Science Museum, Bay Village, Ohio; The University of North Carolina, Charlotte, N.C., and Orem High School, Orem, Utah. They have precision fabrication, straight sides, curved eaves, and the dimensions shown are the inside nominal dimensions, not outside foundation dimensions—therefore more growing space for your money.

Catalog free upon request.

2

THE AMERICAN GINSENG GARDENS
Box 168-D
Flag Pond, TN 37657

PRODUCTS:

ginseng roots
ginseng seed
golden seal roots
golden seal seed

The American Ginseng Gardens
thinks that they may be the only
dealers in the country that can offer
ginseng roots for sale from one year
old to 20 years old. They offer a
very interesting book that tells all
about setting up your ginseng gard-
en and how to go about all the
things that are necessary to maintain it. The American Ginseng
Gardens offer special collections
for beginners. They also have a list
of buyers for marketing ginseng.

Book $3.95

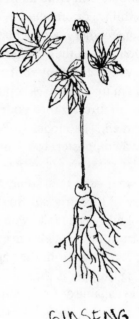

GINSENG

AMERIND-MacKISSIC, INC.
P.O. Box 111
Parker Ford, PA 19457

PRODUCTS:

compost shredder
garden tillers
log chippers
power sprayers

Amerind-MacKissic, Inc., manufactures high quality gardening and lawn care products, including compost shredders,
grinders, chippers, log chippers, power sprayers and garden

AMERIND-MacKISSIC, INC. (Cont'd)

tillers. Many are available as attachments for lawn and garden tractors. Their products are sold under the trade name of "Mighty Mac". The Mighty Mac Model 12-P shredder-chipper will grind all of the prunings or branches a homeowner may encounter. Don't burn these materials, says the company, but grind them up and use as top mulch or till directly into your garden. The model 12-P is used

COMPOST SHREDDER - GRINDER

as a composter, too. The popular PS-300 series of Mighty Mac sprayers are designed to fill the needs of every home-owner—and then some. Some of the PS-300 specifications are: 3 h.p. Briggs & Stratton 4-cycle engines; durable 200 mil polyethylene tank—won't corrode or scale out; hypro twin piston pump—delivers up to 3 gpm and 300 psi; positive direct drive from the engine. The Mighty Mac Model 21PT Log Chipper is the answer to the needs of people who want the capability to chip up to 5" logs without paying the price for a heavy-duty, commercial machine. Any wood, wet or dry, up to 5" diameter can be chipped at a rate of at least 3 feet per minute.

Brochures free.

ANNAPOLIS VALLEY PEAT MOSS CO., LTD.
Berwick, Nova Scotia, Canada

PRODUCTS:

sphagnum peat moss

They have sphagnum peat moss in various sizes pack-aged in plastic bales. They have three brands of peat

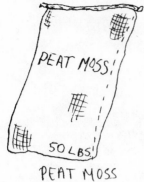

PEAT MOSS

moss: Bluenose, Canada and Beaver. The different brands have no different physical or chemical characteristics. Sphagnum peat moss is all organic and of light texture, with water holding capacity of up to 20 times its own weight. It is an excellent soil conditioner and additive for plants. Brochures free.

ARMSTRONG ASSOCIATES
P.O. Box 94
Kennebunk, ME 04043

PRODUCTS:

carnivorous plants   terrarium supplies

Armstrong Associates are suppliers of the Venus Fly Trap growing kit, which consists of the Fly Trap bulb, sphagnum moss in polybag, colorful label, growing directions and a 5" tall clear dome over a 3½ inch plastic pot growing container. They also have the "Keep America Beautiful Tree Growing Kit" with White Pine or Norway Spruce tree seeds, growing directions and growing cubes and tray. There are Carnivorous Plant Terrarium Kit-dome terrariums with three different carnivorous plants as well as others offered in the catalog. They are the world's largest specialists in carnivorous plants that lure and catch and eat insects.

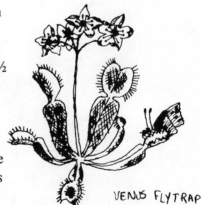

VENUS FLYTRAP

Catalog 25¢.

ARMSTRONG NURSERIES, INC.
P.O. Box 473
Ontario, CA 91761

PRODUCTS:

apple trees	peach trees
apricot trees	pear trees
cherry trees	persimmon trees
dwarf citrus trees	plum trees
fig trees	pomegranate trees
grape vines	prune trees
jujube trees	roses
nectarine trees	strawberry plants

APPLE

In their 86th year Armstrong has many items other than the roses they are famous for. There are seven pages of fine fruit trees, berries and some hard-to-find vegetables. You can always depend on Armstrong for sturdy, vigorous, number 1 field-grown roses, individually selected and handled, carefully packed and shipped.

Catalog free.

ATLAS TOOL & MFG. CO.
5151 Natural Bridge Road
St. Louis, MO 63115

PRODUCTS:

rotary mowers
rotary tillers
shredder-baggers

The Atlas Tool & Mfg. Co. makes lawn and garden power equipment. Their model 10-2130 rotary mower has a 3½ h.p. Briggs & Stratton engine. Pull-up recoil starter with automatic choke. It has a 21" austempered steel blade, 8" steel wheels with semi-pneumatic tires and shielded ball bearings. Atlas Tool & Mfg. Co.'s model 16-5001 shredder-bagger has a 5 h.p. 4-cycle gas engine with a recoil starter. It has three 18" austempered steel blades ¼ inch thick, eight heavy-duty breaker bars, and will shred branches up to 1 inch in diameter. The Atlas tiller model 12-5021 has a 5 h.p. engine with recoil starter. It has two forward speeds and power reverse. It has a tilling width of 26 inches. There are accessories available to fit several of these pieces of equipment.

LAWN MOWER

Brochure free.

BARZEN OF MINNEAPOLIS, INC.
455 Harrison St. N.E.
P.O. Box 1123
Minneapolis, MN 55413

PRODUCTS:

agricultural field chemicals
agricultural field seeds
bird feeders
bird food
bird houses
fertilizers
lawn care items
lawn seed

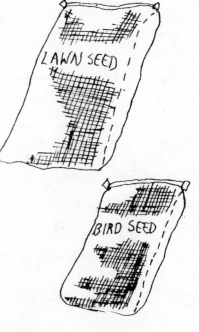

LAWN & BIRD SEED

Barzen of Minneapolis, Inc., has, in their catalog, items covering a rose care program, azalea, camelia and gardenia program, tree care program, flower and bulb program, instant fertilizers, lawn care program, special problem solvers, insect control program, weed control program, disease control program, vegetable care program and gardening aids. Their products are sold under the name of Ferti-lome. They feature just about everything you need to bring your yard up to snuff.

Catalog free.

BETTER LIFE ENTERPRISES, INC.
1462 John Street
Whiting, IN 46394

PRODUCT:

Mulch Away Adapters

Better Life Enterprises, Inc., sells by mail a low cost, practical Mulch Away Adapter for rotary lawn mowers. Their Mulch Away Adapters eliminate the need for hand feeding mulchers. If one desires to bag leaves for garbage disposal, the savings in plastic bags can be great. With a rotary lawn mower equipped with their unit, they were able to compress 12 bags of dry leaves into one bag. The Mulch Away Adapter can be used with any rotary mower having at least one and one-eighth inch clearance between lawn mower deck and mower blade. It eliminates raking leaves and actually fertilizes your yard each time you mulch leaves.

Brochures free.

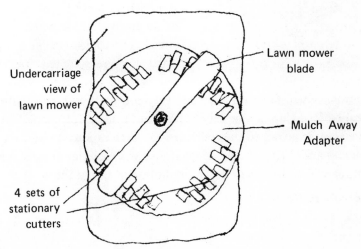

Undercarriage view of lawn mower

Lawn mower blade

Mulch Away Adapter

4 sets of stationary cutters

MULCH AWAY LAWN MOWER ADAPTER

BIG TOMATO GARDENS
B. Quisenberry, Mgr.
Syracuse, OH 45779

PRODUCTS:

tomatoes, table
tomatoes, yellow

TOMATO

The Big Tomato Gardens raise nothing but tomatoes. They feature eight specialties. Three of their specialties are rather unusual. The tomato called Gold Medal is a large, early yellow, streaked red; firm and smooth tomato. It has very little acid. The yellow with streaks and blotches of red makes them very attractive and a gourmet's joy when sliced. The tomato called Tasty Evergreen, when ripe, is still green color inside; outside turns brown. Medium large and very productive. The tomato called Red Cup is uniquely hollow and is ideal for stuffed tomatoes. It grows to the right size—as large as 3 to 4 inches across and 2 to 3 inches deep. If all eight varieties grow as the three we've described do, it would be fun to try them.

Brochure free.

BIO-CONTROL CO.
10180 Ladybird Drive
Auburn, CA 95603

PRODUCTS:

ladybugs
praying mantis

This company ships live ladybugs and Chinese praying mantis egg cases. The species of ladybugs that they sell is Hippodamis Convergens or the common ladybug. The egg cases are of Tenodera Aridifolia Sinensis. The amounts of ladybugs are from ½ pint to 1¼ gallons. The ladybugs average 75,000 to one gallon. In the late spring they ship only the hardy young ladybugs and they may be stored if desired and then released as needed throughout the summer season. The ideal temperature is 32 to 36 degrees. You may store them in the home re-frigerator or walk-in cold storage. The older ladybugs,

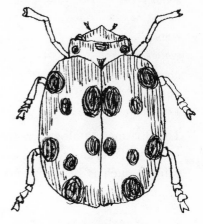

LADYBUG

which are shipped from Jan. 1st to early May, should be re-leased on the evening of the same day received. Their arrival should be timed so that there is some immediate natural feeding. The Chinese Praying Mantis egg cases come in 3, 5 or 8 and up to 50 and 100 cases. There are about 200 eggs per case. They do not guarantee hatching, however, but some tests indicate a 75 to 90 percent hatchout. One attaches or hangs the egg case to a bush, hedge, limb or anything 2 or more feet above the ground. A needle with white thread may be run through the outer surface of the egg case, but not so deep as to damage the eggs, then hung easily where desired. This hanging or swinging helps keep birds and other predators

BIO-CONTROL CO. (Cont'd)

away from the cases. Oiling the upper part of the swing will help keep ants away. High air pollution may have adverse effects on hatching and survival. They also have a wholesale price list. Brochures free.

BOATMAN NURSERY & SEED CO.
South Maple Street
Bainbridge, OH 45612

PRODUCTS:

annuals	ground covers
berries	hedges
bulbs	nut trees
evergreens	roses
flowering shrubs	trees, flowering
fruit trees	trees, shade
grape vines	vegetables

The Boatman catalog is crammed with many varieties of nursery plants and seeds. They have many varieties of stock offered, such as 17 kinds of dwarf apple trees, 26 kinds of peach trees, 6 different pecan trees, 28 kinds of tomatoes, and 15 kinds of strawberries. Boatman's says they have roots in the good earth of Southern Ohio. They expect to be doing business for many years in the same way at the same place. Mr. Boatman says in a brief note in his 1975 catalog that all indications are that this spring will see severe shortages in some seed, plants and trees—particularly those that grow good things to eat. Already they are getting the price increases for the fall of 1975 and spring of 1976. Fertilizer, fuel and everything

CATNIP

12

BOATMAN NURSERY & SEED CO. (Cont'd)

needed for growing is going up. They have increased their cooler space, and installed equipment to handle orders faster. Also they now "baby" their trees and plants by wrapping the roots for shipping. They use a special moisture-holding material like a paper diaper!

Catalog free.

BRITTINGHAM PLANT FARMS
Box 2538
Salisbury, MD 21801

PRODUCTS:

asparagus
blueberry plants
grape vines
raspberry plants
strawberry plants

Brittingham Plant Farms is celebrating their 30th year in business. They grow their own strawberry plants on 100 acres. They grow other plants (as listed), but primarily specialize in strawberry plants. While Brittingham Plant Farms do not claim to be the largest plant nursery or the oldest,

STRAWBERRIES

they do claim to grow the finest strawberry plants and they guarantee them to grow. Their catalog has two pages devoted to instruction for growing strawberry plants alone.

Catalog free.

BRONWOOD WORM FARMS
P.O. Box 28
Bronwood, GA 31726

PRODUCTS:

earthworms

Bronwood Worm Farms sell large hybrid
redworm breeders, standard size redworm
breeders, medium size hybrid redworms,
bed-run redworms, African nightcrawler
fishworms and gray nightcrawlers in lots of
up to 100,000 worms. They enclose complete instructions with each order and the
instructions were completely revised in
1971. The revised instructions show that it
is easier and cheaper to raise earthworms
than was once thought, and that the beds
are prepared differently than they once
were.

Instructions free.

WORMS

BURGESS SEED & PLANT CO.
P.O. Box 218
Galesburg, MI 49053

PRODUCTS:

almond trees
anise
apple trees
apricot trees
artichoke
asparagus
azaleas
balm
basil, sweet
beans, dry
beans, green
begonias
blackberries
blueberry plants
boysenberry plants
broccoli
brussels sprouts
butternut trees
cabbage
cactus
cantaloupes
caraway
carrots
cauliflower
celery
cherry trees
chestnut trees
chives
coriander
corn
crapemyrtle
crownvetch
cucumbers
dahlias
daphne
dewberries
dill
eggplant
endive
fig trees

filbert trees
fuchsias
garden huckleberry
garlic
geranium
gladiolus
grape vines
ground cherry
ground covers
hazelnut trees
herbs
himalayan cherry
holly
horseradish
house plants
hydrangea, tree
kale
kohlrabi
lavender
leek
lemon tree
lettuce
lime tree
maple trees
marjoram, sweet
mexican heather
michigan banana
mini vegetables
mint
mulberry trees
muskmelons
mustard
nectarine trees
new guinea vine
okra
onions
orange tree
parsley
parsnip
paw paw

peach trees
peanuts
pear trees
peas
pecan trees
peppermint
peppers
perennials
persimmon trees
plum trees
popcorn
pumpkins
pussy willow

radishes
raspberry plants
rhubarb
rosemary
roses
rutabaga

sage
salsify
savory, summer
spearmint
spinach
squash
strawberry plants
sweet potatoes
swiss chard
tampala
thyme
tomatoes, paste
tomatoes, table
tomatoes, yellow
tropical plum
turnips
vegetable spaghetti
vine peach
walnut trees
watermelons

Burgess has over 60 years of service and achievement. Breeding and research is conducted by skilled horticulturists who are constantly creating new and better varieties. The quality of their older varieties is scientifically maintained at a high level or is actually improved. Their goal is to supply you with the finest seeds, plants, nursery stock and bulbs that science can produce. Their constant aims are superior flavor, productiveness, attractive appearance, hardiness and resistance to disease and to drought. Year after year Burgess grows their seeds, bulbs, shrubs, plants and trees in the Blizzard Belt where they have to hustle in order to reach maturity. Burgess says this

CARROTS

BURGESS SEED & PLANT CO. (Cont'd)

just naturally means they bear fruit quicker and become more hardy. Once these ancestral urges become the natural characteristic, they have an early bearing, hardier variety.

Catalog free.

W. ATLEE BURPEE CO.
Warminster, PA 18974

PRODUCTS:

achillea
acroclinium
african violets
ageratum
alyssum
amaranthus
amaryllis
anchusa
anemone
anise
anthemis
antirrhinum
aquilegia
arabis
arctotis
asparagus
asparagus fern
asters
astilbe
aubrieta
azaleas
baby blue eyes
baby's breath
bachelor's button
balsam
barberry
basil, ornamental
basil, sweet
beans, dry
beans, green
beets
begonia
bellis perennis

bells of ireland
bignonia
bird houses
bird feeders
blackberry plants
blacy-eye cowpeas
black-eyed susan vine
bleeding heart
bletilla
blueberry plants
blue cup flower
blue lace flower
blue salvia
borage
boysenberry plants
brachycome
briza maxima
broccoli
browalla
brussels sprouts
burning bush
butterfly flower
cabbage
cactus
caladium
calceolaria
calendula
california poppy
calla lilies
calliopsis
campanual
canary creeper
candytuft

canna
cantaloupe
canterbury bells
cape daisy
caraway
cardinal climber
carnation
carrot
catmint
catnip
cauliflower
celeriac
celery
celery cabbage
celosia
celtuce
centaurea
cerastium
cheiranthus
chicory
chinese cabbage
chinese forget-me-not
chinese lantern
chives
christmas cherry
christmas pepper
chrysanthemum
cineraria
clarkia
clematis
cleome
climbing flowers
clover, white
cobaea
cockscomb
coleus
collards
columbine
cornflower
corn, ornamental
corn, pop
corn, sweet

cosmos
cowpea
cress
crownvetch
cucumber
curlycress
cyclamen
cynoglossum
cypress vine
dahlia
daisy, english
daisy, gloriosa
daisy, painted
daisy, shasta
daisy, tahoka
dandelion
day-lily
delphinium
dianthus
didiscus
digitalis
dill
dimorphotheca
dusty miller
eggplant
elderberries
elephant's ear
endive
english daisy
eschscholtzia
euphorbia
evergreens
everlasting flowers
fava bean
fennel
ferns
fertilizers
feverfew
finocchio
flax
flower plants
fordhook spinach

forget-me-not
forget-me-not, chinese
forget-me-not, summer
four o'clock
foxglove
french endive
fruit trees
gaillardia
garden aids
garlic sets
gazania
seranium
gerbera
geum
gladiolus
globe amaranth
gloriosa daisy
gloriosa lily
gloxinia
godetia
gomphrena
gourds, ornamental
grape vines
grass, lawn
grass, ornamental
ground covers
gysophila
hedges
helianthemum
helianthus
helichrysum
heliotrope
helipterum
hemerocallis
herbs
heuchera
hibiscus
hollyhock
honesty
horehound
horseradish roots
house plants

iberis
iceland poppy
impatiens
iris, bearded
ismene
ivy
job's tears
kale
kitchen aids
kniphofia
kochia
kohlrabi
larkspur
lathyrus
lavender
lawn grass
leek
lettuce
lilac
lilies
lily-of-the-valley
lima beans
limonium
linaria
linum
lobelia
love-in-a-mist
lunaria
lupine
lychnis
magic lily
malabar spinach
maltese cross
mangels
marigolds
marvel-of-peru
mathiola
matricaria
melons
mexican sunflower
mignonette
mimosa
montbretia

moonflower
money plant
morning glory
mushroom spawn
muskmelon
mustard greens
myosotis

nasturtium
nemesia
nemophila
nepeta
nicotiana
nierembergia
nigella
night-scented stock
nut trees
okra
onions
oriental poppy
oxalis
oyster plant
pansy
parsley
parsnip
peach bells
peanuts
peas
pelargonium
penstemon
peonies
peppers
pepper, ornamental
perennial sweet pea
periwinkle
petunias
phlox
pincushion flower
pinks
plant supports
polyanthus
popcorn
poppy

poppy, shirley
portulaca
pots, hanging baskets
primrose
primula
pumpkin
pyrethrum
quaking grass
radish
ranunculus
raspberry plants
red hot poker
rhododendron
rhubarb
rock cress
romaine
rosemary
roses
rudbeckia
rutabaga
sage
saintpaulia
salad garden
salpiglossis
salsify
salvia
satin flower
scabiosa
scarlet sage
schizanthus
sea lavender
seed tapes
sensitive plant
shamrock
shasta daisy
shrubs, flowering
siberian wallflower
snapdragon
snow-in-summer
snow-on-the-mountain
soybean, edible
sprayers and dusters

spider plant
spinach
squash
statice
stock
strawberry plants
strawberry seed
strawflowers
sultan's balsam
summer poinsettia
summer savory
sunflower
swan river daisy
sweet alyssum
sweet corn
sweet marjoram
sweet pea
sweet sultan
sweet william
sweet wivelsfield
swiss chard
tagetes
tahoka daisy
tampala
terrariums
thunbergia
thyme
tigerflower
tigridia
tithonia
tomato, paste

tomato, table
tomato, yellow
torenia
transvaal daisy
trees, dwarf fruit
trees, standard fruit
trees, flowering
trees, nut
trees, shade
tritoma
trumpet vine
tuberose
turnip
vegetables, winter
velvet flower
verbena
vinca
vines
viola
violet plants
wallflower
watercress
watermelon
wishbone flower
wisteria
woodland plants
xeranthemum
yucca
zinnias
zucchini

W. ATLEE BURPEE CO. (Cont'd)

The motto for the W. Atlee Burpee Co. is "Burpee Seeds Grow". For gardeners all over the world, Burpee has led the way with seeds of vegetables and flowers in many varieties.

PETUNIA

Burpee probably features more hybrids and has probably perfected more hybrids than any other seed company. This year Burpee introduces Burpee's Ambrosia Hybrid Cantaloupe along with several others. There are far too many varieties with which everyone is familiar to name them all, but some of them are: Burpee's Big Boy Tomato, Burpee Hybrid Zucchini Squash, Burpeana and M & M Hybrid Cucumbers, Burpee Hybrid Crenshaw Melon, F-1 Hybrid Zenith Zinnias, and Burpee's Ruffled Jumbo Zinnias. They also produce the familiar Fordhook seeds that are known all over. Burpee also has a guarantee which states that they guarantee seeds, bulbs, roots, nursery stock and garden supplies to the full amount of the purchase price and you can have your money back, or a replacement, anytime within a year if you are not satisfied with the results. Burpee will celebrate 100 years in the business of breeding and growing for the home gardener in 1976.

Catalog is free.

D. V. BURRELL SEED GROWERS CO.
P.O. Box 150
Rocky Ford, CO 81067

PRODUCTS:

ageratum
alyssum
asparagus
asters
balsam
beans, green
beets
bells of Ireland
broccoli
brussels sprouts
cabbage
calendula
candytuft
canterbury bells
carnation
carrots
cauliflower
celery
celosia
chinese cabbage
chinese forget-me-not
chrysanthemum
clarkia
coleus
coreopsis
cosmos
corn, sweet
cucumbers
dahlia
delphinium
dianthus
digitalis
dill
eggplant
endive
eschscholtzia
gaillardia
geranium

gloriosa daisy
gypsophilia
hollyhock
larkspur
lettuce
lobelia
marigold
marvel of Peru
melons
muskmelon
mustard
nasturtium
okra
onions
pansy
parsley
parsnip
peas
petunia
peppers
periwinkle
phlox
popcorn
poppy
portulaca
pumpkin
radishes
rutabaga
salsify
shasta daisy
snapdragon
spinach
squash
stocks
sunflower
sweet peas
sweet william
tithonia

D. V. BURRELL SEED GROWERS CO. (Cont'd)

tomatoes, sauce
tomatoes, table
tomatoes, yellow

verbena
zinnia

The D. V. Burrell Seed Growers Co. has the 4th generation members of the Burrell family now active in operating the firm. They specialize in high quality garden seeds for commercial market growers and the more serious home gardener. The company states that mail orders receive prompt handling, with over 95% of their orders shipped the day they are received. They also

LIMA BEANS

feature many gardening aids, including garden weeders not usually seen in other catalogs. These weeders are used by commercial vegetable growers. D. V. Burrell Seed Growers Co. is celebrating their 75th year in the business.

Catalog free.

CALIFORNIA GREEN LACEWINGS
P.O. Box 2495
Merced, CA 95340

PRODUCTS:

fly parasites
lacewings
trichogramma (egg parasite)
Zoecon Pherocon kits

Raising and selling beneficial insects is rather unusual. The California Green Lacewings raise and supply beneficial in-

CALIFORNIA GREEN LACEWINGS (Cont'd)

GREEN LACEWING

sects for biological and integrated insect control programs. Biological control may be defined as a method of pest control that relies on natural enemies (predators, parasites and pathogens) to suppress pest populations. The Zoecon Pherocon kits are synthesized sex lure kits available for codling moths, oriental fruit moth, red-banded leaf roller, and the apple maggot fruit fly. These kits provide a means by which growers can monitor insect population as a guide to the timing of spray applications for certain insects.

Information free.

CARINO NURSERIES
P.O. Box 538
Indiana, PA 15701

PRODUCTS:

arborvitae	ground cover
Canadian hemlock	hedges
Christmas trees	larch
firs	nut trees
flowering plants	Penn-Sylvan planting stock
flowering shrubs	pines
flowering trees	shade trees
forest trees	spruces

Carino Nurseries offer a great number of evergreen types of trees. They have a smaller number of flowering shrubs, vines,

CARINO NURSERIES (Cont'd)

etc., for sale as well. These plants are all offered at wholesale prices, which is great if you plan to put in a great number of trees or start a Christmas tree farm. Carino Nurseries participates in the Penn-Sylvan tree improvement program. This program is designed to select genetically superior strains of pines, spruces and firs for use as Christmas trees. Only stock grown from seeds which have been found to be superior is accepted into the program. In addition to the detailed study on performance predictions, the data on physical traits will include a recommended grading standard for the nurseryman.

WHITE SPRUCE

Catalog free.

CLEAR CREEK FARMS, INC.
5300 Clark Road
Paradise, CA 95969

PRODUCTS:

castings/worm manure
Power Plant
Red Hybrid Earthworm

The Clear Creek Farms operate an earthworm hatchery and market earthworms to a worldwide market. Their grower organization spreads from the Mexican border to Vancouver

CLEAR CREEK FARMS, INC. (Cont'd)

EARTH WORMS

and as far east as Arkansas. The castings or worm manure are formulated into a potting soil called Power Plant. The company states that "it is easy to raise earthworms—they require no expensive equipment, and take little space. Earthworms flourish on all kinds of waste organic material such as animal manures, or plant sources. There is no noise, no odor, no disease, and you can raise them anywhere. While the company has no catalog, they state that they will be happy to hear from anyone and will answer any questions you might have concerning the raising of earthworms.

CONCERN, INC.
2233 Wisconsin Ave. N.W., Room 210
Washington, DC 20007

PRODUCTS:

environmental calendars

The sponsors of these calendars (of which there are two) are the Audubon Naturalist Society of the Central Atlantic States, Inc., and Concern, Inc. The Living Garden 1975 calendar is written "with the conviction that the purpose in gardening is to create, not to destroy." To this end, it encourages natural controls. Prepared and reviewed by experts, the calendar is geared to the home gardener's cycle of the seasons with monthly hints

THE CONCERN CALENDAR

for a more natural approach to gardening. The Concern Calendar for 1975 is a guide which suggests positive ways for

27

CONCERN, INC. (Cont'd)

you to affect your environment. . . such as January: "how to be a thoughtful user of household energy"; April: "wild eating, tame planting", and November: "food for thought. A guide to nutrition." Any net benefits from the sales of these calendars and additional contributions will be used to further research and educational programs in the environmental field.

Calendars $3.00 each plus postage.

COUNTRYSIDE GENERAL STORE
130 E. Madison Street
Waterloo, WI 53594

PRODUCTS:

cyclone seeder
ladybugs
organic plant protectant
seeder

GARDEN SEEDER

The Countryside General Store has hard-to-find items and tools for homesteading, gardening, farming, etc. Their catalog has grown to be the production it is because people along the way have asked them about many things they couldn't find locally. The catalog is interesting, if for nothing else, for the rare and unusual items offered which you just don't see anywhere else.

Catalog $1.00

DADANT & SONS, INC.
Hamilton, IL 62341

PRODUCTS:

beekeeping supplies

Dadant & Sons offers a full
line of beekeepers' supplies.
They manufacture and sup-
ply basic wooden goods, protective beeware, and honey
house equipment for the beginning beekeeper and the
commercial beekeeper. They
offer complete hobby packs
for the beginning beekeeper,
including everything they
need to start with bees. In
addition they supply bulk

QUEEN BEE

packed items for large commercial beekeepers. Beekeeping,
besides being a fascinating hobby, can be rewarding mone-
tarily. One can easily find an outlet for the honey, and there
is an increasing use of honey in cooking, as a substitute for
sugar. Bees are also an indispensible pollinator in orchards
and certain vegetable crops.

Catalog free

DANHAVEN FARMS
P.O. Box 2038
Vancouver, WA 98661

PRODUCT:

Elimination of Moles, Gophers and Ground Squirrels (publication)

The Danhaven Farms for the past nine years have marketed a written report on the containment or elimination of moles, gophers and ground squirrels. They seldom, if ever, receive a request for a refund. They do guarantee satisfaction in all their ads. They sell the manual for $3.00. The Danhaven Farms say their methods do work, and there is more than one method contained in their report.

MOLE

There are some for organic farming, some for chemical elimination, and also some for mechanical means. The Danhaven Farms are a highly reputable firm and stand behind their information four-square. To their knowledge, no one else is selling anything similar at this time.

Report $3.00.

DeGIORGI COMPANY, INC.
Council Bluffs, IA 51501

PRODUCTS:

abronia
abutilon
acacia
acanthus
achillea
aconitum
acroclinium
adonis
agrostema
agrostis
allium
aloes
alonsea
alyssum
amaranthus
anagalis
anchusa
anemone
annobium
anpelopsis
anthemis
antigonon
antirhinum
aquillegia
arabis
arcotis
arenaria
aristolochia
armeria
artichoke
asciepia
asparagus
asperula
aster
aubretia
austrian pine
babtisia
baby's breath
bachelor's button
balm

balsam
balsam pear
bartonia
basil
beans, dry/green
beets
begonia
bellis
bells of Ireland
bent grass
bird of paradise
bittersweet
black-eyed susan
bleeding hearts
blue bonnet
blue bottle
blue grass
blue lace flower
balloon vine
borage
boston ivy
brachycome
briza
broccoli
broccoli raab
browalla
brussels sprouts
cabbage
cactus
calceollaria
calendula
california poppy
callopsis
campanula
canary bird vine
candytuft
canna
canteloupe
caragana
caraway

cardinal climber
cardoon
carnation
carrots
castor oil bean
cassia
catananche
catnip
cauliflower
celastrus scandens
celeriac
celery
celosia
centaurea
cerastium
chamomile
cheiranthus allioni
chelone
cherry, christmas
cherry, jerusalem
chervil
chicory
chinese lantern
chives
chop suey
christmas pepper
christmas rose
chrysanthemum
cineraria
cinnamon vine
cirsuim japonecuni
clarkia
clematis
cleome
cobea
cockscomb
coleus
collard
colorado blue spruce
columbine
colx
coreopsis
coriander

cornflower
corn knives
corn salad
corn, sweet
cornus
coral bells
cosmos
cotula
cotyledon
cowslip
cow peas
cress
crucianella
cucumber
cup and saucer
cuphea
cyclamen
cynoglosum
cyperus
cypress vine
dahlia
daisy, african
daisy, english
daisy, painted
daisy, pyrethrum
daisy, shasta
datura
delphinium
devil in the bush
dianthus
diascia
dicentra
dictamnus
didiscus
digitalis
dill
dimorphteca
dog tooth violet
doronicum
dracanea
dusty miller
echeveria
echinops

DeGIORGI COMPANY, INC. (Cont'd)

echium
edelweiss
eggplant
endive
eremurus
erigeron
erinus
eryngium
erysimum
erythrina
erythronium
escarole
eschscholtzia
eucalyptus
euphorbia
everlasting

felicia
fennel
ferns
feverfew
flame flower
forget me not
four o'clock
foxglove
funka-lily
gaillardia
garlic
gentiana
geranium
gerbera
gesneria
geum
gilia
gladiolus
globe amaranth
gloriosa daisy
gloxinia
godetia
gomphrena
gourds
grasses
grasses, ornamental

grass hook
grevillea
gumbo
gypsophila
hardy phlox
helenium
helianthemum
helianthus
helichrysum
heliopsis
herbs
hesperis
hibiscus
hieracium
hollyhock
horseradish
houchera
hunnemania
hyacinth bean
hypericum
iberis
ice plant
immortelle
impatiens
indian corn
indian pink
inula
ipomea
iris
irish lace
jacaranda
jack in the pulpit
jacobea
jerusalem cherry
job's tears
joseph's coat
kalanchoe
kale
kentucky blue grass
kochia
kohlrabi
kudzu
lace flower

lady slipper
lagurus
lantana
larkspur
lathyrus
lavatera
lavender
lawn grass
layia
leek
leptosiphon
lettuce
lillium
linaria
linum
lobelia
lunaria
lupinus
lychnis
lythrum

mad wort
marguerite
marigold
martynia proboscidea
marvel of peru
mathiola bicornis
matricaria
maurandia
meadow rue
mesembryanthemum
michaelmum daisy
mignonette
mimosa
mimulus
mina
mini, baby rose
monarda
monkey flower
monkshood
morning glory
moon flower
mourning bride

mullein pink
mung bean
mushrooms
muskmelons
mustard
myosotis
naegelia
nasturtium
nemesia
nemophlia
nepeta
nicotiana
nierembergia
nigella
oenothera
okra
onion
oregano
oyster plant
oxypetalum
painted tongue
panicum
pansy
papaver
parsley
parsnip
passion flower
peanuts
peas
peat pots
pennisetum
pentstemon
pepper
perilla
petunia
phacella
phlox
phygelius
physalis
physotegia
pinks
platycodon
plumbago

poinclana
polemonium
polyanthus
polygonum
popcorn
poppy
portulaca
pot marigold
primula
pumpkin
pyrethrum
queen anne's lace
radiehetta
radish
ranunculus
red hot poker
reseda
rhodante
rhubarb
ricinus
rock cress
rosemary
rose moss
rudbeckia
rutabaga
rye grass
sage
salad, rocket
salpigiosis
salsify
salvia
santolina
sanvitalla
savory
saxifraga
scarlet runner
schizanthus
scythes
scorzonera
sea holly
sea lavender
sea pink
sedum

sempervivum
sesame
senecio
sensitive plant
shamrock
shasta delay
sickles
silene
similax
snapdragon
snapdragon, climbing
snapdragon, hardy
snow in summer
solanum
sorrel
soy bean
sparachetti
special mixtures
spergula
spinach
spruce
squash
stachys
star of bethlehem
statice
stipa
stocks
stokesia
strawberry
straw flower
sunflower
sun plant
sweet alyssum
sweet basil
sweet corn
sweet fennel
sweet peas
sweet peas, hardy
sweet rockets
sweet sultan
sweet violet
sweet william
sweet wivelsfield

swiss chard	uniola
tagetes	valeriana
tahoka daisy	verbascum
tendergreen	verbena
thalicrum	veronica
thermopsis	viburnum carlesi
thunbergia	vinca
thyme	viola
thymus	violet
tithonia	virginian stock
tomato, paste	viscaria
tomato, sauce	viscaris
tomato, table	waldmeister
tomato, yellow	wallflower
torch lily	watermelon
torenia	watercress
trollius	wistaria
trumpet vine	wood rose
tunica	wormwood
turnip	xeranthemum
turnip broccoli	yucca
umbrella plant	zinnia

The DeGiorgi Company was started in 1905. This company prepays shipment of all seeds to any point in the United States, Hawaii, Alaska and Canada; except airmail and F.O.B.

ABUTILON (FLOWERING MAPLE)

The DeGiorgi Company has many outstanding and unusual types of novelty and specialty vegetables and flowers, some of which are evergreen tree seeds, Parisian carrots which are nearly spherical, and a new vegetable gourd which is also edible. They also feature some hard to find tools such as European scythes and the straight snaths to be used with the scythes. They have Austrian corn knives also. Their prices are lower than any

DeGIORGI COMPANY, INC. (Cont'd)

we have seen. The articles on the many varieties of flowers and vegetables are very interesting and can be of extreme help for the novice gardener.

Catalog is 35¢.

DESERT PLANT CO.
P.O. Box 880
Marfa, TX 79843

PRODUCTS:

cactus

This company offers many types of cactus. Some of them are very unusual looking and many are quite beautiful. The cactus plants are grown in the great desert regions of Texas and Mexico and are several years old, although the Desert Plant Co. has no way of determining a definite age of the cactus plant. The plants have been grown where the annual rainfall is less than twelve inches per year. Cactus will adapt themselves to most regions and most environments with the following provisions: do not over-water them, cactus plants should be given good drainage, and all cactus plants must have plenty of sunlight. Most of the cactus offered in their catalog bloom, and the flowers are quite attractive. Desert Plant Co. also sells in quantity lots.

PRICKLY PEAR CACTUS

Catalog $1.00.

DIAMOND INTERNATIONAL CORP.
P.O. Box 1070—Apiary Dept.
West 16th Street
Chico, CA 95926

PRODUCTS:

acid, carbolic crystals
aluminum paint
bee brushes
bee escape boards
bee escapes
bee hive paint
bee hives
bees and queens
bee smokers
bee veils
benzaldehyde
blow torch
bottoms, hive
brand capping melter
branding irons
brood chamber, slide out
brushes
cage, queen
calcium cyanide
cans, honey
cappings drier
cappings melter
capping scratcher
cap remover
carbolic acid crystals
carbolic covers
cell protector
chlordane dust
clamps, hose
cleats
comb honey equipment
coveralls and bee suits
covers, hive
crayon
crayon holder
cyanogas
division boards
dry brow

electric uncapping knives
embedder, wire
entrance guard
escapes, bee
excluders
extractors, honey
extractors, wax
eyelets, metal
eyelet tool

feeders, bee
follower boards
foundation bee-comb
foundation fasteners
frames, brood and honey
frame grips
frames, nailed
frame parts
frame rests, flat tins
frame spacers
frame wire
fumigants
gates, honey
generator, steam
gloves, bee
glove sleeves
grafting tool, automatic
guard, entrance
helmet
hive bodies (supers)
hive bomb
hive bottoms
hive covers
hive paint
hives, bee
hive scrapers
hive tools
honey bear
honey extractors

honey gate
honey jars
honey labels
honey pumps
honey strainers and material
hose, steam
inner covers
introducing cage, sureway
knives, uncapping
labels, honey
label paste
marking crayon
metal eyelets
nails
needles, transferring
nulomoline
observation hive
package bees and queens
paint
paradichlorobenzene (PDB)
phenol
plastic case foundation
plastic coating
pollen substitutes
pollen trap
power uncapping machine
pump control tank
pump, honey
queen and drone traps
queen bees
queen cage
queen excluders
queen marking cage
queen rearing tools
rope
rubber stamp

sample jars and cartons
section holders
section honey boxes
section press
section scraping knife
section spreader
separators
smokers, bee
spacers, frame
spiral cage
springs, super
staples
steam generator
steam uncapping knives
sting kill
stoller frame spacer
strainer cloth
sulfathiozole
supers
super springs
sureway introducing cage
terramycin
tins, flat
tools, hive
transferring needle
uncapping equipment
veils, bee
wasp killer
wax and wood cell cups
wax melters
wax tube fastener
wire, frame
wiring embedder
wraps, comb honey
yeast

Diamond International Corp., Apiary Dept., has a complete line of beekeeper's supplies. They also buy crude beeswax and honey. They also manufacture their own beecomb foun-

DIAMOND INTERNATIONAL CORP. (Cont'd)

BEE

dation and wooden ware. When you want to buy or sell established colonies of bees, write them giving the number of colonies or equipment that is of interest to you. They maintain a free bulletin board. If you have 100 pounds or more of beeswax and want 100 pounds or more of any of the foundation, an exchange price will apply. Diamond International Corp. will be happy to explain this upon request. At the same time they will furnish shipping tags for your convenience in shipping your beeswax to them. Be sure to tell them the kind and quantity of foundation desired. Space in their catalog does not permit listing all the items that they handle. If you do not find your needs listed, write them. If they do not have it, they can usually get it.

Catalog free.

DRESDENN, INC. (DIVISION OF LAIDLAW)
200 N.E. Adams
Peoria, IL 61602

PRODUCT:

seed sprouter

This seed sprouter is a new seed sprouting system from Switzerland. The basic unit consists of three seed sprouting trays, a base moisture-collecting tray, a lid, and three water

DRESDENN, INC. (DIVISION OF LAIDLAW) (Cont'd)

SPROUTER

syphons. A specific amount of specially selected seeds is spread evenly over the grooved trays. Slowly pour about a pint of water into the top tray. Excess water will travel the grooves in the upper tray, exit through the syphon and descend to the next tray. At each level the seeds in each tray will absorb just the right amount of moisture for germination. The excess water is collected in the bottom tray. Most sprouts are ready to be harvested and used within 2 to 5 days. With the sprouter they will send you three single-serving packages of seed to get you started. In addition, you receive a detailed, illustrated instruction booklet complete with exciting, tasteful, original recipes for your enjoyment.

Brochures free.

ENVIRONMENTAL DYNAMICS
P.O. Box 996
Sunnymead, CA 92388

PRODUCTS:

greenhouses
hydroponic units

GREENHOUSE

Hydroponic gardening is soilless vegetable growing. Environmental Dynamics manufactures hobby greenhouses and hobby hydroponic units. They supply various hydroponic kits plus a 12 lesson course in hydroponics. They also supply accessories pertaining to greenhouse requirements, such as ventilation systems, cooling systems and benches, etc. They have two catalogs that will soon be in print, the New

41

ENVIRONMENTAL DYNAMICS (Cont'd)

Greenhouse Accessory Catalog and the Hydroponic Catalog. They supply automatic control systems which are pre-wired and ready to plug in. Environmental Dynamics has Gro-Lux lighting systems as well.

Greenhouse literature free.
Accessory catalog is 50¢.

EVANS PLANT COMPANY
Box 38
Ty Ty, GA 31795

PRODUCTS:

beet plants	eggplant plants
broccoli plants	lettuce plants
brussels sprouts plants	
cabbage plants	onion plants
cauliflower plants	pepper plants
collard plants	tomato plants

The Evans Plant Company grows and ships field grown standard and hybrid varieties of vegetable plants to all areas of the United States. Their plants are grown in an open field and exposed to all types of weather conditions, which, the company states, makes them excellent for transplanting in fields or home gardens. This company has 47 years experience in the plant growing business.

Brochure free.

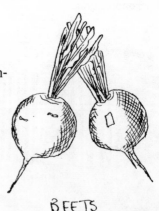

BEETS

FARMER SEED & NURSERY COMPANY
Faribault, MN 55021

PRODUCTS:

allium
apple trees
apricot trees
asparagus
azaleas
beans, dry
beans, green
beets
begonia
bleedingheart
blueberry plants
blue grass
broccoli
brussels sprouts
buckwheat
bulbs
cabbage
cabbage plants
cannas
carrot
cauliflower
celery
cherry trees
chrysanthemums
clematis
clover
crocus
cucumber
currants
daffodils
dahilas
dill
dwarf apple trees
eggplant
evergreens
fall bulbs
fertilizers
flowering crabapple
garlic
geraniums

gladiolus
gooseberries
gourds
grape vines
grass seed
ground cherry
ground covers
hedge plants
herbs
horse radish
hotkaps
huckleberry
hyacinths
iris
ivy
kale
kohlrabi
lawn grass
lettuce
lilacs
mangels
marjoram
midget vegetables
muskmelons
mustard
narcissus
onion seed
onion sets
parsley
parsnip
peanuts
pear trees
peas
peat pots
peonies
peppers
perennials
petunia plants
phlox plants
plum trees

FARMER SEED & NURSERY COMPANY (Cont'd)

pop corn
potatoes
pumpkin
radish
raspberry plants
rhododendron
rhubarb
roses
rutabaga
sage
salsify
shade trees
shrubs
sphagnum moss
spinach

squash
strawberry plants
sugar beets
sweet corn
sweet potato plants
swiss chard
tomato plants
tomatoes, sauce
tomatoes, table
tree lilac
tulips
turnips
vines
watermelons

CANTELOPE

Since 1888, Farmer Seed & Nursery Co. has been serving home gardeners. They originated and continue to emphasize Midget Vegetables for the northern home gardener. They have an extensive list of midget vegetables that are both early in maturity and do not consume very much space. They offer a complete horticultural and agricultural service through mail order and through their retail garden center outlets. Their seeds and nursery stock are selected and bred for the northern tier of states and southern provinces of Canada. They are extremely hardy and adapted to this area, although they will do well in more southern locations. The color pictures and the general outlay of their catalog are extremely well done and present a very attractive catalog.

Catalog free.

FERNDALE GARDENS
Nursery Lane
Faribault, MN 55021

PRODUCTS:

almond tree
andromeda
anemones
anthurium
artichokes
asparagus
azaleas
baby's breath
bamboo
begonias
bird of paradise
bittersweet
blackberry plants
blueberries
blue stokesia
bush apricot
bush cherry
cactus
camellias
carnations
chain tree
chestnut tree
christmas roses
coffee tree
coronilla
cyclamen
dawn redwood
dianthus
dogwood
dwarf iris
dwarf maple
earthworms
elderberry
empress tree
evergreen holly

ferns
fig tree
flowering crabapple
freesias
gardenia
geranium
ginseng roots
gladiolus
heath
juniper
lady bugs
lavender
lemon tree
lily of the valley
lime tree
lythrum
madeira vine
nectarine tree
norfolk island pine
orange tree
peach tree
peanuts
pear tree
plum tree
praying mantis
pyrethrum
raspberry plants
rhubarb
roses
shallots
strawberry plants
strawberry paradise tree
sweet peas
violets
wildflowers

FERNDALE GARDENS (Cont'd)

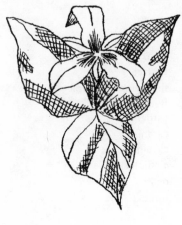

Without an index it is hard to make sure everything is listed for this company, but they do offer many fascinating items for sale. Among the items offered are giant ranunculus, orchids, a flower called "The White Pearl of the Incas", a tri-colored dogwood, and a flowering crabapple tree with five colors on just one tree. These are just to name a few of the unusual and rare items offered by Ferndale Gardens.

Catalog free.

TRILLIUM
(WILDFLOWER)

FERTILE HILLS ORGANIC FARMS
Route 1, Box 134-C
Hurdle Mills, NC 27541

PRODUCTS:

organic hybro-tite (potassium)
organic rock phosphate

Fertile Hills Organic Farms sells organic rock phosphate and organic hybro-tite (potassium) by the ton or by 50 pound bags. The company is regional to the states of Virginia, North Carolina and South Carolina. They also sell organic produce from May through September.

Fertilizer & produce information free. Booklets $1.50.

ORGANIC
ROCK
PHOSPHATE

50 LBS.

HENRY FIELD SEED & NURSERY CO.
Shenandoah, IA 51602

PRODUCTS:

ageratum
ajuga
althea
alyssum
amaranthus
amaryllis
annual flowers
apple trees
apricot trees
arborvitae
artemisia
ash trees
asparagus
asters
astilbe
azaleas
baby's breath
bachelor buttons
balloon flowers
balsam
barberry
beans, dry
beans, green
beets
begonias
bells of Ireland
birch trees
bittersweet
blackberry plants
bleeding hearts
blueberry plants
blue flax
boysenberry plants
Bradford pear trees
broccoli
brussels sprouts
burning bush
bush cherries
buttercups
butterfly bush

cabbage
cactus
caladium
calla lilies
candytuft
cannas
canterbury bells
carnations
carrots
castor oil beans
cauliflower
celery
cherry trees
chinese elm trees
chinese lantern
chives
chrysanthemums
citron
clematis
cockscomb
coleus
collards
columbine
coral bells
coreopsis
corn, sweet
cosmos
cottonwood trees
crab apple trees
crepe myrtle
crownvetch
cucumbers
currants
dahlias
daisies
dawn redwood
delphinium
deutzia gracillis
dewberries
dianthus

dill
dogwood
dogwood, red twig
dwarf lace plant
eggplant
elderberries
elm trees
euonymus shrubs
evergreens
ferns
fig trees
flowering trees
forget-me-not
forsythia
four o'clock
fruit trees
fruit trees, dwarf
gaillardias
garlic
geraniums
gerbera
ginkgo trees
gladiolus
golden elder
golden rain tree
gooseberries
gourds
grape vines
ground cherry
ground cover
hackberry
hedges
hemerocallis
hen & chicken plants
herbs
hibiscus
·high bush cranberry
hollyhocks
honeysuckle
horseradish
hostas
huckleberries
hybrid elm

hydrangeas
impatiens
iris
ivy
japanese pagoda tree
kale
kohlrabi
korean boxwood
larkspur
lavender
lawn seed
leek
lettuce
lilacs
lilies
lily of the valley
linden
locust
loosestrife
lupines
lythrum
magnolia
maple trees
marigolds
midget vegetables
mimosa
mint
mock orange
monarda
money plant
morning glory
mung beans
mushroom spawn
muskmelons
mustard
nasturtiums
nectarine trees
nitragin
nut trees
okra
onions
pachysandra
pampas grass

HENRY FIELD SEED & NURSERY CO. (Cont'd)

pansy
parsley
parsnips
paw paw
peach trees
peanuts
pear trees
peas
penstemon
peonies
peppers
perennials
persimmon trees
petunias
phlox
pineapple lily
pink almond
pinks
pin oak tree
plumbago
plum trees
polygonum cuspidatum
popcorn
poplar trees
poppy
portulaca
potatoes
potentilla
primrose, Missouri
privet
pumpkins
purple leaf bush
purple leaf plum
pussywillow
pyracantha, Kazan
pyrethrum
quince, flowering
radishes
ranunuculus
raspberry plants
red bud
red oak tree
rhododendrons

rhubarb
ribbon grass
rosa multiflora
rose moss
roses
rose tree of China
Russian olive
rutabaga
ruta blue mound
sage
salsify
salvia
sedum
sensitive plant
service berry
shamrock
shellflower
shrubs
silver lace vine
smoke bush
snapdragons
snow ball
spinach
spirea
squash
strawberry plants
strawflowers
sunflowers
sunshine shrub
sweet peas
sweet potatoes
sweet william
swiss chard
sycamore
tamarix
thermopsis
thyme
tithonia
tobacco
tomatoes, table
tomatoes, yellow
tree hydrangea
tritoma

trumpet vine
tuberose
turnips
verbena
viburnum, fragrant
vinca minor
vines
violets
voo doo lily

watermelons
weigela
willow, fantail
willow trees
wisteria
yarrow
yucca
zinnias
zoysia

The Henry Field Seed & Nursery Co. carries a complete line of garden seeds, plants, and gardening aids. They have a rather large selection of trees offered. They have the 5-in-1 apple trees as well as a good number of fruit trees. Henry Field also offers windbreak and shade trees and decorative trees with colorful foliage or blossoms.

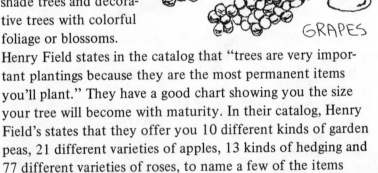

GRAPES

Henry Field states in the catalog that "trees are very important plantings because they are the most permanent items you'll plant." They have a good chart showing you the size your tree will become with maturity. In their catalog, Henry Field's states that they offer you 10 different kinds of garden peas, 21 different varieties of apples, 13 kinds of hedging and 77 different varieties of roses, to name a few of the items offered.

Catalog free on request.

FISCHER GREENHOUSES
Oak Avenue
Linwood, NJ 08221

PRODUCTS:

african violets
gesneriads
greenhouse supplies

A FRICAN VIOLETS

Fischer Greenhouses have and offer the best collection of domestic and foreign introductions of African violets. They offer 100 selections which are carefully screened before being offered. They also feature several terrariums which are guaranteed to grow, an 8-piece indoor gardener kit, many varieties of pots and pot hangers, plus foggers and humidifiers among their many items.

African violet catalog 15¢.
Indoor garden aids catalog 25¢.

THE FMALI CO.
P.O. Box 1072
Santa Cruz, CA 95061

PRODUCTS:

ginseng roots
ginseng seeds
goldenseal roots

The Fmali Company offers a complete line of ginseng preparations and roots. They represent four of the major ginseng companies. The Fmali Company offers a special selection of wild American botanicals and a small selection of other Chinese botanicals. Besides the herbs and roots they also have a nice selection

GINSENG

THE FMALI CO. (Cont'd)

of Chinese sundries such as analgesic balms, books and hair products. They will give bulk prices on quantities of 25 pounds to a ton of the wild goldenseal root or powdered root. Catalog is free.

FMC CORPORATION, OUTDOOR POWER EQUIPMENT DIVISION
215 South Park Street
Port Washington, WI 53074

PRODUCTS:

riding and walking mowers
rotary tillers
snow throwers
utility and garden tractors

FMC manufactures the Bolens line of outdoor power equipment. The Bolens mulching mower cuts grass and then recuts

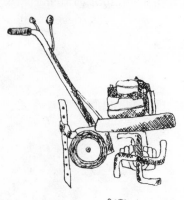

ROTO-TILLER

clippings into a fine mulch that decomposes quickly with no thatch buildup. The no discharge chute design virtually eliminates hazardous flying debris. With no clippings to clean up, the consumer doesn't have to bag or rake mowing debris. Recent studies by leading turf specialists report the nitrogen return factor from mulched grass can reduce the amount of fertilizer required to maintain healthy lawns. The Bolens rugged two-stage Snowthrowers come in 5, 7 and 8 h.p. models, with clearing widths of 24", 26" and 32". It has an adjustable differential for maximum traction, and a safety-grip clutch control. If you let go, the drive disengages automatically, preventing forward or backward motion. Their other products are fully covered in their attractive brochures.

Brochures free.

DEAN FOSTER NURSERIES
Route 2
Hartford, MI 49057

PRODUCTS:

climbing strawberry vine
strawberry plants

Dean Foster Nurseries carries a complete line of garden plants and offers a wholesale and retail mail order service. The Dean Foster Nurseries originated the world famous Robinson strawberry variety. They import from France the original Mount Everest Climbing Strawberry Vine.

Catalog free.

STRAWBERRIES

FRED'S PLANT FARM
Route 1
Dresden, TN 38225

PRODUCTS:

sunflower seed
sweet potato plants

sweet potatoes
tobacco
tobacco seed

SWEET POTATO

Fred's Plant Farm is owned and operated by Fred Stoker and has been in business for 27 years. Their brochure states that they bed 3,000 bushels of seed and produce 5 million plants from April 20-July 1 of sweet potatoes alone. They also state that they can furnish you with any kind of chewing or smoking tobacco. Their motto is, "Sell a good product, advertise it, and satisfy the customer".

Brochures free.

FRENCH TEXTILES CO., INC.
835 Bloomfield Ave.
Clifton NJ 07012

PRODUCT:

"Birds Off" mesh

"Birds Off" mesh is a knitted polypropylene mesh that is available in various sizes and is spread over fruit trees, grape vines, berry beds and vegetables to protect them from marauding birds. It is easy to use, light weight, can be used season after season, is rot and mildew proof, and has been tested for years and really does the job. It comes in sizes from

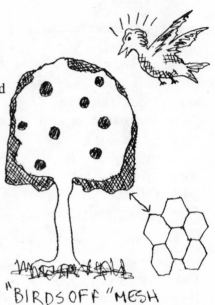

"BIRDS OFF" MESH

4½ feet x 36 feet up to 18 feet x 21 feet, Large commercial acerage sizes are also available on request. "Birds Off" allows rain, sun and air to penetrate, while it frustrates feathered freeloaders.

Brochures free.

GALLANTS HERB PRODUCTS, INC.
R.F.D. 2
Albion, PA 16401

PRODUCTS:

garlic
garlic ointment

GARLIC

This company offers a rather unusual look into the world of garlic. They have an old Italian variety sold as a seed for planting and table stock to restaurants, stores and individuals. Formulated garlic ointment is also sold to be used to remedy numerous physical ailments. They state that their garlic is organically grown, cross-bred 12 years to develop specific large bulbs and plump cloves that are easier to separate and peel, and is of stronger quality than ordinary garlic, with a higher percentage of sulfides that are more effective when used as a remedy for any of the numerous physical ailments that garlic can cure or prevent from developing. They are registered with the Pennsylvania Department of Registration and sold as Certified Gallants Garlic with instructions as to how, when and where to plant, harvest and storage, etc.

Catalog $1.50.

GALT RESEARCH INCORPORATED
R.R. 1, Box 245
Trafalgar, IN 46181

PRODUCT:

Dipel Biological Insecticide

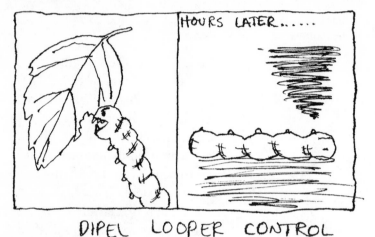

DIPEL LOOPER CONTROL

Galt Research Incorporated offers Dipel biological insecticides. It is not harmful to man, fish, birds, bees, beneficial insects or pets. It is very effective in the garden for cabbage looper and other leaf-eating insects. It is approved by the Environmental Protection Agency as completely safe. Since Dipel is exempt from residue tolerance, you may use it right up to the moment of harvest. Your harvest crews can work in the field immediately after application. Because Dipel is not a dangerous chemical, you do not need special clothing or have to follow special precautions when mixing and applying. Dipel, says Galt Research Incorporated, is storable for months on end. It also doesn't matter if it is freezing or at 110 degrees. It is a wettable powder and therefore doesn't lose its strength while being stored. Dipel can be applied by ground or aerial equipment, or as a locally-formulated dust, or as a spray.

Brochure free.

GARDEN WAY MFG. CO.
Dept. 54454
102nd Stree and 9th Avenue
Troy, NY 12180

PRODUCTS:

power composter
rotary tiller

Troy-Bilt Roto Tiller and Power Composter is so easy to handle, you guide it with just one hand. You will never again

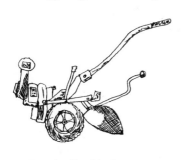

TROY-BILT ROTO-TILLER

be shaken and jolted by a common rotary tiller that has its revolving blades in front and no power to its wheels. The Troy-Bilt Roto Tiller and Power Composter has its revolving blades in the rear and powered wheels, which means you can guide it with just one hand. You do not walk behind it, you walk beside it, leaving no wheel marks or footprints. The unique tines dig deeply, more evenly. You can till for hours without fatigue. These are sold direct, saving the buyer at least $100 if sold through a dealer. Off-season discounts. Furrowing, snow removal and other attachments available.

Catalog free.

GARDEN WAY RESEARCH
Dept. 54434
P.O. Box 26
Charlotte, VT 05445

PRODUCT:

garden cart

Garden Way Garden Carts and general purpose garden carts are perfectly balanced on two huge bicycle-style wheels to roll easily over lawns and gardens. They are uniquely designed to carry up to 400 pounds with little effort. These are also available in do-it-yourself kit form. For basic gardening uses, these large capacity carts cannot be beat for carrying huge loads of compost, manure, grass clippings, hay and nearly anything for your garden. The top-of-the-line cart, the model 26, is the largest cart available today in the United States.

GARDEN WAY CART

Catalog 50¢.

GIRARD NURSERIES
Box 428
Geneva, OH 44041

PRODUCTS:

arborvitae

azaleas

baby evergreen and shrubs

bonsai trees

broadleaf evergreens

canadian hemlock

cypress

evergreen seeds

firs

flowering shrubs

french hybrid lilacs

junipers

ornamental trees

pines

rhododendrons

shade trees

spruces

yews

GIRARD NURSERIES (Cont'd)

AZALEA

Girard Nurseries grow over 100 acres of nursery stock, including many usual and unusual types of trees as well as the shrubs and plants they grow. They have originated many new plants to the trade, such as Girard's Leucothoe "Rainbow", Girard's Hemlock "Gracilis Nana", and Girard's Sarbaronia Brel. They are now releasing to the trade a new strain of evergreen azalea in pinks, reds and whites which they think is much superior to many azaleas on the market today.

Catalog free.

GRO-MORE GREENHOUSES
P.O. Box 154
Orinda, CA 94563

PRODUCTS:

greenhouse accessories
greenhouses

Alden Mills is the founder of Gro-More Greenhouses. He says his Gro-More greenhouses are without question the best dollar-for-dollar buy on the market today. There is no foundation needed for installing these greenhouses. The Gro-More greenhouses may be added onto. They have extension kits in four foot lengths. You can add on forever. They are easily assembled, easily moved, with construction taking only

GRO-MORE GREENHOUSE

half a day. If you want to move it, merely pull the anchor stakes and lift it to its new location. Gro-More greenhouses are sold factory direct, thus eliminating the middle-man to raise the price. Gro-More greenhouses are available in two models. Both use the same frame, but with different coverings.

Brochure free.

GURNEY SEED & NURSERY CO.
Yankton, SD 57078

PRODUCTS:

african violets
ageratum
almond, flowering
almond, garden
althea
alyssum
amaryllis
annual flowers
anthurium
apple trees
apricot trees
arborvitae
artemisia
artichokes
ash trees
asparagus
asters
azaleas
baby's breath
bachelor button
balloon flower
balsam
bamboo
barberry
beans, dry
beans, green
beauty bush
beets
begonias
bells of ireland
birch trees
bird of paradise

bittersweet
blackberry plants
bleeding heart
bluebells
blueberry plants
bonemeal
bonsai
boston ivy
boxwood
boysenberry plants
broccoli
brussels sprouts
buffalo berries
burning bush
bush cherries
buttercup
butterfly bush
butternut
cabbage
cactus
caladium
calla lilies
candytuft
cannas
canterbury bells
caraway
carnations
carrots
catnip
cauliflower
celeriac
celery

celosia
cherry trees
chestnut trees
chickens
chicory
chives
choke cherries
chrysanthemum
citron
citrus plants
clarkia
clematis
cockscomb
coleus
collards
columbine
comfrey
compost kit
coral bells
coreopsis
corn, field
cornflower
corn, sweet
cosmos
cotton
crab apple trees
cress
crowder peas
crownvetch
cucumber
currants
dahlias
daisies
day lilies
delphinium
dewberries
dill
dogwood
dried blood
dusty miller
dwarf fruit trees
eggplant
elderberries

elm trees
endive
escarole
evergreens
evergreen shrubs
everlasting flowers
fennel
ferns
fertilizers
field seeds
fig trees
flax
forget-me-not
forsythia
four-o-clocks
foxglove
fuchsias
gaillardia
gardenia
garlic
geraniums
gerbera
ginseng roots
gladiolus
gloxinias
godetia
gooseberries
gourds
grape vines
grass, ornamental
grass seeds
ground cover
gypsophila
hanging baskets
hanging plants
hazelnut trees
hedges
hemerocallis
herbs
hickory
holly
hollyhocks
honeysuckle

horehound
horseradish
hotkaps
house plants
huckleberries
hydrangeas
impatiens
iris
ivy
junipers
kale
kohlrabi
larkspur
lavender
lawn seed
leek
lettuce
lilac
lilies
lily of the nile
lily of the valley
lobelia
locust
loganberries
loosestrife
luffa sponge
lupines
magnolia
mangels
maple trees
marigold
mignonette
miniature roses
mints
mock orange
morning glory
mulberries
mushroom
muskmelons
nasturtium
nectarine
nicotiana
nitragin

nut trees
oak trees
okra
onions
orchids
oriental vegetables
pansies
parsley
parsnip
paw paw
peach trees
peanuts
pear trees
peas
peat bogs
pecans
penstemon
peonies
peppers
perennial seeds
persimmon
petunias
philodendron
phlox
pimento
pinks
plum trees
popcorn
poplar trees
poppies
portulaca
potatoes
primrose
privet
pumpkins
purple plum trees
pussy willows
pyrethrum
quince
radishes
raspberry plants
redwood trees
regal lilies

resurrection plant
rhododendrons
rhubarb
rock garden plants
rosemary
rose, multiflora
roses
rutabaga
sage
salpiglossis
salsify
salvia
sand cherries
sea lavender
sedums
shade trees
shallots
shamrock
shell flower
shrubs
shrubs, evergreen
silver king
silver lace vine
snapdragon
snowballs
soybeans
spinach
spirea
squash
statice
stocks
strawberry plants
strawflower
sultana

sumac
summer savory
sunflowers
sweet basil
sweet marjoram
sweet peas
sweet potatoes
sweet sultan
sweet william
swiss chard
tamarix
terrariums
thyme
tobacco plant
tomatoes, paste
tomatoes, table
tomatoes, yellow
trumpet vine
tuberoses
turnips
vegetables, giant
verbena
vinca
vines
violets
walnut trees
water lilies
watermelon
weigela
willows
wine grapes
yews
yucca
zinnias
zucchini

Gurney is 109 years old and their catalog is chock full of many common and unusual types of planting stock for the

LAVENDER

gardener. One of the most popular things that Gurney's offers is their special offer for kids called Gurney's Giant Jumble Packet, which is sold to children for one cent. The child simply encloses the penny with the parent's order and states that he or she wishes the special offer of the Jumble Packet. Gurney's also offers many specially-priced items throughout the catalog.

Among the many rather unusual items offered you will find blue potatoes, almost-blue zinnias, an early-maturing honeydew-type melon, and Gurney's famous mystery package. Gurney has many varieties of fruits, vegetables and flowers that are not offered by any other catalog. Much of the Gurney nursery stock is developed where the temperature ranges from 105 above to 35 below, thus, Gurney says, creating a better, tougher, hardier stock.

Catalog is free.

BEN HAINES COMPANY
Dept. 75 LP 4
1902 Lane
Topeka, KS 66604

PRODUCTS:

cactus	succulents
ferns	yucca
sage	

Ben Haines Co. is a rather unusual company as they offer many cacti and succulents that are cold climate and can take minus 20 to 40 degrees. Mr. Haines can custom order many items you may need or want. He also sells wholesale as well as retail. Mr. Haines has a pictorial book of cold

CACTUS

climate cacti and succulents for $3.25, as well as a South African frost tender list for $1.10.

Price list 40¢.

HAMMAN
Route 5, Box 176
Escondido, CA 92025

PRODUCT:

comfrey

Comfrey is the common name of a group of old-world perennial herbs from the genus Synphytum of the Borage family.

COMFREY

They have been thought to be of medicinal value. A few are used in borders for the interest of their large, hairy foliage. The foliage is much more beautiful than the small, purplish, blue or yellow flowers. Comfrey is easily grown in any good garden soil and is tolerant of shade. It is said that one should remove the flower stalks of those grown for their foliage and propogate by division, root-cuttings or by seed. Mr. Hamman had an accident and was out of the comfrey business for 120 days with a broken hip, but is now operating once again. His are crown cuttings and are guaranteed to grow.

Booklet $1.00

JOSEPH HARRIS CO., INC.
Moreton Farm
Rochester, NY 14624

PRODUCTS:

african daisy
ageratum
alyssum
amaranthus
antirrhinum
aquilegia
arabis
artificial soils
asparagus seed
aster
aubretia
baby's breath
bachelor button
balsam
basil
basil, ornamental
beans, dry
beans, fava
beans, field
beans, green
beets
begonia
begonia seed
bellis
bells of ireland
blanket flowers
blue flax
blue salvia
borage
borecole
broccoli
brussels sprouts
burning bush
cabbage
calendula
california poppy
candytuft
cantaloupe
canterbury bells
cape marigold

capsicum
captan
carnation
carrots
castor oil beans
cauliflower
celeriac
celery
celosia
centaurea
chicory
chinese cabbage
chinese forget-me-not
chrysanthemum
cleome
clock vine
clover, white
cockscomb
coleus
collard
columbine
coreopsis
cornflower
corn, salad
corn, sweet
cos lettuce
cosmos
creeping zinnia
cress
crown vetch
cucumbers
cynoglossum
dahlia seed
daisy, african
daisy, gloriosa
daisy, painted
daisy, shasta
delphinium, annual
delphinium, hardy
dianthus

diazinon
digitalis
dill
dimorphotheca
domestic rye grass
doronicum
dusty miller
eggplant
endive
english daisy
eschscholtzia
euphorbia
fava beans
fennel
fertilizers
field beans
finocchio
flowering cabbage
flowering tobacco
forget-me-not
four o'clock
foxglove
french endive
french marigold
gaillardia
garlic
gazania
geraniums
gladiolus
gloriosa daisy
gomphrena
gourds
grass, lawn
ground cherry
gumbo
gypsophila
helenium
helichrysum
heliotrope
herbs
hibiscus
hollyhocks

honesty
hotkaps
iberis
iceland poppy
impatiens
ipomea
jewels of opar
kale
kidney beans
kochia
kohlrabi
lady slippers
larkspur, annual
larkspur, hardy
lathyrus
lavatera
lavender
lawn grass
leek
leopard's band
lettuce
lima beans
linum, hardy
lobelia
lunaria
lupines, hardy
mallow
manzate
marigolds
marjoram
marvel of peru
melons
mignonette
molucella
moonflower
morning glory
moss rose
moss, sphagnum
mushrooms
muskmelons
mustard
myosotis

nasturtium
nicotiana
okra
onion
onion sets
onion plants
oriental poppy
ornamental basil
ornamental pepper
painted tongue
pansy
parsley
parsnip
peas
peppers
periwinkle
petunia
phlox, annual
pincushion flower
pinks
polyanthus
poor man's orchid
pop corn
poppy, california
poppy, iceland
poppy, oriental
poppy, shirley
portulaca
pot marigold
primrose
pumpkin
pyrethrum
radish
ricinus
rock cress
romaine
rudbeckia
rutabaga
rye grass, domestic
rye grass, perennial
sage
salpiglossis
salvia
sanvitalia

scabiosa
scarlet sage
schizanthus
sevin
shasta daisy
shell flower
silver dollars
snapdragon
snow on the mountain
soil test kits
solanum
sphagnum moss
spider plant
spinach
spinach beet
squash
statice
stocks
strawflowers
summer cypress
summer savory
sunflower
sweet marjoram
sweet peas
sweet sultan
sweet william
swiss chard
tagetes
thunbergia
thyme
tithonia
tomatoes, paste
tomatoes, table
tomatoes, yellow
tuberous begonia
turnip
verbena
vinca rosea
viola
watercress
watermelon
witloof chicory
zinnia
zucchini

JOSEPH HARRIS CO., INC. (Cont'd)

Located in Rochester, New York, the Joseph Harris Co., Inc., offers a complete selection of seeds for the home gardener. They have many varieties of flowers and vegetables. The Joseph Harris plant breeders have made many exclusive introductions in both vegetables and flowers.

VINCA (PERIWINKLE)

Catalog free.

HEISE'S WAUSAU FARMS
Route 3
Wausau, WI 54401
PRODUCTS:

ginseng capsules
ginseng powder
ginseng root

Heise's Wausau Farms state that ginseng has a history of more than 1,500 years. It is a perennial belonging to the eggplant species. Ginseng requires up to seven years' growth. They also tell that it requires absolute attention, complete care, is extremely particular to geographic and climate conditions and likes a clean atmosphere, cool weather and well drained acid soil formed by hardwood compost. All of the ginseng products they sell are grown on their farms in Wausau, Wisconsin, and these gardens are open for public visitation from June 25 to Sept. 25 each year.

Brochures free.

THE HOUSE PLANT CORNER, LTD.
Box 5000
Cambridge, MD 21613

PRODUCTS:

greenhouse supplies
house plants

The House Plant Corner, Ltd., stresses that plants need the proper light, as well as all other aspects of proper care. This seems to be the most outstanding failure of all new growers. Their catalog has all of the items needed to properly care for your house-plants, as well as all of the green-house supplies you need. They have many kinds of pots—from poly pots to clear plastic ones al-lowing you to watch the root development of your plants and

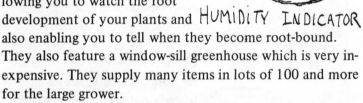

HUMIDITY INDICATOR

also enabling you to tell when they become root-bound. They also feature a window-sill greenhouse which is very in-expensive. They supply many items in lots of 100 and more for the large grower.

Catalog 25¢.

HYDROPONIC SOCIETY OF AMERICA
P.O. Box 516
Brentwood, CA 94513

PRODUCT:

hydroponic information

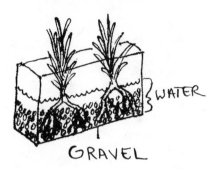

GRAVEL

HYDROPONIC GROWING

Their scientific, commercial and hobby techniques are of hydroponic growing. Hydroponics is the growth of plants without soil. Plants are grown in gravel, or some other inert medium, and are fed with a nutrient solution periodically during the day. Using this technique, plants do not require conventional soil and hence can be grown anywhere a gravel pot can be placed.

Yearly subscriptions are $24.00.

INTER-STATE NURSERIES
Hamburg, IA 51644

PRODUCTS:

achillea	birch trees
ajuga	bittersweet
almond, flowering	blackberry plants
althea	bleeding heart
amaryllis, hardy	blueberry plants
annuals	boxwood, korean
apple trees	boysenberry plants
apricot trees	bridal wreath
artemisia	buddleias
ash trees	burning bush
asparagus	caladium
asters	calla lilies
azaleas	candytift
barberry	cannas
beauty bush	canterbury bells
begonias	cardinal shrub

carnations, hardy
caryopteris, azure
cherry, kwanzan flowering
cherry trees
chestnut, chinese
chrysanthemum
clematis
columbine
crab, flowering
crape myrtle
crown vetch
currants
dahlia
daisy, shasta
day lilies
delphinium
dianthus
dogwood
elm, chinese
elm, hamburg
euonymus
euphorbia
evergreens
ferns
firethorn
forsythia
fruit trees
geranium alpinum
gerbera
gladiolus
gooseberries
grape vines
grass, fountain
ground covers
gypsophilas
hedges
helenium
heuchera
hibiscus
hollyhock
honeusuckle
horseradish
hosta

hydrangea
hypericum
iberis
iris
ivy
lilac
lilies
lily of the valley
linden
locust trees
lythrum
magnolia
maple trees
mock orange
nectarine trees
nitragin
oak trees
olive, russian
pachysandra
peach trees
pear trees
pecan trees
peonies
perennials
phlox
plantain lily
platycodon
plumbago
plum trees
polygonum
poplar trees
potentilla
primrose
privet
pyrethrum
quince trees
ranunculus
raspberry plants
redbud
rhubarb
rosa multiflora
roses
ruta blue mound

INTER-STATE NURSERIES (Cont'd)

salix
salvia
sedum
shade trees
shrubs
silver lace vine
smoke tree
snowball
spirea
stokesia
strawberry plants
sweet peas
sycamore

tamarix
tree roses
tritoma
tuberoses
veronica
viburnum
vinca minor
vines
violet
walnut trees
weigela
willows
wintergreen
yucca

This is Inter-State's 57th year in the nursery business. They started their nursery at Hamburg in 1919, growing and selling at wholesale to other nurseries. In 1931 they decided

WINTERGREEN

that they would sell their nursery stock direct-to-you, so they issued their first catalog. The Inter-State Nurseries are owned and operated by the Sjulins (a Swedish name, pronounced "Showlin"). They are aided by their sons and a very fine organization. They have over 2,000 acres of fine soil which is ideal for growing nursery stock. It sometimes gets down to 20 degrees below zero in the winter, assuring hardiness in their stock. The most important facts, according to Inter-State, are that behind this firm are several life-times of nursery experience, a huge selection of the best varieties, plus some of the best nursery soil. They are located in an ideal location, almost the center of the United States. They are a fine organization that is always looking ahead for better varieties and improved methods, and they have a sincere desire and effort to please and satisfy their customers.

Catalog free.

JACKSON & PERKINS CO.
Medford, OR 97501

PRODUCTS:

african daisy
ageratum
alyssum
asparagus
asters
baby's breath
bachelor buttons
balsam
beans, green
beets
begonias, fibrous
bells of ireland
berries
broccoli
brussels sprouts
bulbs
cabbage
cactus
calendula
candytuft
carnation
carrots
cauliflower
celery
celosia
cleome
coleus
collard
cornflower
corn, sweet
cosmos
dahlia
delphinium
dianthus
dimorphotheca
dusty miller
eggplant
endive
fruit trees
gazania
geranium

gloriosa daisy
gourds
grape vines
gypsophila
helianthus
herbs
hollyhock
impatiens
kale
kohlrabi
larkspur
lettuce
lobelia
marigolds
melons
mustard greens
nasturtiums
okra
onions
pampas grass
pansy
parsley
parsnip
peas
peppers
petunias
phlox
portulaca
primula
pumpkins
radishes
rhubarb
roses
rudbeckia
salvia
scabiosa
snapdragon
spinach
squash
stocks
strawflowers

sunflower	turnips
sweet peas	verbena
sweet william	vinca rosea
swiss chard	viola
tomatoes, table	zinnia

Jackson & Perkins is 103 years old. They are known just about everywhere for the roses they grow and introduce each year. They are not as well known for the other flower and vegetable seeds they also produce and offer in their attractive catalog. The headquarters for the company is in Medford, Oregon, while the roses are grown in Wasco, California. The catalog featuring flower and vegetable seeds is a separate catalog

PANSY

from the one that offers the roses and other items. The rose catalog is called "Roses '75," while the other catalog offered is called "Seedbook." Seedbook concentrates heavily on hybrid flower and vegetable seeds.

Both catalogs free on request.

JARDIN DU GOURMET
W. Danville, VT 05873

PRODUCTS:

flower seeds
garden aids
vegetable seeds

This firm has its main headquarters in Beaufort-en-Vallee, France. Their distribution center in the United States is Jar-

CARROTS

din du Gourmet. The main company (Vilmorin-Andrieus, S.A.) distributes flower seeds and vegetable seeds for gardeners and seed merchants and equipment for gardens. They have reliable seeds for growers. This company features new French specialties of Vilmorin varieties. They have the famous carrot "Nantes" and Tim-Tom. They have melons of the Charentais type Vedrantais, paper Esterel, Lavatera "Tanagra," Aubrietia "Rois Des Rouges" and Clarkia "Bali".

Catalog 50¢.

JOHNNY'S SELECTED SEEDS
N. Dixmont, ME 04932

PRODUCTS:

beans, dry	herbs
beans, green	kale
beets	leek
broccoli	lettuce
brussels sprouts	melons
burdock	onions
cabbage	parsley
carrots	parsnip
cauliflower	peppers
chinese cabbage	popcorn
corn, drying	radishes
corn, sweet	rice
cucumbers	rutabaga
dandelion	scorzonera
eggplant	spinach
endive	squash
ginseng seeds	sunflower seed
greens	tomato, table
	turnips

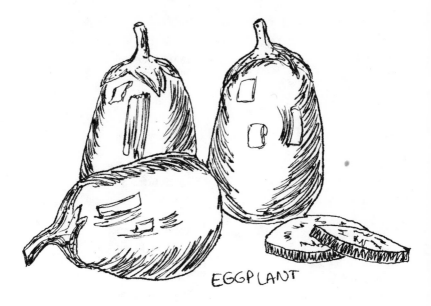

EGGPLANT

Johnny's Selected Seeds have changed their name from Johnny Apple Seeds as the result of a trademark dispute with Johnny Appleseed's, North Beverly, Massachusetts, a firm with which they are in no way connected except by the universal ties affecting all of humanity. If you've wondered where Johnny Apple Seeds went, here they are! This is only their second selling season. Johnny's Selected Seeds' work is based upon the idea that good food is the basis of our well being and quality seeds are the most fundamental step in creating good food. They also feel that quality can be consistently upgraded by selecting the most promising strains, and also by raising seed crops on small acreages with ecologically sound agricultural practices. Their seeds are organically grown. They do not list maturity dates, because they feel there is too great a variation due to differences in soil type, fertility, latitude, temperature, exposure, etc. They feature a "Johnny's Seed Swap", which is rather interesting to read about in their catalog.

Catalog free.

J. W. JUNG SEED CO.
Randolph, WI 53956

PRODUCTS:

ageratum
air fern
alpine currant
alyssum
amaryllis
anchusa
apple trees
apricot trees
aquilegia
artemesia
ash trees
asparagus
asters
autumn olive, cardinal
azalea mollis
baby's breath
bachelor button
balsam
barberry
basil
beans, dry
beans, green
beauty bush
beets
begonias
begonia seed
bells of ireland
birch
bittersweet vine
bleeding heart
blueberry plants
blue bird flower
blue lace flower
borecole
broccoli
brussels sprouts
burning bush
bush bittersweet
bush cherry
butterfly bush

butterfly plant
cabbage
cactus
caladiums
calendula
california poppy
calla lily
canary bird vine
candytuft
cannas
canterbury bells
cardinal climber
cardinal shrub
carnations
carrots
castor oil bean
cauliflower
celery
celery cabbage
celosia
centaurea
cherry tree
china rose tree
chinese chestnut
chinese lantern
chives
chrysanthemum
chrysanthemum seed
citron
clarkia
clematis
cleome
clover
clove pinks
cockscomb
coleus
corn
cosmos
cotoneaster
cottonwood
cranberry, dwarf

cranberry, high bush
cress
crocus
crownvetch
cucumber
currant
daffodils
dahlias
daisy
datura
daylilies
delphinium
dill
dogwood
eggplant
endive
evergreen bittersweet
evergreens
everlasting flower
ferns
festuca glauca
field beans
flowering crab apple
flowering kale
forsythia
four o'clock
funkia
gaillardia
garlic
gas plant
geranium seed
gladioli
gloriosa daisy
gloxinia
gooseberry
gourds
grape hyacinths
grapes
grass seed
ground cherry
ground covers
hedges

herbs
heuchera
hibiscus
high hedge
hollyhock
honeysuckle
horseradish
house plant seed
huckleberry
hyacinths
hydrangea
impatiens
iris
ivy
kochia
kohlrabi
larkspur
lavaters
lawn grass
leek
lettuce
liatris
lilacs
lilies
lily seed
lily of the valley
locust trees
love in a mist
lunaria
lupines
lychnis
lythrum
mangels
maple trees
marigolds
mexican lily
mignonette
missouri primrose
mock orange
morning glory
muskmelon
mustard
mystery lily

nasturtium
nicotiana
nigella
ninebark
okra
onions
oxallis
pansy
parsley
parsnip
peach trees
peanuts
pear trees
peas
peonies
pepper
petunias
phlox
pinks
platycondon
plum trees
popcorn
poplar trees
poppies
portulaca
potatoes
potentilla
primrose
privet
pumplin
pussy willow
pyrethrum
quince, flowering
radish
rainbow flowers
rainbow indian corn
ranunculus
raspberries
red leaf plum
rhubarb
roses
russian olive
rutabaga

sage
salsify
salvia
satin flower
scabiosa
scarlet runner bean
scilla
sedum
seed corn
shallots
shasta daisy
snapdragon
snowberry
snowdrops
snow on the mountain
spider plant
spinach
spirea
squash
stocks
strawberries
summer poinsettia
sunflower
sweet peas
sweet william
swiss chard
tamarix
tithonia
tomatoes, paste
tomatoes, table
tomatoes, yellow
tritoma
trumpet vine
tuberoses
tulips
tulip poppy
tulips
turnip celery
velvet flower
verbena
vinca minor
vinca rosae
walnut trees

watermelon
weigela
willow trees
wisteria

yews
yucca
zinnias

From 1907 to 1975 the J. W. Jung Seed Co. has progressed in serving home gardeners. There are few things you can purchase in which you place as much confidence in the company with whom you are dealing as you do when you purchase

TITHONIA (MEXICAN SUNFLOWER)

seeds. No one can tell just by looking at a seed whether or not it will grow and whether or not it will produce a satisfactory product. From the time that the J. W. Jung Seed Co. was started the policy was, and still is, to sell quality products at fair and reasonable prices. At the Jung Farms they grow a wide assortment of seeds, plants, bulbs, shrubs and trees, and also carry on extensive trials to insure that their customers receive new and improved products as they become available. Visit their garden center in Randolph, Wisconsin. They are open daily except Sundays 8 to 5 from March to June. From June through February they are open weekdays 8 to 12 and 1 to 5, and Saturday 8 to 12. No Sundays. In their store, in addition to all the catalog items, you will find additional varieties of plants, bulbs, larger sizes of trees and evergreens, bedding plants and vegetables. There is a staff of experts to answer your questions.

Catalog free.

THE WALTER T. KELLEY COMPANY
Clarkson, KY 42726

PRODUCTS:

aprons
bee escapes
bee pins
bees
bellows
boilers
bottom boards
branding iron
brush
cages
capping melter
capping scratcher
comb foundation
comb honey cutter
electric knives
extractors
frame cleaner
frame nailing device
frame spacers
gloves
helmet hat
hives
hive tool
honey gates

honey pump
nails
observation hives
package bees
plastic bottom boarnd and
    covers
pollen trap
queens
smokers
steam generator
super elevator
super fixtures
super springs
supers
uncapping knives
uncapping machine
veils
wax mould pan
wax press
wax seperator
wax tube fastener
wax working
wire
wiring device

All beekeeping equipment can be supplied here, complete with the hive, bees and the necessary bottling and labeling supplies needed. They do not have dealers, but keep their prices down by selling direct to the beekeeper at wholesale factory prices. On page 6 of their catalog they list a beginner's outfit, which includes the bee hive and necessary sting-proof equipment needed by the beekeeper. They also will buy wax. Write for price

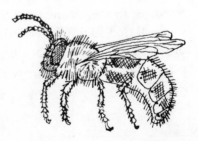

BEE

82

THE WALTER T. KELLEY COMPANY (Cont'd)

quotations. They also have the rather unusual Straw Skeps which are used for display at honey stands, fairs, etc.

Catalog free, book $1.00 postpaid.

BUD KINNEY WORM FARM
Route 1, Box 438-T
Chico, CA 95926

PRODUCT:

redworms

Bud Kinney sells redworms for gardens, fishing and worm farm starters. He says that there is a fantastic market and demand for the redworm business, and that it is the best way to improve soil. He has redworms in quantities of up to 100,000, and also bin size supplies of redworms are available. He has a live delivery guarantee.

Price sheet available free.

KITAZAWA SEED COMPANY
356 W. Taylor Street
San Jose, CA 95110

beans, green	japanese greens
burdock	melon, bitter
chinese cabbage	mustard
cucumber	radish, japanese
eggplant	sugar peas

Kitazawa Seed Co. has an interesting brochure. While they do not have a large selection of seeds, what they do have are unusual or rare

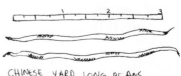

CHINESE YARD LONG BEANS

types of vegetables. If you have been looking for seeds of

KITAZAWA SEED COMPANY (Cont'd)

many oriental vegetables to grow for your own use, this
would be the place to look.

Brochure free.

HERMAN KOLB, BEE HOBBYIST
Box 183
737 West Main
Edmond, OK 73034

PRODUCT:

observation bee hives

This is the first really inexpensive and practical bee hive
designed especially for the close study of these social insects.
A great help in every class-
room for the study of na-
ture. Because bees have
been a benefit to man for
ages, there is an abun-
dance of literature available for scientific study.
It is possible for these
small hives to last indef-
initely under ideal con-

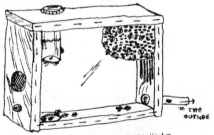

OBSERVATION BEE HIVE

ditions. No gloves, protective clothing or smoker needed.
Simple installation—requires only that a 5/8th inch hole
be provided to the outside. The hive is ready to go when you
receive it. Just extend the entrance tube outdoors. This hive
comes complete and includes: hive with fertile queen and
worker bees, entrance tube, foundation comb, feeder, cover
and complete instructions for starting and caring for the
colony.

Brochures free.

THOMAS B. KYLE, JR.
SPRING HILL NURSERIES CO.
110 Elm St.
Tipp City, OH 45371

PRODUCTS:

almond, flowering
almond trees
amaryllis
angel flower
anthemis
apple trees
apricot trees
artemisia
artichokes
ash trees
asparagus
aster
astilbe
azaleas
baby's breath
barberry
baskets of gold
begonia
bellflower
birch trees
bittersweet
blackberries
black-eyed susans
bleeding heart
bluebells
blueberry plants
blue moon flowers
bonsai
boxwood
boysenberries
burning bush
caladium
campanula
candytuft
cardinal flower
carnations
chartreuse shrub

cherry, bush
cherry, flowering
cherry trees
chinese lantern
christmas rose
chrysanthemums
citrus plants
clematis
columbine
coral bells
cotoneaster
crab, flowering
crepe myrtle
cyclamen
dahlias
daisies
daylilies
delphinium
dewberries
dogwood
dwarf fruit trees
elderberries
elm trees
euonymus
evergreen
ferns
feverfew
fig trees
firebush
forget-me-not
forsythia
foxglove
fuchsia
gaillardia
geranium
ginkgo
gladiolus

grape vines
hedge
hen & chickens plants
hibiscus
holly
hollyhocks
honeysuckle
horseradish
hosta
houseplants
hydrangea
hypericum
iris
ivy
juneberries
lady's slipper
lavender shrub
lemon fluff
lilacs
lilies
lily of the valley
linden
live forever
locust
lupines
lythrum
magic flower
magnolia
maltese cross
maple trees
mimosa
mock orange
mulberry
multiflora hedge
nectarine trees
nut trees
oak trees
olive trees
orange glory flower
orchid, hardy
pansy
peach trees
peanuts

pear trees
perennials
persimmon trees
phlox
pinks
plate o'gold
plum trees
poplar trees
poppy
potentilla
primrose
pyrancantha
rain tree
raspberry plant
redbud
red hot poker
rhododendron
rhubarb
rose of sharon
roses
sarvistree
sedum
smoke tree
snowball
snow-on-the-mountain
spirea
stokesia
strawberry plants
sumac
sweet gum
sweet peas
sweet shrub
sycamore
tree peonies
trinity flower
tuberose
verbena
veronica
vines
violets
weigelia
willow
witchhazel
yucca

THOMAS B. KYLE, JR. (Cont'd)

BLUE SPRUCE
(SEEDLING)

This company says you will find exactly what you want in Spring Hill's colorful, value-packed spring and fall catalogs, including dwarf fruit trees, nut and shade trees, hedges, ground covers, vines, shrubs, bulbs, evergreens and house plants. Buy direct from the grower and save. Hundreds of Red Circle Specials will save you money. Founded in 1849, Spring Hill is one of America's largest and most reliable mail order nurseries. Enjoy the convenience of credit card shopping, or if you're in a hurry, phone (800) 228-2042 and order toll-free.

Catalog free.

LAKELAND NURSERIES SALES
340 Poplar Street
Hanover, PA 17331

PRODUCTS:

almond trees
apple trees
artichokes
asparagus
azaleas
baby's breath
bamboo
begonias
blackberries
black walnut tree
bleeding heart
blueberry plants
blueberry tree
buckeye tree
bush apricot
bush cherry
butternut trees
cactus
caladium
camellias
cannas
carnation
carpathian walnut tree
chain tree
cherry tree
chincherinchee
chinese tree wisteria
christmas rose
cobra lily
coffee tree
coronilla
cyclamen
dawn redwood
dogwood
dutchman's pipe vine
dwarf maple
dwarf pear tree
earthworms
edelweiss
elephant ears
evergreen holly

LAKELAND NURSERIES SALES (Cont'd)

ferns
fig trees
flamingo flower
flowering crab apple
gardenia
gas plant
geranium
ginseng roots
gladiolus
gloxina
hazelnut tree
heath
herbs
hibiscus
horseradish
ladybugs
lemon tree
lilies
lily, climbing
lily of the valley
lime tree
longberries
miniature roses
nectarine trees
norfolk island pine
onion sets
orange tree
orchid lily
orchids
pampas grass
pansy
paw paw
peachtarine tree

peach tree
peanuts
pear trees
pecan trees
persimmon trees
phlox
pineapple plant
plum bush
plum/prune tree
plum trees
pony tail palm
prayer plant
praying mantis
primrose
privet
purple winter creeper
raspberry plants
redwood burl
reed, giant
rhubarb
roses
scarlet beauty tree
shallots
strawberries
strawberry paradise tree
sweet pea
transvaal daisies
tree roses
tree tomatoes
watermelon
weeping willow
wild flowers
"WIN" garden

THYME

Not having an index makes it difficult to list all of the things that Lakeland Nurseries sells. They have some very unusual and hard to find items. They have a tree called "Fruit Cup Tree". It is one single tree with four different fruits budded on it. The four fruits

88

LAKELAND NURSERIES SALES (Cont'd)

are peaches, apricots, plums and nectarines. They also offer a "WIN" garden, which is several assortments offered very reasonably to grow food for yourself and your family to help on your grocery bills. These two things are just a sample of the many things shown in this catalog that you won't find anywhere else.

Catalog free.

LAWSON'S NURSERY
Route 1, Box 61
Ball Ground, GA 30107

PRODUCTS:

apple trees
ornamental trees
pear trees

This company specializes in dwarf and semi-dwarf apple trees. They offer a few pear and ornamental trees also. They have quite a large list of apple trees and offer especially old fashioned types of apples hard to find anywhere else. The Lawsons claim that they have driven hundreds of miles getting some of the varieties they offer. Some of the varieties come from trees over

APPLE

100 years old, and those trees are still bearing without ever being sprayed. Some of the varieties they offer include: Black Twig, Grannie Smith, Old Fashioned Yellow Horse "Hoss", and "20-Ounce Pippin".

Brochure free.

LEAHY MANUFACTURING CO.
406 W. 22nd Street
P.O. Box 451
Higginsville, MO 64037

PRODUCTS:
bee supplies
poultry incubators

BEE HIVE

The Leahy Manufacturing Co. has four pages of bee supplies, such as hives, supers, covers, hive stands, frames, comb honey sections, super foundations and wired foundations. They also have a number of poultry items, such as egg cases, debeakers, brooders and incubators, etc.

Brochures free.

HENRY LEUTHARDT NURSERIES, INC.
Montauk Highway
East Moriches, Long Island, NY 11940

PRODUCTS:

apple trees
apricot trees
blueberry plants
cherry trees
crabapple trees
currants
espalier apple trees
espalier flowering crabapple trees
espalier peach trees
espalier pear trees

filbert nut trees
gooseberries
grape vines
nectarine trees
peach trees
pear trees
plum trees
quince trees
raspberries

ESPALIER FRUIT TREE

This is a rather unusual company, as not only do they sell the usual grapes and berries, but all their fruit trees are either dwarf or semi-dwarf. They also feature Espalier fruit trees. These are trees trained to grow FLAT against walls and fences. Their catalog shows several photographs of trees trained in this way, and they are really quite beautiful. Henry Leuthardt states in his catalog that the culture of Espaliers is an old art based on the application of a principle of plant growth known as "sap flow control". Hence, the choice of understock is important for the fruit trees' later training. A dwarfing rootstock of a type with a small root system is chosen. This limits the size of the tree that is grafted on it, slows its growth, and encourages early bearing. The forms into which Espaliers are fashioned are determined by the natural growth habit of the kind of fruit tree, even of the particular variety. Training, like the effect of rootstock, further slows sap flow and gives better distribution. His catalog goes much further into the story of these fruit trees and into many details of growing fruit trees.

Catalog 25¢.

CONNIE MAHAN'S ANNELID ACRES
Box 6132
University, AL 35486

PRODUCTS:

earthworms

This company ships earthworms by mail order. These are not the common burrowing garden variety, but rather top-feeding redworms which are ideal for composting. They consume only organic materials and can accomplish wonders in a compost pit or under an organic mulch in a garden. A fuller description is given in the leaflets. They also sell redworm eggs. They furnish complete instructions for composting with earthworms. By their method, kitchen wastes can be turned into compost, and the process can be carried on all year round as it is completely odorless. In climates with cold winters, composting can be done indoors in a basement, an unused room, or "you can even do it in the kitchen".

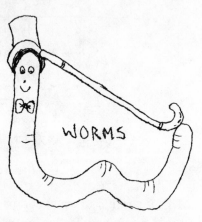

Leaflets free.

EARL MAY SEED & NURSERY CO.
Shenandoah, IA 51603

PRODUCTS:

artichokes
asparagus
asters
beans, dry
beans, green
beets
begonias
bleeding heart

bone meal
broccoli
brussels sprouts
cabbage
caladium
calla lilies
cannas
carnations

92

carrots
cauliflower
celery
cherries
chives
clematis
cockscomb
columbine
compost bin
corn cutter
corn, sweet
cosmos
cucumbers
currants
dahlias
delphinium
dill
dwarf fruit trees
elms (hybrid)
endive
evergreens
ferns
fertilizer
flowering shrubs
flowering trees
fungicides
garlic
geranium food
geraniums
gladiolus
grapes
hedges
herbs
hominy corn
horseradish
house plants
iris
kale
kohlrabi
larkspur
lawn seed
leeks
lettuce

lilies
magnolias
maple trees
marigolds
mole killer
morning glories
mulch
muskmelons
mustard
nasturtiums
netting
okra
onions
pansy
parsley
parsnips
peach trees
peanuts
pear trees
peas
peat moss
peat pots
peppers
petunias
popcorn
poppy
potatoes
pumpkin
radishes
ranunculus
rhubarb
rootone
roses
rutabaga
sage
salsify
salvia
seedling trees
shrubs
snapdragons
soil test kits
spinach
squash

EARL MAY SEED & NURSERY CO. (Cont'd)

strawberry plants
sunflower
sweet peas
sweet potatoes
swiss chard
tobacco
tomatoes, sauce
tomatoes, small

tomatoes, table
tomatoes, yellow
turnips
tuberoses
verbena
vines
watermelons
weed killers
zinnias

PEAS

This company has been sending seeds and nursery stock all over the United States since 1919. The Earl May Seed & Nursery Co. guarantees their products. If you are not satisfied with the results of the seed or nursery stock, they will replace it any time within the first growing season. This company offers a great many types of seeds and plants, as well as many gardening aids and miscellaneous items of interest to the gardner. This is also one of the only companies found where you can get a pea and bean sheller.

Catalog is free.

McGREGOR GREENHOUSES
1195 Thompson Ave. (Box 36)
Santa Cruz, CA 95063

PRODUCTS:

exhaust fan
greenhouse heater
greenhouses

greenhouse thermostat
humidifier

McGregor Greenhouses makes greenhouses in several sizes for the home gardener or nurseryman. They have two basic types, the free-standing and the attached models. Their greenhouses are completely precut and require a weekend to assemble. They have all-bolted framework, and they always have extensions available to expand growing room. McGregor Greenhouses also supplies intensive vegetable growing methods with all their greenhouses. The free-standing models come in 4, 8, 12 and 16 foot sizes,

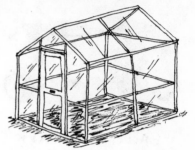

GREENHOUSE

while the attached models come in 4 and 8 foot sizes. As houseplants and terrariums are more popular than ever, they have added a section that tells you how to propogate and sell the most popular house plants. Some of their customers report they have paid for their greenhouses with the house plants they have started and sold locally.

Brochure free.

C. W. MICHAELS CO.
590 New Albany Road
Moorsetown, NJ 08057

PRODUCT:

"The Garden Straddler"

"The Garden Straddler" is a new garden aid (a mobile seat) that enables a gardener to sit in comfort as he or she moves it over rows of vegetables to plant, thin, weed, harvest, etc. It can also be used alongside flower beds and berry bushes. It can be moved either forward or backward. "The Garden Straddler" can aid all gardeners, young and old, but it has proven to be extremely useful to senior gardeners, especially those handicapped with knee, back and hip problems. As a result of the inquiries and orders recieved as a result of the publicity on "The Garden Straddler", Mr. C. W. Michaels has been surprised by the number of gardeners who have knee, back, hip and other more severe handicaps. These gardeners deserve a lot of encouragement as they are determined to garden despite their handicaps. The comments contained in the brochure are just a very small sample of the problems that his customers and potential customers have. "The Garden Straddler" moves easily on four seven-inch diameter wheels. Clearance over the rows is 16 inches high and 20 inches wide. It weighs only 15 pounds. When cold weather comes, "The Garden Straddler" can be carried inside and used for cleaning, painting, waxing and scores of other bending and stooping jobs.

GARDEN STRADDLER

Brochure free.

J. E. MILLER NURSERIES, INC.
Canandaigua, NY 14424

PRODUCTS:

cherry trees
dwarf fruit trees
garden aids
grape vines
ground covers
nut trees

ornamental trees
shade trees
small fruits & berries
standard fruit plants
strawberry plants

Miller Nurseries is a family-owned and operated business. They try to do business on a friendly basis and personally wish to serve all of their customers. Ed Miller started a small mail-order business in 1936 to serve folks who might like a few grapes for home use. In 1940 his brother George joined the growing business. The two of them learned grape culture from their father. Their farm is on the sunny slopes of Canan-

PLUMS

daigua Lake, and the mail-order business is now operated by Ed, George and their sons. The younger generation has brought a new and progressive outlook to the farm and business of selling their products, but still they keep their standards of personal, efficient service, offering all of their customers the best stock and a square deal.

Catalog free.

MOTHERS GENERAL STORE
P.O. Box 506
Flat Rock, NC 28731

PRODUCTS:

garden cultivator   soil test kits   survival garden

Mother's General Store was established in late 1971 to accomplish the following goals: They hope to gather into one central supply house a line of the old-time tools that are becoming increasingly difficult to otherwise locate. They also intend to make readily available by mail all the do-more-with-less, latest technology products that the modern homesteader needs and wants. They also aspire to create a market for

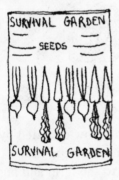

SURVIVAL GARDEN

"cottage industry" merchandise—items that individuals, families, co-ops and communes (perhaps even you or your group) can manufacture at home or in your own shop. Most of all, they hope to generate a profit, ALL OF WHICH will be turned over to Mother's Research Center. This center will soon be established to further wrestle with the problems of ecological living and alternate life-styles. Mother's General Store catalog has many items of interest, as well as many items you didn't think you could find any more or weren't even made any more. It would be worth having just to read it and find out what is available.

Catalog 35¢.

J. MULLIN, NURSERY
1173 Doylestown Pike
Quakertown, PA 18951

PRODUCT:

diatomaceous earth insecticides

J. Mullin, Nursery, has a very interesting insecticide. It is re-
fined from a special type of diatomaceous earth, which is
made up of the microscopic skeletal remains of tiny algae
plants called diatoms. These
tiny, sharp-edged shells of
diatoms kill insects mechanic-
ally, as opposed to chemical-
ly. The waxy outer surface of
the insect is scratched and
punctured by these tiny shells.
The insects then die from
dessication or dehydration
when their vital juices are al-
lowed to escape. There are

DIATOMACEOUS EARTH
MAGNIFIED 7000X

three types of these Perma-Guard insecticides: the D-20,
which kills roaches, ants and other insects looking for a home
in your home; the D-21, which is for garden plants and will
not harm the birds that eat the bugs or the beneficial earthworms, and the D-32, which is effective against fleas, ticks
and lice. Bug-free pets are happier, states the brochure!

Brochure free.

MUSSER FORESTS, INC.
Route 119 North
Indiana, PA 15701

PRODUCTS:

broadleaf evergreens
evergreen seedlings
evergreen transplants
ground covers
hardwood seedlings

hardwood shrubs
hedges
landscape evergreens
landscape ornamentals
perennials

Evergreen and hardwood seedlings and transplants, rooted cuttings such as rhododendrons, azaleas, junipers, arborvitae, Japanese yew, etc., ground covers, landscape ornamentals, container-grown plants and perennials are some of the

DOUGLAS FIR

items offered by Musser Forests. According to them, they are the largest nursery of the kind in America. Through scientific culture, the seedlings develop the strong, compact mass of fine roots and sturdy plants characteristic of Musser stock. New techniques in fertilization, spraying and handling are studied and tested to assure healthy, disease-free seedlings. The most modern equipment and methods are employed for the greatest possible efficiency and economy.

Catalog free.

NEW YORK STATE FRUIT TESTING COOPERATIVE
  ASSOCIATION
Geneva, NY 14456

PRODUCTS:

apple trees
blackberry plants
blueberry plants
cherry trees
crab apple trees
elderberries

grape vines
nectarine trees
ornamental apple trees
peach trees
pear trees
plum trees
strawberry plants

NEW YORK STATE FRUIT TESTING
COOPERATIVE ASSOCIATION (Cont'd)

The New York State Fruit Testing Cooperative Association propogates new fruit varieties and virus-free clones and makes them available to anyone interested in trying them. The New York State Fruit Testing Cooperative Association was organized in 1918 for the purpose stated above. No funds have ever been appropriated for the support of this Association, and therefor a sufficient charge must be made for nursery stock to cover ex-

PEACH

penses. The Association has grown steadily with a membership today of about 5,000, representing 50 states and many foreign countries.

Catalog free.

NICHOLS GARDEN NURSERY
1190 North Pacific Highway
Albany, OR 97321

PRODUCTS:

beans, dry	garlic
beans, green	ginseng roots
beets	herb plants
broccoli	herbs
brussels sprouts	lettuce
cabbage	mushrooms
canteloupe	novelty vegetables
carrots	onions
cauliflower	ornamental corn
corn	ornamental gourds
cucumbers	parsley
dried herbs and spices	peas
eggplant	peppers
everlasting flowers	pumpkins
flower seeds	radishes
	salsify

spinach
squash
tomatoes, paste
tomatoes, table

tomatoes, yellow
turnips
watermelons

ROSEMARY

Herb seeds and rare and unusual vegetable seeds are featured in this garden catalog. They also have herb plants, herb teas and miscellaneous garden aids. The Nichols Garden Nursery is located in Oregon's famous Willamette Valley. Nichols has been in the seed and nursery business for a quarter of a century. Their purpose during those years has been to bring people closer to nature through gardening. Nothing can equal the sense of accomplishment of growing hundreds of pounds of vegetables from a few ounces of seeds. They are also concerned with those seeking ways of making a supplementary income from their gardens. Nichols continues to mimeograph their catalog because the huge job of making over 200,000 catalogs means year-round work for their more than twenty employees with no lay-offs during the slack periods. Nichols says no matter how hard they try, they are not perfect. As long as it's necessary to have people put up orders, the possibility of human error exists. Having ordered from this firm, we must say they have yet to make a mistake, but at least Nichols admits that it is possible.

Catalog 25¢.

L. L. OLDS SEED COMPANY
P.O. Box 1069
Madison, WI 53701

PRODUCTS:

achillea
acroclinium
ageratum
agrostemma
alfalfa
almond, flowering
alyssum
amaranthus
amaryllis
anchusa
anemone
anise
antirrhinum
apple trees
aquilegia
arabis
arctotis
armeria
asparagus
asters
bachelor button
balm
balsam
barberry
basil
beans, dry
beans, green
beets
begonia
bellis monstrosum
bells of ireland
bentgrass
bittersweet
black-eyed peas
bluegrass
bone meal
borage
brachycome
bridal wreath

broccoli
browallia
brussels sprouts
bulbs
burning bush
cabbage
cabbage plants
cactus
caladium
calendula
california poppy
calla lily
calliopsis
candytuft
canna
canterbury bells
captan
caraway
carnations
carrot
castor beans
catnip
cauliflower
celeriac
celery
celosia
centaurea
cherry trees
chervil
chicory
chinese lantern
chives
chrysanthemum
cineraria
citron
clarkia
cleome
clover
cobaea scandens

cockscomb
coleus
collards
coral bells
coreopsis
coriander
corn, sweet
cosmos
cress
crocus
cucumber
cuphea
currants
daffodills
dahlia
daisy
datura
delphinium
dianthus
diazinon
dictamnus
didiscus
digitalis
dill
dolichos
doronicum
dowpon
eggplant
endive
english daisy
everlasting flowers
fertilizers
fescues
florence fennel
flowering crab
forget-me-not
forsythia
four o'clock
foxglove
fruit trees
gaillardia
garlic
geranium

geum
ginseng roots
gladiolus
gloxinia
godetia
gomphrena
gourds
grape vines
grass seeds
grevillea
ground cherry
gypsophila
hedge plants
helianthus
helichrysum
heliotrope
herbs
heuchera
hibiscus
hollyhock
honeysuckle
horehound
hot caps
huckleberry
hyacinths
hydrangea
iberis
impatiens
ipomea
ismene calathina
job's tears
kale
kochia
kohlrabi
lantana
larkspur
lathyrus
lavender
lawn seed
leek
lettuce
liatris
lilacs

lily
linaria
linum
lobelia
lunaria
lupinus
lythrum
mangels
marigold
marjoram
matthiola
mignonette
mimosa
mint
moonflower
morning glory
moss rose
muskmelon
mustard
narcissus
nasturtium
nemesia
nicotiana
nigella
nitragin
nursery stock
okra
onions
oregano
oriental vegetables
oxalis
pansy
parsley
parsnip
peach trees
peanuts
pear trees
peas
peat pots
penstemon
peonies
pepper
perennial flowers

periwinkle
petunia
philadelphus
phlox
plum trees
popcorn
poppy
portulaca
potatoes
primula
privet
prunus
pumpkin
pyrethrum
quince, oriental
radish
raspberry plants
red hot poker
rhubarb
ricinus
rosemary
rose multiflora
roses
rudbeckia
russian olive
rutabaga
rye grass
sage
salpiglossis
slasify
salvia
saponaria
scabiosa
schizanthus
shrubs
snapdragon
snowball
snowberry
snow on the mountain
soil test kits
solanum
sphagnum moss
spinach

L. L. OLDS SEED COMPANY (Cont'd)

sprayers
squash
statice
stocks
strawflowers
sugar beets
summer savory
sunflowers
sweet fennel
sweet peas
sweet potatoes
sweet william
swiss chard
thunbergia
thyme
tithonia
tobacco

tomato, paste
tomato, table
tomato, yellow
torenia
tuberose
tulips
turnips
verbena
vetch
viburnum
vinca
vines
viola
wallflower
watermelon
weigelia
zinnia

The L. L. Olds Seed Company is in their 88th year of selling and supplying gardeners with the many varieties of vegetable and flower seeds and plants.

They have opened a new 40,000 square foot office and warehouse facility at 2901 Packers Avenue, Madison, Wisconsin. There they have a warehouse and seed processing plant, mail order department, retail garden center, and their general offices—all under one roof. During the spring plant-

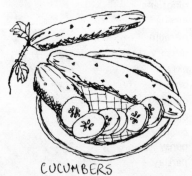

CUCUMBERS

ing season they are open 7 days a week. They now prepay shipment of all garden seeds, bulbs, plants, flower seeds and shrubs offered in their catalog in the continental U.S.A. for those who mail order seed, etc. They also have a section of gardening aids featured in their catalog.

Catalog free.

PACIFIC COAST GREENHOUSE MFG. CO.
430 Burlingame Avenue
Redwood City, CA 94063

PRODUCTS:

greenhouse coolers
greenhouse fans
greenhouse heaters
greenhouse humidifiers
greenhouses

GREENHOUSE

Pacific Coast Greenhouse Mfg. Co. manufactures greenhouses and all the necessary equipment to operate and maintain them. They have greenhouse installations in many places, including Golden Gate Park, San Francisco, California: one 18 feet by 93 feet and one 18 feet by 72 feet; and at the University of California, Davis, California: two 30 feet by 100 feet and one 18 feet by 30 feet. Pacific Coast Greenhouse Mfg. Co. makes greenhouses in sizes from 3 feet long by 6 feet 3½ inches wide up to 102 feet long by 18 feet 3½ inches wide. These are prefabricated models. The company will also answer any requests for special greenhouses you may need. They have been producing greenhouses for more than 40 years. They also have the automatic Frisco fogger humidifier, complete with controls.

Catalog free.

GEO. W. PARK SEED CO., INC.
Greenwood, SC 29647

PRODUCTS:

abutilon
acacia
acanthus
achillea
achimenes
aconitum
acroclinum
adonis
african violet
agapanthus
agathaea
ageratum
agrostis
allium
aloe, tiger
alostroemeria
althea
alyssum
amaranthus
amaryllis
amazon lily
ammobium
amsonia
anaphalis
anchusa
androsace
anemone
anthemus
anthurium
antigonon
antirrhinum
aphanostephus
aphelandra
aquilegia
arabis, rock cress
aralia
arctotis
arenaria
armeria
arnica
asclepias

asparagus fern
asphodelus
aster, annual
aster, perennial
astilbe
aubretia
avena
azalea
baby's breath
baby blue eyes
bachelor button
balsam
baptisia
bartonia
basil
begonia
belamcanda
bellflower
bellis
bells of ireland
bergenia
beverly bells
bignonia
bird of paradise
blackberry lily
bleeding heart
bletilla
bougainvillea
bouvardia
brachycome
briza
browallia
buddleia
bupthalmum
butter daisy
butterfly lily
cabbage, flowering
cactus
caladium
calandrinia

calceolaria
calendula
calla lily
calliopsis
camelia
campanula
candytuft
canna
canterbury bells
capiscum
carnation
castor oil bean
cassia
catananche
celosia
celsia
centaurea
centratherum
cerastium
cheiranthus
chelone
chrysanthemum
cineraria
cladanthus
clarkia
clary
clematis
cleome
clianthus
clitoria butterfly
clivia
cobaea
cobra orchid
cockscomb
coffea
coleus
columbine
convallaria
coral bells
cordyline
coreopsis
cornflower
corn, ornamental

coronilla
corydalis
corynocarpus
cosmo
cotton, ornamental
cotyledon
crepe myrtle
crepis
crossandra
crotalaria
croton
crown vetch
cunonia
cuphea
cyclamen
cynoglossum
cyperus
cypress vine
cyphomandra
cytisus broom
dahlborg daisy
dahlia
daisy, english
daisy, painted
daphne
darlingtonia
datura
daylily
delphinium
dianthus
dicentra
dichondra
dictamnus
didiscus
digitalis
dimorphotheca
dodecatheon
dombeya
doronicum
dryas
dusty miller
echeveria
echinops

echium
eggplant, ornamental
emilia
episcia
eranthis
eremurus
erigeron
erinus
eryngium
erythrina
erythronium
eschscholtzia
eucalyptus
eucharis
eucomis
eupatorium
euphorbia
eutoca
everlastings
exacum
fatsia, aralia
felicia
ferns
ficus
flag of spain
flax, linum
forget-me-not
four o'clock
foxglove
franklinia
freesia
fuchsia
funkia, hosta
gaillardia
galtonia
garden mixtures
gazania
gentian
geranium
gerbera
gesneria
geum, avens
gilia

gladiolus
globularia
gloriosa daisy
gloriosa lily
glory flower
gloxinia
godetia, satinflower
gomphocarpus
gomphrena
gourds
grass, lawn
grass, ornamental
grevillea
gypsophilia
harpephyllum
heather
hedychium
helenium
helianthemum
helianthus
helichrysm
heliopsis
heliotrope
helipterum
helleborus
hemerocalis
herbs
herniaria
hesperis
heuchera
hibiscus
hollyhock, althea
hop
hosta
hoya
hunnemannia
hyacinth
hypericum
hypoestes
iberis
ice plant
impatiens
incarvillea

ipomoea

iris, flag

ismene

jacaranda

jacobinia

jasione

jasmine, yellow

jewels of opar

job's tears

kalanchoe

kale, flowering

kochia, cypress

kudzu vine

laburnum

lantana

larkspur

latania

lathyrus

lavatera

lavender

layia

lazy daisy

leontopodium

leucanthemum

lewisia

liatrus, gayfeather

lilium, lily

lily of the valley

linaria, toadflax

liriope

living stones

lobelia

lofus

lunaria

lupine

lychnis, campion

lycoris

lythrum

machaeranthera

madeira vine

maltese cross

malva, mallow

manaos beauty

mandevillea

marble vine

marguerite

marigold, tagetes

martynia

mathiola

matricaria

maurandia

meconopsis

merion blue grass

meryta sinclair

mesembryanthemum

michaelmas daisy

microsperma

mignonette

mimosa

mimulus

mirabilis

momordica

monarda

montbretia

morning glory

musa banana

myosotis

naegelia

nasturtium

nemesia

nemophila

nepeta, catmint

nertera

nicandra

nicotiana

nierembergia

nigella

oenothera

opuntia

orchis, orchid

ornithogalum

oxalis

oxypetalum

paeony

palms

pampas grass

pansy, heartease
passiflora
pelargonium
pentapetes
pentas
pentstemon
peperomia
pepper, ornamental
perilla
periwinkle, vinca
petunia
philodendron
phlox
phygelius
physalis
physostegia
pilea
pineapple lily
pinks
pitcher plant
platycodon
plumbago
poinciana
poinsettia
polemonium
polka dot plant
polygonum
poppy
portulaca
potentilla
primrose
primula
pseudopanax
punica
pyrethrum
queen anne's lace
ramonda
ranunculus
rechsteiner
rhodanthe
rhododendron
rhoicissus
ricinus

romneya
rose, rosa
royal red bugler
rudbeckia
sagina
saintpaulia
salpiglossis
salvia
sanguinaria
santolina
sanvitalia
saponaria
saxifraga
scabiosa
scarlet sage
schefflera
schizanthus
sedum
sempervivum
sensitive plant
shamrock
shasta daisy
shrubs
sidalcea
silene
sinningia
smilax
snapdragon
solanum
spider flower
sprekelia
stachys lanata
star of texas
statice
stephanotis
stocks, gilliflower
stokesia
strawberry
strawflower
strelitzia
streptocarpus
succulents
sultana

sunflower
sweet pea
sweet william
tahoka daisy
talinum
tetranema
teucrium
thalictrum
thea tea
thermopsis
thistle
thrift
thunbergia
thyme
thymus
tigridia
tobacco, flowering
torenia
touch-me-not
tradescantia
transvaal daisy
trillium
tritoma
trollius

trumpet flower
tuberose
valeriana
vegetables
venidium
venus fly trap
verbascum
verbena
verbesina
veronica
vines
viola
wahlenbergia
wallflower
waterlily
wild flowers
wisteria
wood rose
xeranthemum
yucca
zephyranthes
zinnia
zoysia

In their 107th year of dependable service, the George W. Park Seed Company is a family tradition. Park's believes that by experience and love of this profession, they are able to provide you with the finest seeds, plants and gardening accessories and service in their industry. George W. Park truly believed and lived his creed: "Your success and pleasure

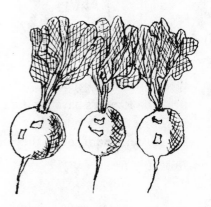

RADISHES

are more to Park than your money". While this policy did not make him rich in worldly goods, he was rich in friends. George W. Park left a challenging heritage to his sons. Catalog free.

113

QUALITY SEED GARLIC
Earle & Hazel Renno
2929 Friendly Grove Road
Olympia, WA 98506

PRODUCTS:

elephant garlic
red german garlic

This is a family-owned business specializing in garlic growing
and selling. Red German garlic was developed to its present
stage by Earle Renno. This garlic was brought from Germany

GARLIC

to Olympia in 1908 by an old
German saloonkeeper on a
visit to his childhood home.
He died in 1940 and his wife
gave Earle Renno about a doz-
en clusters that he had kept
planted in the rose bed. The
last inside husk is red, so Mr.
Renno called it Red German
Garlic. He has developed this
garlic to where three clusters

to the pound is not uncommon. They also raise and sell
Elephant garlic, which is the largest and mildest of the gar-
lics. The Renno's have produced a cluster of Elephant garlic
weighing two pounds. They say the larger the bulb, the larger
the cluster, and it seems they are out to prove it.

Brochure free.

RABBIT HOP NURSERY
Route 2, Box 1086
Rabbit Hop Road
Spruce Pine, NC 28777

PRODUCTS:

apple trees
broom corn seeds

job's tears
sunflower seed

English cider apple trees are grown and sold by this nursery. These are the same cider apples used in the making of the famous English cider. The trees grow very well in North Carolina. Also available are Kingston Black, Yarlington Mill, Nehou, Dabbinett and Medaille d'Or on semi-dwarf roots that are two years old. Rabbit Hop Nursery also features the old time broom corn seed, job's tears and large sunflower seeds.

Details free.

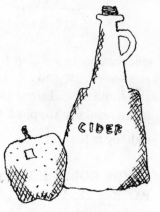

CIDER APPLES

REDWOOD DOMES
P.O. Box 666
Aptos, CA 95003

PRODUCTS:

air inlet vents
cooling exhaust fans
greenhouse heaters

greenhouse humidifier
greenhouses
growing benches
summer shade cloths

Developed over a period of 20 years, these geodesic-shaped greenhouses are really beautiful. The assembly is simple and

REDWOOD DOMES (Cont'd)

DOME GREENHOUSE

precise. They have a patented aerodynamic design which provides healthier growing conditions because it allows superior air circulation. They can be placed anywhere, and being round in shape, the greenhouses need no orientation to sun changes. The catalog shows the different sizes of greenhouses being used for such things as an artist's studio, as a warehouse and as a vacation cabin. The company will also build special sized Dome Greenhouses to fit your needs if the regularly supplied sizes do not meet your requirements.

Catalog is free.

CLYDE ROBIN SEED CO., INC.
P.O. Box 2855
Castro Valley, CA 94546

PRODUCTS:

abelia	amelanchier
abies	anemone
abronia	angelica
acacia	anthocephalum
acamptopappus	apocynum
acer	aquilegia
achillea	arbutus
achlys	archontophoenix
aconitum	arctomecon
actaea	arctostaphylos
adansonia	arenia
adenostoma	argemone
adiantum	armeria
agastache	arnica
agave	aruncus
ailanthus	artemisia
alberta	asclepias
albiziz	aster
allium	athyrium

atriplex
baccharius
baeria
baileya
belamcanda
berberis
betula
bloomeria
bolusanthus
brachychiton
brodiaea
callirhoe
callistemon
callitris
calochortus
calodendrum
calycanthus
calyptridem
camassia
camellia
campanula
campsis
caragana
carthamus
cassia
castillija
ceanothus
cedrus
celastrus
cercidium
cercis
cercocarpua
chamaecyparis
cheilanthes
cherianthus
chilopsis
chimaphila
chlorogalum
chorizanhe
chrysanthemum
chrysothamnus
cimicfuga
cirsium

cistus
clarkia
clematis
collinsia
colvillea
comarstaphylis
coreopsis
corethrogyne
cornus
cotoneaster
cowania
crocidium
cryptomeria
cupressus
cynara
cynoglossum
cypripedium
cytisus
dais
dalea
darlingtonia
datura
daubentonia
delphinium
dendromecon
dicentra
digitalis
dimorphotheca
dodecatheon
dudleya
dyssodia
echinacea
echinocactus
elaeagnus
emmenanthe
encelia
ephedra
epilobium
eremocarpus
erigeron
eriodictyon
eriogonum
eriophyllum

erysimum
erythronium
eschscholtzia
eucalyptus
euonymus
eustoma
fallugia
felicia
ferocactus
foeniculum
fouquieria
fragaria
franseria
fraxinus
fremontia
fremontodendron
fritillaria
gaillardia
galvezia
garrya
gaultheria
gentiana
geum
gilia
gillium
ginkgo
gliricidia
haplopappus
helenium
helianthemum
helianthus
helleborus
heracleum
heteromeles
heuchera
hibiscus
holodiscus
horkelia
hovenia
hunnemannia
hypericum
ilex
ilmus

ipomea
iris
isomeris
jacaranda
jatropha
juncus
juniperus
kalmia
koelreuteria
lagerstroemia
lagurus
lathyrus
laurus
lavandula
lavatera
layia
leontopodium
lepechinia
lespedeza
leucadendron
leucaena
leucospermum
leucothoe
lewisia
liatris
libocedrus
lilium
limnanthes
linaria
linum
liquidambar
liriodendron
lobelia
lonicera
luetkea
lunaria
lupinus
madia
mahonia
marrubium
melia
mentzelia
mespilus

mimulus
mirabilis
monardella
morus
myrica
nandina
narthecium
nemophila
nicotiana
nigella
nolina
oenothera
orchid
orthocarpus
paeonia
paliurus
papaver
parkinsonia
pedicularis
peltophorum
penstemon
perideridia
phacelia
philadelphus
pholistoma
phyllodoce
physocarpus
picea
pinus
pittosporum
platanus
platystemon
podalyrica
podocarpus
polystichum
potentilla
primula
prunus
pseudotsuga
pueraria
purshia
raillardella
raillardia
rhamnus

rhododendron
rhodotypos
rhus
ribes
rosa
rudbeckia
rumex
salvia
samanea
sambucus
sanguinaria
sanguisorba
saponaria
schotia
sciadopitys
scutellaria
senecio
shepherdia
sidalcea
silene
sisyrinchium
smilacina
solidago
sophora
sorbus
spartium
spathodea
sphaeralcea
spiraea
sporobolus
strelitzia
symphoricarpos
syringa
tanacetum
taxus
tellima
thalaspi
thalictrum
thespesia
thuja
tithonia
tofieldia
torreya

trachycarpus
trichostema
trillium
tsuga
ulec
umbellularia
valeriana
venegasia
veratrum
verbascum
vernonia
viburnum
vida
viola

virgilia
vitis
washingtonia
wisteria
woodsia
wyethia
xerophyllum
xylococcus
yucca
zauschneria
zelkova
zephyranthes
zigadenus
zizyphus

ACACIA-MIMOSA

The Clyde Robin Seed Co., Inc., has a very beautiful catalog showing many of the wild flowers, trees and plants they have to offer. Their catalog has everything listed under its scientific plant name. They do this because it is the only way of correctly describing the seeds of the plants which they offer. They have tried to use the ONE most common name before each plant, but common names are of little value when some flowers have OVER fifty! Their catalog is put together on the order of a garden book, for there are instructions on the growing and care of the different plants shown.

Catalog $1.00.

F. W. SCHUMACHER CO.
Sandwich, MA 02563

PRODUCTS:

abies
acacia
acer
aesculus
ailanthus
albizzia
alnus
amelanchier
amorpha
ampelopsis
arctostaphylos
aristolochia
aronia
asimina
azalea
bauhinia
berberis
betula
broussonetia
buddleia
butea
buxux
callicarpa
calluna
calycanthus
camellia
campsis
cargana
carpinus
carrisa
carya
casses
catalpa
ceanothus
cedrus
celastrus
celtis
cephalotaxus
ceratonia
cercidiphyllum
cercis

chaenomeles
chamaecyparis
chamaerops
chimonanthus
chionanthus
cinnamomum
citrus
cladrastis
clematis
clerodendron
clethra
cleyera
colutea
cordyline
cornus
corylus
cotinus
cotoneaster
cowania
crataegus
cryptomeria
cupressus
cydonia
cytisus broom
davidia
delonix
diospyros
disanthus
dolichos
elaeagnus
enkianthus
erythrina
eucalyptus
euonymus
evodia
exochorda
fagus
fatsia, aralia
feijoa
firmiana
franklinia

fraxinus
gaultheria
genista
ginkgo
gleditsia
grevillea
gymnocladus
halesia
hamamelis
hibiscus
hippophae
hovenia
hydrangea
hypericum
ilex
juglans
juniperus
kalmia
kerria
koelreuteria
kolkwitzia
laburnum
lagerstroemia
larix
laurus
lespedeza
leucothoe
libocedrus
ligustrum
liquidambar
liriodendron
lonicera
maackia
macadamia
maclura
magnolia
mahonia
malus
mespilus
milia
morus
myrica
nandina

nyssa
olea
ostrya
oxydendrum
paeonia
parkinsonia
parthenocissus
passiflora
paulownia
phellodendron
phoenix
picea
pieris
pinus
pittosporum
platanus
plumbago
podocarpus
poinciana
prunus
pseudolarix
pseudotsuga
pueraria
pyracantha
pyrus
quercus
rhamnus
rhododendron
rhododendron hybrids
rhodotypos
rhus
robinia
rosa
sapium
schinus
sciadopitys
sequoia
shepherdia
sophora
sorbus
spartium
stewartia

styrax
symphoricarpos
syringa
tamarix
taxodium
taxus
thevetia
thuja
tilia
trachycarpus
tsuga

ulex
ulmus
vaccinum
viburnum
vitex
vitis
washingtonia
weigela
wisteria
yucca
zelkova

SWISS STONE PINE

The F. W. Schumacher Co. specializes in offering seeds of hundreds of types of trees, rhododendron and azalea. They feature fruit stock seeds as well as many seed specialties. All their seeds are offered cleaned unless they are dried berries or dried hips. Although plants grown from seed of horticultural varieties often yield superior plant material in comparison to those grown from nondescript seed, F. W. Schumacher wishes to emphasize that seeds of such varieties or hybrids, with few exceptions, cannot be expected to come true to name. The seed lots are carefully inspected on arrival and tests are made as far as possible. All bulk lots shipped refrigerated.

Catalog free.

SEEDWAY, INC.
Hall, NY 14463

PRODUCTS:

ageratum
alyssum
asparagus
aster
aubrietia
baby's breath
bachelor button
basil, ornamental
beans, dry
beans, green
beets
bells of ireland
broccoli
brussels sprouts
cabbage
cabbage, savory
calendulas
canterbury bells
carnations
carrots
cauliflower
celery
chinese cabbage
cockscomb
coleus
columbine
corn, ornamental
corn, sweet
cosmos
cress
dahlias
daisy, english
daisy, painted
daisy, rudbeckia
daisy, shasta
delphinium
eggplant
endive
firebush
four o'clock

gladiolus
gourds
herbs
hollyhocks
horseradish
kale
kohlrabi
larkspur, regal
lettuce
lupines
marigolds
morning glories
muskmelons
nasturtiums
okra
onion plants
onion seeds
onion sets
pansies
parsley
peas
peppers
petunias
phlox
pinks
poppies
portulaca
primrose
pumpkin
radishes
rhubarb roots
rutabaga
salsify
salvia
scabiosa
snapdragons
spinach
squash, summer
squash, winter

statice
strawflowers
sunflowers
sweet peas
sweet william

swiss chard
tomatoes, table
tomatoes, yellow
turnips
watermelons
zinnias

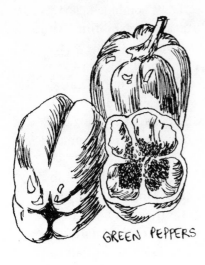

GREEN PEPPERS

Seedway, Inc., is located in Hall, New York, and list themselves as "the home of quality seeds." Besides offering a variety of flower and vegetable seeds and a few plants, they have a special price list for commercial buyers. They have a nice selection of gardening aids offered, including garden stakes, hotkaps, black plastic mulch, garden seeders, insecticides and fungicides, as well as sprayers.

Catalog is free.

SHASTA CANYON NURSERY
P.O. Box 924
Anderson, CA 96007

PRODUCTS:

strawberry plants

They grow California varieties of strawberry plants and offer them to customers in multiples of 25 plants. All their plants come packaged with complete growing instructions. They have three outstanding California varieties available. Tioga is

STRAWBERRIES

the most popular strawberry among commercial berry growers. More Tioga plants are grown in California each year than all other varieties combined. The fruit is large and firm, with exceptional flavor. Yields are normally high. Tioga is very reliable in its fruit production, and this outstanding variety adapts well to a wide range of growing conditions. The Fresno variety is second in commercial popularity, and is itself a superb strawberry. The berries are attractively shaped, flavor is good and fruits process well. Fresno generally peaks in production later than Tioga and is a good choice to plant with the earlier varieties to extend the period of fruit production. Sequoia is the earliest of the California varieties offered. The berries are large, dark and exceptionally sweet. This variety is ideal for the home gardener who wants to enjoy the old-fashioned strawberry flavor. Fruit production is also excellent with Sequoia. Shasta Canyon Nursery has supplied the finest commercial fruit growers with nursery stock for over 30 years. California strawberry plants are appreciated throughout the world as the very best available.

Catalog free.

SHIELDS PUBLICATIONS
P.O. Box 472
Elgin, IL 60120

PRODUCT:

earthworm books

Shields Publications publishes books on how to raise earthworms and how earthworms can help us in many ways. This includes the use of earthworms in organic gardening. They distribute 12 books, which are: Raising Earthworms for Profit, Profitable Earthworm Farming, Raising the African Nightcrawler, How to Sell Earthworms by Mail, Larger Red Worms, ABC's of the Earthworm Business, The Worm Farm, Earthworm Feeds and Feeding, A-Worming We Did Go, Earthworm Selling & Shipping Guide, With Tails We Win, and Let an Earthworm be Your Garbage Man. Shields Publications do not know of anyone else who specializes in earthworm books, as they do. They offer a complete line of earthworm books covering any phase of earthworm culture that a person may be interested in developing.

Brochures free.

R. H. SHUMWAY SEEDSMAN
Rockford IL 61101

PRODUCTS:

african violet plants	asparagus roots
african violet seeds	asparagus seeds
alfalfa	aster plants
alfalfa tea	banana tree
anemone bulbs	beans, dry
anemone seeds	beans, green
apple trees	beets
artichokes	begonia bulbs

begonia plants
birch trees
blackberries
blueberry plants
boysenberries
broccoli plants
broccoli seed
brussels sprouts plants
brussels sprouts seed
cabbage plants
cabbage seed
cactus plants
caladium bulbs
calla lilies
canna bulbs
carnation plants
carrots
cauliflower plants
cauliflower seed
celery
celeriac
cherry trees
chicory
chives
chrysanthemum plants
citron
clover
coleus plants
collards
compost kit
corn, field
corn, hybrid
corn, salad
corn, sweet
cow peas
cress
crowder peas
cucumbers
currants
dahlia
dandelion
date trees
dwarf fruit trees

eggplant
elephant ears
elm trees
endive
evergreens
ferns
fertilizer
fescues
field seed
fig tree
flower seeds
fly trap plant
fuchsias
garden huckleberry
garlic
geranium
gladiolus
gloxinia
gooseberries
gourds
grape vines
greenhouses
ground cover
hedges
herbs
horseradish roots
hotcaps
house plants
ivy
kale
kohlrabi
lespedeza
lettuce
lilies
lily, hardy
lily of the valley
lily seed
madeira vines
magnolia
mangel
mango melon
maple trees
melons

millet
milo maize
mole & gopher killer
mushroom spawn
mustard
mustard spinach
nectarine trees
nitragin
nut trees
oak trees
okra
okra, vine
onion plants
onion seeds
onion sets
oxalis
parsley
parsnip
pasture mixture
peach trees
peanuts
pear trees
peas
peat pots
peonies
pepper plants
peppers
perennial plants
persimmon tree
philodendron
peporomia
phlox plants
popcorn
pumpkin

radish
ranunculus
rape
raspberry plants
reed canary grass
rhubarb
roses
rutabaga
salsify
shade trees
sphagnum moss
spinach
spirea
squash
strawberry plants
sugar beets
sugar cane
sugar sorghum
sunflower
sweet potato plants
swiss chard
timothy
tobacco
tomato, paste
tomato plants
tomato, table
tomato, yellow
tuberoses
turnips
velvet plant
vines
violet plants
watermelon
young berries

This company is now 105 years old. They offer a great variety of all types of fruits, vegetables and flowers, etc.

R. H. SHUMWAY SEEDSMAN (Cont'd)

They also have special low
wholesale prices (not prepaid)
for market gardeners. They
feature a nice selection of
house plants as well. There
are five generations of seeds-
men's and nurserymen's
knowledge combined in this
company. Their catalog is
illustrated with many very

HOREHOUND

nice drawings and photographs of the items offered for sale.

Catalog is free.

SILVER FALLS NURSERY
Star Route, Box 55
Silverton, OR 97381

PRODUCTS:

abelia	ferns
ajuga	firs
almond, flowering	heath
arborvitae	heather
azaleas	hemlock
barberry	holly
beech	juniper
birch	larch
bittersweet	mahonia
bridal wreath	maple trees
brooms	oak trees
cedars	oregon grape
cherry, flowering	pines
cotoneasters	pyracantha
crabapple trees	quince, flowering
cypress	sequoias
dogwood	spruce

Silver Falls Nursery has azaleas for bonsai in several colors.
This should create an interesting piece of bonsai. They ship

PIN OAK

trees and shrubs for landscaping and bonsai, all bare-root. They have grown or assembled the trees and shrubs that are in the greatest demand. You can purchase several trees or shrubs of these sizes for the price of one only a year or two older. Their trees are listed by specialists as suitable subjects for bonsai, and are so labeled in the tree and shrub descriptions in their catalog. If you desire them and so indicate in your order, they will, whenever possible, select stock which could lend itself to bonsai.

Catalog free.

D. B. SMITH CO.
414 Main Street
Utica, NY 13503

PRODUCT:

air sprayers

D. B. Smith Co. manufactures high-density polyethylene compressed air sprayers for use in applying insecticides, fertilizer liquids, weed control chemicals, etc. Such features as corrosion resistance, light weight, and that they are colorful and easy to use, put these sprayers years ahead of others. Their sprayers are manufactured to eliminate service problems. You can use these sprayers for all of

COMPRESSED AIR SPRAYER

D. B. SMITH CO. (Cont'd)

the ordinary spray jobs, such as flower beds, rose gardens,
vegetable gardens, shrubs, trees, lawns, etc.

Catalog free.

SPRING HILL FARM
36 Spring Hill Road
East Sandwich, MA 02537

PRODUCTS

beans, green
beets
broccoli
brussels sprouts
cabbage
carrot
cauliflower
chinese cabbage
corn, sweet

lettuce
melons
onions
radish
spinach
squash
swiss chard
tomato, table
watermelon

CORN

Spring Hill Farm is a small seed
company, and although they
now carry a very basic line of
vegetables, they will be expand-
ing. Their prices warrant sending
for their brochure. The brochure
tells what one packet of seed
will produce, giving the number
of feet (for row crops) or the
number of hills or plants you
can expect from the one packet.

Brochure free.

STARK BRO'S NURSERIES
Louisiana, MO 63353

PRODUCTS:

apple trees
apricot trees
asparagus
blackberries
blueberry plants
cherry trees
chestnut trees
crab apple trees
flowering trees
grape vines
hedges
hickory
nectarine trees

peach trees
pear trees
pecan trees
peonies
plum trees
prune trees
quince trees
raspberry plants
rhubarb
shade trees
strawberry plants
walnut trees

In 1816 James Stark moved to Missouri, taking apple scions to plant along the Mississippi River, and thus began the Stark Bro's heritage. Ever since, new generations of Starks have continued this pioneer spirit. It is equally amazing that in 1893 Clarence Stark realized the genius in Luther Burbank. Working with Stark Bro's, Luther Burbank decided, before his death, that Stark Bro's would be where he left his nursery plant discoveries. There are ten locations listed where trees and plants are grown for Stark Bro's. They offer assortments suited to the size of the land you have available for planting, and market orchard assortments, as well as single tree sales.

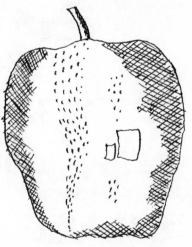

APPLE

Catalog is free.

STEELE PLANT CO.
Box 191
Gleason, TN 38229

PRODUCTS

broccoli plants
brussels sprouts
cabbage plants

cauliflower plants
onion plants
sweet potato plants

For the last two years the Steele Plant Company has been selected to furnish the sweet potato plants for George Washington's Mount Vernon vege-

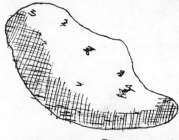

SWEET POTATO

table garden. They also were selected to grow and ship sweet potato plants for the largest and best established plant, seed and nursery mail order companies. They have the new varieties of sweet potatoes, as well as the older varieties that were popular many years ago. Their onion, cabbage, brussels sprouts and cauliflower plants are grown and shipped for them by a plant grower that serves the largest seed and nursery mail order companies in the world.

Brochure free.

STOKES SEEDS, INC.
Box 548, Main Post Office
Buffalo, NY 14240

PRODUCTS

adiantum
african daisy
ageratum
alyssum
amaranthus
angel's trumpet
antirrhinum
aquilegia
arabis

armeria
asparagus
aster
aubretia
bachelor button
balsam
basil, ornamental
beans, dry
beans, green

beets
beets, novelty
begonia
bell flower
bellis perennis
bells of ireland
brachycome
broccoli
browallia
brussels sprouts
burning bush
cabbage
cactus
calceolaria
calendula
calliopsis
campanula
candytuft
cantaloupe
carnation
carrot
castor oil plant
cauliflower
celeriac
celery
celosia
celtuce
centaurea
cheiranthus
chicory
chinese cabbage
christmas cherry
christmas pepper
chrysanthemum
cineraria
citron
clarkia
cleome
cobaea
coleus
collards
columbine

coreopsis
cornflower
corn, ornamental
corn salad
corn, sweet
cosmos
creeping zinniz
cress
crossandra
cucumber
cyclamen
cynoglossum
cyperus
dahlia
daisy, english
daisy, painted
dandelion
datura
delphinium
dianthus
digitalis
dimorphotheca
doronicum
dracaena
dusty miller
eggplant
endive
escarole
eschscholtzia
euphorbia
everlastings
ferns
feverfew
floss flower
forget-me-not
foliage
four o'clock
foxglove
freesia
fuschia
gaillardia
garden huckleberry

STOKES SEEDS, INC. (Cont'd)

gazania
geranium
gerbera
geum
gloriosa daisy
gloxinia
godetia
gomphrena
gourds
grevillea
ground cherry
helianthemum
helianthus
helichrysum montrosum
heliotrope
hemerocallis
herbs
heuchera
hibiscus
hollyhock
iberis
ice plant
impatiens
ipomea
iris
kalanchoe
kale
kochia
kohlrabi
lady slipper
larkspur
lathyrus
lavandula
lavatera
lavender
leek
lettuce
linaria
linum
lobelia
lunaria
lupines
marigold

marvel of peru
matricaria
matthiola
melon zucca
mesembryanthemum
mignonette
mimosa
mimulus
money plant
moonflower
morning glory
mushroom spawn
muskmelon
myosotis
nasturtium
nemesia
nemophila
nicotiana
nierembergia
nigella
okra
onion seeds
onion sets
ornamental grasses
ornamental tree seed
painted tongue
palm
pansy
parsley
parsnip
peanuts
peas
pepper
petunia
phacelia
philodendron
phlox
physalis
pinks
polygonum
popcorn
poppy
portulaca

primrose
primula
pteris
pumpkin
pyrethrum
radish
rainbow rock cress
rieinus
rock cress
rock garden mix
rudbeckia
rutabaga
saintpaulia
salpiglossis
salsify
salvia
santolina
sanvitalia
scabiosa
scarlet runner bean
schefflera
schizanthus
sedum
sensitive plant
shamrock
shasta daisy
smilax
snapdragon
snow in summer
spider flower
spinach

squash
statice
stocks
stokesia
strawberry plants
strawflower
sunflower
sweet peas
sweet william
swiss chard
thrift
thunbergia
tithonia
tobacco
tomato, paste
tomato, table
tomato, yellow
torenia
tritoma
turnip
ursinia
verbena
veronica
vinca rosea
violas
violet
virginia stock
wallflower
watercress
watermelon
zinnia

Stokes, in an effort to climate-test new varieties, for more than 40 years have maintained extensive flower and vegetable seed trials. Their main business for many years has been greenhouse growers. They deal with market gardeners, and know

STOKES SEEDS, INC. (Cont'd)

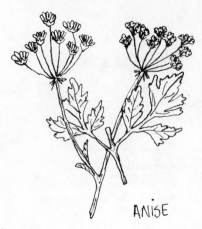

ANISE

that these growers rely on Stokes for high quality seeds and special strains to produce their valuable crops and also for prompt service throughout the season. Stokes has been under the same management for 45 years and their business is based on customer confidence and trust, resulting in many satisfied and loyal customers in all parts of Canada and the United States. As their seed is harvested, it is properly milled and in some cases sized for precision seeding. Stokes stores it in one of the largest humidity- and temperature-controlled seed storages in North America, with an area of 90,000 cubic feet. This season they will have nearly all their packages printed with complete growing instructions for both the professional and the amateur grower. Each year they grow thousands of annuals for their own trials, the All America Trials, and more than half a mile of annual flower beds which lead to the gates of Stokesdale. They welcome hundreds of visitors to inspect their seed farms and flower and vegetable trials during July and August.

Catalog free.

SUDBURY LABORATORY, INC.
572 Dutton Road
Sudbury, MA 01776

PRODUCTS:

fertilizer   soil test kits

Sudbury Laboratory, Inc., is well known for the soil test kits they make and sell to home gardeners everywhere. Sudbury states that these are the only simple and inexpensive home

SUDBURY LABORATORY, INC. (Cont'd)

garden soil test kits available.
This company also sells seed
starter cubes, some of which
are treated with liquified seaweed. The soil test kits de-
termine PH, and deficiencies
in nitrogen, phosphorus, potash,
etc. Sudbury also sells Sudbury Sea-Power, which is a
new product for them. It is a
liquified seaweed packed with
55 natural, vital trace elements,

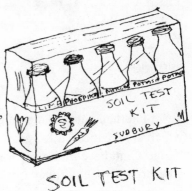

SOIL TEST KIT

minerals and vitamins essential for the healthy growth of all
vegetables, flowers, house plants and shrubs. They offer
"Chaperone" aerosol repellents for cats and dogs. Indoors, it
protects your furniture and outdoors, it protects gardens,
shrubs, outdoor furniture, buildings and car wheels from
dog and cat nuisance.
Brochures free.

SUNSTREAM
P.O. Box 484
Pittsburgh, PA 15230
PRODUCTS:

beekeeping supplies

packaged bees and queens

BEES

This is Pennsylvania's largest
and finest bee supply center.
They carry publications from
foreign countries, printed in
English. They have a complete
line of beekeeping supplies.
They offer several products
that other manufacturers do
not, such as three honey plant
seeds and planters containing
seeds for ready germination. Their catalog price is refunded
with the first $5.00 order.   Catalog 50¢.

TERRA-PHERNALIA, EARTH-ORIENTED IMPORTS
P.O. Box 504
Milbrae, CA 94030

PRODUCT:

inflatable greenhouses

Terra-Phernalia has inflatable greenhouses in four sizes
which are engineered for growers of flora who are on limited
budgets and have limited space for growing. Also for those
who do not wish permanent
installations on the space
available. The four sizes offered are: mini, 25" wide x
25" high x 19" long; small,
27" x 29" x 35"; medium,
38" x 36" x 43"; and large,
48" x 45" x 52". All inflation
valves are self-sealing and are
complete with outside weather
seals. The small, medium and

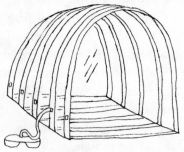

INFLATABLE GREENHOUSE
(WITH PUMP)

large models are ventilated at both ends by use of zippered
end-flaps with snap tie backs. Mini models are likewise e-
quipped, but only on one end. All models are complete with
six reinforced exterior tie down tabs. All models are also
complete with two reinforced interior suspension tabs for
Gro-Lux type lights and come with a reinforced thermometer
ring and electrical cord entry. There are other accessories included as well. Not one single tool is required to erect these
greenhouses. The company says that they are ready to use in
20 minutes after the package arrives.

Catalog free.

THON'S GARDEN MUMS
4815 Oak Street
Crystal Lake, IL 60014

PRODUCT:

chrysanthemums

This is a small family-owned business which breeds and produces Garden Chrysanthemums as a specialty. All of their

CHRYSANTHEMUM

efforts are applied to this one product. To the best of the company's knowledge, there is no other firm in the country devoting all of its efforts to chrysanthemums. Thon's Garden Mums operate one of the most modern horticultural plants in the country. They ship these Garden Chrysanthemums via mail order only. For a small family-owned business they have a beautifully put together catalog with all colored photographs of their varieties of chrysanthemums.

Catalog free.

WILLIAM TRICKER, INC.
7125 Tanglewood Drive
Independence, OH 44131

PRODUCTS:

aquatic plants   goldfish   water lilies

This very interesting catalog has beautiful color photographs of water lilies in colors from an almost iridescent blue to bright red. William Tricker, Inc., is in its 80th year of leadership in the field of water lily and aquatic plant culture. The late William Tricker, originator of water lily culture in the

WILLIAM TRICKER, INC. (Cont'd)

United States, was born in England. After receiving his apprenticeship in botany, he came to the United States in 1885. Upon the death of William Tricker, his son, Charles L. Tricker, took over the management of the business. It increased so rapidly that in 1927 he found it necessary to move his business to

WATER LILY

Saddle River, New Jersey. Charles L. Tricker passed away in 1961. At this time his son-in-law, Wilfred V. Schmidin, took over the management of the company. He has also spent his entire life in the field of horticulture and the growing of aquatic plants. Today they serve not only the United States, but all nations as the world's largest producers of hardy and tropical water lilies and aquatic plants. The history of William Tricker, Inc., is an American success story. They have established an industry for the enjoyment of thousands of people. William Tricker, Inc., feature their own fiber glass pools. They have several shapes available, including some with waterfalls. They also have pumps, lights, heaters, fish food and several types of goldfish. They feature a special pool, plants and goldfish collection which would make any yard much more attractive, and the prices are quite reasonable.

Catalog 25¢.

OTIS S. TWILLEY SEED CO.
Salisbury, MD 21801

PRODUCTS:

ageratum	broccoli
alyssum	cabbage
aster	calendula
balsam	cantaloupes
beets	carnation
beans, green	carrots

cauliflower
celery
celosia
centaurea
coleus
collards
corn, ornamental
corn, sweet
cosmos
cucumber
dahlia
delphinium
dianthus
eggplant
endive
everlasting flowers
geranium
gladiolus
gloriosa daisy
gypsophila
herbs
hibiscus
hollyhock
impatiens
kale
kohlrabi
lettuce
marigold
morning glory
mustard

nasturtiums
okra
onion
ornamental gourds
pansy
parsley
parsnips
peas
peppers
petunia
phlox
portulaca
pumpkin
radish
salvia
snapdragon
spinach
squash
strawflower
sweet pea
sweet william
swiss chard
tomatoes, sauce
tomatoes, table
tomatoes, yellow
turnips
verbena
watermelon
zinnia

CABBAGE

Otis S. Twilley says, "The seed business is my life and work. As a small boy I took great delight in my garden. By the time I was fifteen I had won a great many first prizes at fairs. It has been my good fortune to personally sell seed from the Florida Everglades to New England, from New Jersey to the Midwest. It is a real pleasure to personally know

143

OTIS S. TWILLEY SEED CO. (Cont'd)

so many of you." The Twilley Seed catalog is very well put together and has many interesting little bits of information by Mr. Twilley.

Catalog free.

W. J. UNWIN, LTD.
Impington Lane, Histon
Cambridge CB4 4LE England

PRODUCTS:

abutilon
acacia
achillea
acroclinium
african violet
ageratum
agrostemma
alstroemeria
alyssum
amaranthus
anagallis
anchusa
anemone
angelica
annual flowers
antirrhinum
aquilegia
arabis
aralia sieboldii
arctotis
asparagus
asparagus meyersii
asparagus, ornamental
asparagus plumosus
asparagus sprengeri
aster
aster, perennial
aubergine
aubretia

auricula
baby blue eyes
balm
balsam
barberton transvaal daisy
bartonia aurea
basil
basil, ornamental
beans, broad
beans, dwarf french
beans, runner
beet
begonia
begonia rex
bellis perennis
bells of ireland
bergamot
borage
borecole
broccoli
broom
brussels sprouts
burnet
burning bush
cabbage
cacalia
cactus
calabrese
calceolaria

calendula officinalis
campanula
canary creeper
candytuft
canna
canterbury bells
capiscum
caraway
carnation
carrot
castor oil plant
catmint
cauliflower
celeriac
celery
celosia
centaurea cyanus
centaurea imperalis
chard
cheiranthus
chelone
cherry pie
chervil
chicory
chinese lantern
chives
chrysanthemum
cineraria
cistus
clarkia
clary
cleome
cobaea scandens
cockscomb
coffea arabica
coleus
collections of vegetable seeds
columbine
convolvulus
cordyline
coreopsis
coriander
corn flower

corn salad
cosmea
courgette
cress
cucumber
culinary peas
cyclamen
cyperus
dahlia
daisy
delphinium
dianthus
diascia
digitalis
dill
dimorphotheca
double daisy
dracaena indivisa
eccremocarpus
echium
endive
erigeron
eryngium
eschscholtzia
eucalyptus
euphorbia
everlasting pea
exacum
feathered cockscomb
fennel
ficus bengalensis
flax
forget-me-not
foxglove
freesia
fuchsia
gaillardia
garden pink
garzania
geranium
gerbera
gesneria
geum

gloxinia
godetia
goldenrod
gossypium
gourds
grasses
grass, lawn
grevillea robusta
gypsophila
helenium
helichrysum
heliopsis
heliotrope
hemerocallis
herbs
heuchera
hibiscus
hollyhock
honesty
house plants
hyssop
iberis sempervirens
impatiens
incarvillea
inula
ipomea
jacaranda
jacobaea
jasione
kalanchoe
kale
kniphofia
kochia
kohlrabi
lagerstroemia
larkspur
lavatera
lavender
layia
leek
leontopodium alpinum
leptosiphon
lettuce

liatris
lilium
linaria
linum
livingstone daisy
lobelia
love-in-a-mist
love-lies-bleeding
lupinus
lychnis
lysimachia
lythrum
maize
mallow
marigold
marjoram
marrow
matricaria
mathiola
meconopsis baileyi
melon
mesembryanthemum
mexican sunflower
michaelmas daisy
mignonette
mimosa, acacia
mimosa, pudicia
mimulus
mina lobata
mint
mirabilis
molucella
monarda
morning glory
mushroom spawn
mustard
myosotis
naegelia
nasturtium
nemesia
nemophila
nepeta
nicotiana

nigella
night scented stock
onion
onion sets
ornamental cabbage
ornamental gourds
ornamental grasses
ornamental kale
pansy
parsley
parsnip
pea, everlasting
peas
penstemon
periwinkle
peruvian lily
petunia
phacelia
philodendron
phlox
physalis
pimpernel
pink, garden
polyanthus
poppies
portulaca
pot marigold
primrose
primula
pumpkin
punica granatum
purslane
pyrethrum
radish
red hot poker
rhodanthe
rhubarb
ricinus
rock cistus
rosemary
rose, polyantha
rudbeckia
rue

sage
saintpaulia
salpiglossis
salsify
salvia
salvia horminum
savory
savoy
saxifrage
scabious
schefflera digitata
schizanthus
scorzonera
seaholly
seakale
sea kale beet
sedum
sensitive flower
shallots
shell flower
siberian wallflower
snapdragon
solanum
solidago
sorrel
sparmannia
spider flower
spinach
star of the veldt
statice
stocks
stocks, night scented
stocks, virginian
stonecrop
strawberry
streptocarpus
sugar peas
sunflower
swede
sweet corn
sweet peas
sweet sultan
sweet violet

W. J. UNWIN, LTD. (Cont'd)

sweet william
swiss chard
tagetes
tarragon
thyme
tibetan poppy
tithonia speciosa
tobacco
tobacco plant
tomato
torenia fournieri
tritoma
trollius
tropaeolum
turnip

vegetable marrow
vegetable seed collections
vegetable spaghetti
verbascum
verbena
vinca
viola
violet
virginian stock
viscaria
wallflower
wallflower, siberian
winter cauliflower
xeranthemum
zea japonica
zinnia

This company from England has a catalog full of beautifully colored photographs of the vegetables and flowers they offer.

HYSSOP

Unwin Dahlias are known the world over. In their 1975 message they ask, "What would our great grandparents think about our newer varieties of flowers and vegetables? Would they agree that progress has been made? W. J. Unwin Ltd. are sure that they would, for undoubtedly there has been appreciable improvement, sometimes even spectacular and dramatic. Our forbears knew nothing of the great advantages given to present-day growers by the complete uniformity of habit, colour, size, shape and greater vigour of hybrids." Unwin is right: there certainly have been many improvements made. Unwin is the only seed firm of any size in the country (England)

W. J. UNWIN, LTD. (Cont'd)

which is still a strictly private family limited company. They are quite independent of any other firm or group of firms. The company is still entirely controlled and owned by members of the Unwin family. This company offers many interesting things, and as for the money exchange, perhaps your local bank can be of help to you if you desire to order from Unwin.

Catalog free.

VAN BOURGONDIEN BROTHERS
P.O. Box A
Babylon, NY 11702
PRODUCTS:

amaryllis	hardy perennials
begonias	house plants
caladiums	hybrid lilies
cannas	lily of the valley
clematis	roses
dahlias	small fruits
german iris	tree peonies
gladiolus	vegetables
ground covers	

LILY

Van Bourgondien Brothers has Holland domestic grown bulbs and plants. Their beautifully done catalog shows the flowers all in color plus all the other types of bulbs and plants they offer. They say they have the largest selection of rare and unusual bulbs as well as the general garden items. They have the Voo Doo bulbs that can be flowered without potting during the winter, and if planted outdoors in spring will make a palm-like plant. The flower is yellow-green with purple spots and is rather unusual.
Catalog free.

VARIOUS DESIGNS
Box 336
Montrose, IA 52639

PRODUCTS:

composters
electric smoke house
greenhouses
hand baler

shredder/mulcher
stackable cold frames
walk-in cooler

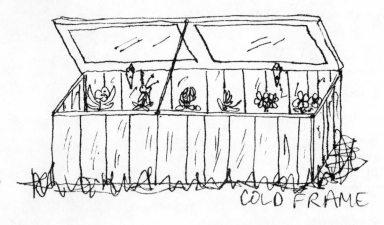

COLD FRAME

Various Designs sell plans by mail order for various designs of garden equipment and some greenhouse plans. They will be having other equipment plans in the near future. Their plans and information are hopefully designed so that even a handy child can make them. The shredder/mulcher is easy to build for your own rotary mower, and does not alter the operation of your mower. They have a 6 foot by 12 foot greenhouse that you can walk around in, and can supposedly be built for UNDER $25.00, and will hold hundreds of plants. Their hand baler allows you to bale your shredded mulch, leaves, grass or hay. Easy to build and will make a bale about one foot square by two feet long that is easy to handle with less waste. Various Designs composters are three different ways to turn your mulch into compost. They also have recipes available for 28 different things you can smoke in the electric smoke house.

Catalog 50¢.

VERMONT-WARE
Richmond Road, P.O. Box E
Hinesburg, VT 05461

PRODUCTS:

town and country carts

Vermont-Ware has been building heavy-duty truck bodies
for the past 20 years, and, as they also did spare-time gardening and working around their place, they had need to move

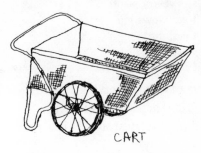
CART

and haul things. They decided
to improve the wheelbarrow,
and finally came up with a
special cart. They say it is easy
to maneuver by women, older
folks, and even children. A
few details that Vermont-Ware
feels will make it one of the
most hard-working and reliable
tools you've ever owned are: large 20" wide-tread semi-
pneumatic tires for easy stair climbing and rolling; functional-
ly place wheels for easy pushing or pulling and balance;
holds two to three times as much as a wheelbarrow; is narrow
enough to fit through doorways; is tight-welded, lightweight
all steel body with wear-resistant finish; and it stores easily—
just hang on a hook or stand on end. Vermont-Ware says
they have been especially pleased to hear about the interesting ways people have found to use their carts.

Brochure free.

WAYNESBORO NURSERIES, INC.
P.O. Box 987
Waynesboro, VA 22980

PRODUCTS:

apple trees   blackberry plants
apricot trees   blueberry plants
asparagus   boysenberry plants

bulbs
cannas
cherry trees
chrysanthemums
dewberries
dwarf fruit trees
evergreens, broadleaved
evergreens, coniferous
fig trees
gladiolus
grape vines
ground covers
hedges
iris
nectarine trees

nut trees
paw paw
peach trees
pear trees
peonies
persimmon trees
plum trees
raspberry plants
rhubarb
roses
shrubs, flowering
strawberry plants
trees, flowering
trees, shade
vines

Since 1922 Virginia's largest growers have been serving planters. Waynesboro Nurseries operate 2,200 acres, of which approximately 1,000 acres are planted in nursery stock. This company states they have one of the most complete lines of plant material in the nursery industry, consisting of fruit trees, berry plants, nut trees, grape vines, flowering and shade trees, evergreens, flowering shrubs, vines, ground covers, bulbs, roses and perennials. Visitors are always welcome at their nurseries. Not only can you look at their vast assortment of plant material and their packing and shipping facilities, you can also pick up and take home your selection of things from them. They also have some garden supplies available that are not listed in their catalog. Waynesboro Nurseries encourage fruit tree plantings consisting of assorted varieties so as to provide for cross pollination.

CHERRIES

Catalog free upon request.

WESTERN MAINE FOREST NURSERY
36 Elm Street
Fryeburg, ME 04037

PRODUCTS:

arborvitae	fir	spruce
balsam fir	hemlock	yew
	pine	

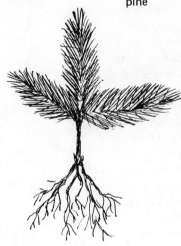

SCOTCH PINE
(SEEDLING)

Western Maine Forest Nursery supplies evergreen stock from 2 to 5 years old which they grow from seed. Even though they have a mail order retail business, their sales are primarily to commercial nurseries, Christmas tree growers, garden centers, etc. Their stock is hardy and is grown in Maine. They are in their 52nd year of growing evergreens for the wholesale and retail trade. They sell their trees in nice sized amounts for the retail market, as well as the wholesale market, because their trees are bundled in lots of 5, 10 on up to 100 or 1,000. Their catalog is very well presented and the trees are shown in color.

Catalog free.

WILSON BROTHERS FLORAL CO., INC.
Roachdale, IN 46172

PRODUCTS:

african violets
begonias
bird of paradise
bougainvillea
cactus
carnation
chenille plant
china bells
christmas cactus
coleus
columnea
crossandra
episcia
fern
flamingo flower
fly trap plant
fuchsia
gardenia
geraniums
goldfish plant
hibiscus
hindu rope

hoya
lantana
lemon tree
lipstick vine
norfolk pine
norse fire plant
orange tree
orchid
passion flower
patience plants
persian carpet
petunias
philodendron
piggy-back plant
roses
shrimp plant
string of hearts
string of pearls
sultana
wax vine
zebra plant

Wilson Brothers Floral Co., Inc., puts out a very colorful catalog showing many varieties of flowering and decorative plants, mainly to be grown in the house or a protected area. They have a very nice selection of gardening aids featured, as well as the plants. They feature several unusual types of house plants, such as the epsicia (vining violets), a very bright colored miniature orchid, and the gooseberry plant.

PRAYER PLANT

Catalog free.

WORLD GARDENS
845 Pacific Ave., Dept. A
Willows, CA 95988

PRODUCTS:

cut flowers
Hawaiian perfumes

tropical plants
tropical seeds

BIRD OF
PARADISE

World Gardens has very unusual plants and seeds for sale. According to them, eighty percent of their seeds and plants for sale are not found in the United States. They have tropical seeds and plants from around the world, and Hawaiian perfumes. Their cut flowers (which are from Hawaii) consist basically of anthuriums, birds of paradise, red ginger, orchid sprays and assorted foliage, and are shipped from March first to December eighteenth of each year. They ship plants and seeds from March first to November tenth (approximately) each year. However, they do ship their perfumes year round. They ship by mail order only.

Catalogs free.

W-W GRINDER CORPORATION
2957 N. Market
Wichita, KS 67219

PRODUCT:

grinder/shredder

All W-W grinder/shredders are equipped to handle dry and
wet materials. The standard ¾" perforated screen furnished
with the grinder/shredder is
for grinding dry and friable
material. Ideal for such materials as dry leaves, straw,
shrub and tree trimmings, or
for finishing compost to pot-
ting-soil consistency. If the
material is exceedingly wet,
every other bar or every other
roller-rod can be removed until the right gaps are provided
to attain the desired grind and at the same time handle the
higher moisture material. All of the W-W grinder/shredders
are manufactured with gray iron cast side, which gives life-
time service to the users.

COMPOST GRINDER/SHREDDER

Catalog free.

MASTER INDEX

ABELIA
  Clyde Robin Seed Co., Inc.
  Silver Falls Nursery
ABIES
  Clyde Robin Seed Co., Inc.
  F. W. Schumacher Co.
ABRONIA
  DeGiorgi Company, Inc.
  Clyde Robin Seed Co., Inc.
ABUTILON
  DeGiorgi Company, Inc.
  Geo. W. Park Seed Co., Inc.
  W. J. Unwin, Ltd.
ACACIA
  DeGiorgi Company, Inc.
  Geo. W. Park Seed Co., Inc.
  Clyde Robin Seed Co., Inc.
  F. W. Schumacher Co.
  W. J. Unwin, Ltd.
ACACIA mimosa (see Mimosa,
  acacia)
ACAMPTOPAPPUS
  Clyde Robin Seed Co., Inc.
ACANTHUS
  DeGiorgi Company, Inc.
  Geo. W. Park Seed Co., Inc.

ACER
  Clyde Robin Seed Co., Inc.
  F. W. Schumacher Co.
ACHILLEA
  W. Atlee Burpee Co.
  DeGiorgi Company, Inc.
  Inter-State Nurseries
  L. L. Olds Seed Company
  Geo. W. Park Seed Co., Inc.
  Clyde Robin Seed Co., Inc.
  W. J. Unwin, Ltd.
ACHIMENES
  Geo. W. Park Seed Co., Inc.
ACHLYS
  Clyde Robin Seed Co., Inc.
ACID, carbolic crystals
  Diamond International Corp.
ACONITUM
  DeGiorgi Company, Inc.
  Geo. W. Park Seed Co., Inc.
  Clyde Robin Seed Co., Inc.   Clyde
ACROCLINIUM
  W. Atlee Burpee Co.
  DeGiorgi Company, Inc.
  L. L. Olds Seed Company
  Geo. W. Park Seed Co., Inc.   Inc.
  W. J. Unwin, Ltd.

157

ACTAEA
  Clyde Robin Seed Co., Inc.
ADANSONIA
  Clyde Robin Seed Co., Inc.
ADENOSTOMA
  Clyde Robin Seed Co., Inc.
ADIANTUM
  Clyde Robin Seed Co., Inc.
  Stokes Seeds, Inc.
ADONIS
  DeGiorgi Company, Inc.
  Geo. W. Park Seed Co., Inc.
AESCULUS
  F. W. Schumacher Co.
AFRICAN daisy (see Daisy, african)
AFRICAN violet plants
  R. H. Shumway Seedsman
AFRICAN violets
  W. Atlee Burpee Co.
  Fischer Greenhouses
  Gurney Seed & Nurseries Co.
  Geo. W. Park Seed Co., Inc.
  W. J. Unwin, Ltd.
  Wilson Brothers Floral Co.,
    Inc.
AFRICAN violet seeds
  R. H. Shumway Seedsman
AGAPANTHUS
  Geo. W. Park Seed Co., Inc.
AGASTACHE
  Clyde Robin Seed Co., Inc.
AGATHAEA
  Geo. W. Park Seed Co., Inc.
AGAVE
  Clyde Robin Seed Co., Inc.
AGERATUM
  W. Atlee Burpee Co.
  D. V. Burrell Seed Growers Co.
  Henry Field Seed & Nursery
    Co.
  Gurney Seed & Nursery Co.
  Joseph Harris Co., Inc.
  Jackson & Perkins Co.
  J. W. Jung Seed Co.
  L. L. Olds Seed Company
  Geo. W. Park Seed Co., Inc.
  Seedway, Inc.
  Stokes Seeds, Inc.

  Otis S. Twilley Seed Co.
  W. J. Unwin, Ltd.
AGRICULTURAL field chemicals
  Barzen of Minneapolis, Inc.
AGRICULTURAL field seeds
  Barzen of Minneapolis, Inc.
AGROSTEMA
  DeGiorgi Company, Inc.
  L. L. Olds Seed Company
  W. J. Unwin, Ltd.
AGROSTIS
  DeGiorgi Company, Inc.
  Geo. W. Park Seed Co., Inc.
AILANTHUS
  Clyde Robin Seed Co., Inc.
  F. W. Schumacher Co.
AIR fern
  J. W. Jung Seed Co.
AIR inlet vents
  Redwood Domes
AIR sprayers
  D. B. Smith Co.
AJUGA
  Henry Field Seed & Nursery
    Co.
  Inter-State Nurseries
  Silver Falls Nursery
ALBERTA
  Clyde Robin Seed Co. Inc.
ALBIZIZ
  Clyde Robin Seed Co., Inc.
ALBIZZIA
  F. W. Schumacher Co.
ALFALFA
  L. L. Olds Seed Company
  R. H. Shumway Seedsman
ALFALFA tea
  R. H. Shumway Seedsman
ALLIUM
  DeGiorgi Company, Inc.
  Farmer Seed & Nursery Com-
    pany
  Geo. W. Park Seed Co., Inc.
  Clyde Robin Seed Co., Inc.
ALMOND, flowering
  Gurney Seed & Nursery Co.
  Inter-State Nurseries

158

Thomas B. Kyle, Jr. — Spring
Hill Nurseries Co.
L. L. Olds Seed Company
Silver Falls Nursery
ALMOND, garden
Gurney Seed & Nursery Co.
ALMOND tree
Burgess Seed and Plant Co.
Ferndale Gardens
Thomas B. Kyle, Jr. — Spring
Hill Nurseries Co.
Lakeland Nurseries Sales
ALNUS
F. W. Schumacher Co.
ALOES
DeGiorgi Company, Inc.
ALOE, tiger
Geo. W. Park Seed Co., Inc.
ALONSEA
DeGiorgi Company, Inc.
ALPINE currant
J. W. Jung Seed Co.
ALSTROEMERIA
Geo. W. Park Seed Co., Inc.
W. J. Unwin, Ltd.
ALTHEA
Henry Field Seed & Nursery
Co.
Gurney Seed & Nursery Co.
Inter-State Nurseries
Geo. W. Park Seed Co., Inc.
ALTHEA hollyhock (see Holly-
hock, althea)
ALUMINUM paint
Diamond International Corp.
ALYSSUM
W. Atlee Burpee Co.
D. V. Burrell Seed Growers Co.
DeGiorgi Company, Inc.
Henry Field Seed & Nursery Co.
Gurney Seed & Nursery Co.
Joseph Harris Co., Inc.
Jackson & Perkins Co.
J. W. Jung Seed Co.
L. L. Olds Seed Company
Geo. W. Park Seed Co., Inc.
Seedway, Inc.
Stokes Seeds, Inc.

Otis S. Twilley Seed Co.
W. J. Unwin, Ltd.
AMARANTHUS
W. Atlee Burpee Co.
DeGiorgi Company, Inc.
Henry Field Seed & Nursery Co.
Joseph Harris Co., Inc.
L. L. Olds Seed Company
Stokes Seeds, Inc.
W. J. Unwin, Ltd.
AMARYLLIS
W. Atlee Burpee Co.
Henry Field Seed & Nursery Co.
Gurney Seed & Nursery Co.
J. W. Jung Seed Co.
Thomas B. Kyle, Jr. — Spring
Hill Nurseries Co.
L. L. Olds Seed Company
Geo. W. Park Seed Co., Inc.
Van Bourgondien Brothers
AMARYLLIS, hardy
Inter-State Nurseries
AMAZON lily
Geo. W. Park Seed Co., Inc.
AMELANCHIER
Clyde Robin Seed Co., Inc.
F. W. Schumacher Co.
AMMOBIUM
Geo. W. Park Seed Co., Inc.
AMORPHA
F. W. Schumacher Co.
AMPELOPSIS
F. W. Schumacher Co.
AMSONIA
Geo. W. Park Seed Co., Inc.
ANAPHALIS
Geo. W. Park Seed Co., Inc.
ANAGALIS
DeGiorgi Company, Inc.
W. J. Unwin, Ltd.
ANCHUSA
W. Atlee Burpee Co.
DeGiorgi Company, Inc.
J. W. Jung Seed Co.
L. L. Olds Seed Company
Geo. W. Park Seed Co., Inc.
W. J. Unwin, Ltd.

ANDROMEDA
Ferndale Gardens
ANDROSACE
Geo. W. Park Seed Co., Inc.
ANEMONE
W. Atlee Burpee Co.
DeGiorgi Company, Inc.
Ferndale Gardens
L. L. Olds Seed Company
Geo. W. Park Seed Co., Inc.
Clyde Robin Seed Co., Inc.
W. J. Unwin, Ltd.
ANEMONE bulbs
R. H. Shumway Seedsman
ANEMONE seeds
R. H. Shumway Seedsman
ANGEL flower
Thomas B. Kyle, Jr. — Spring
Hill Nurseries Co.
ANGELICA
W. J. Unwin, Ltd.
ANGEL'S trumpet
Stokes Seeds, Inc.
ANGETICA
Clyde Robin Seed Co., Inc.
ANISE
Burgess Seed and Plant Co.
W. Atlee Burpee Co.
L. L. Olds Seed Company
ANNOBIUM
DeGiorgi Company, Inc.
ANNUAL flowers
Henry Field Seed & Nursery
Co.
Gurney Seed & Nursery Co.
W. J. Unwin, Ltd.
ANNUAL larkspur (see Larkspur,
annual)
ANNUAL phlox (see Phlox, annual)
ANNUALS
Boatman Nursery & Seed Co.
Inter-State Nurseries
ANPELOPSIS
DeGiorgi Company, Inc.
ANTHEMIS
W. Atlee Burpee Co.
DeGiorgi Company, Inc.
Thomas B. Kyle, Jr. — Spring

Hill Nurseries Co.
Geo. W. Park Seed Co., Inc.
ANTHOCEPHALUM
Clyde Robin Seed Co., Inc.
ANTHURIUM
Ferndale Gardens
Gurney Seed & Nursery Co.
Geo. W. Park Seed Co., Inc.
ANTIGONON
DeGiorgi Company, Inc.
Geo. W. Park Seed Co., Inc.
ANTIRHINUM
DeGiorgi Company, Inc.
W. J. Unwin, Ltd.
ANTIRRHINIAN
Geo. W. Park Seed Co., Inc.
ANTIRRHINUM
W. Atlee Burpee Co.
Joseph Harris Co., Inc.
L. L. Olds Seed Company
APHANOSTEPHUS
Geo. W. Park Seed Co., Inc.
APHELANDRA
Geo. W. Park Seed Co., Inc.
APOCYNUM
Clyde Robin Seed Co., Inc.
APPLE trees
Armstrong Nurseries, Inc.
Burgess Seed and Plant Co.
Farmer Seed & Nursery Com-
pany
Henry Field Seed & Nursery
Co.
Gurney Seed & Nursery Co.
Inter-State Nurseries
J. W. Jung Seed Co.
Thomas B. Kyle, Jr. — Spring
Hill Nurseries Co.
Lakeland Nurseries Sales
Lawson's Nursery
Henry Leuthardt Nurseries, Inc.
New York State Fruit Testing
Cooperative Association
L. L. Olds Seed Company
Rabbit Hop Nursery
R. H. Shumway Seedsman
Stark Bro's Nurseries
Waynesboro Nurseries, Inc.

APRICOT trees
  Armstrong Nurseries, Inc.
  Burgess Seed and Plant Co.
  Farmer Seed & Nursery Company
  Henry Field Seed & Nursery Co.
  Inter-State Nurseries
  J. W. Jung Seed Co.
  Thomas B. Kyle, Jr. — Spring
    Hill Nurseries Co.
  Henry Leuthardt Nurseries, Inc.
  Stark Bro's Nurseries
  Waynesboro Nurseries, Inc.
APRONS
  The Walter T. Kelley Company
AQUATIC plants
  William Tricker, Inc.
AQUILEGIA
  W. Atlee Burpee Co.
  Joseph Harris Co., Inc.
  Geo. W. Park Seed Co., Inc.
  Clyde Robin Seed Co., Inc.
AQUILLEGIA
  DeGiorgi Company, Inc.
  J. W. Jung Seed Co.
  L. L. Olds Seed Company
  Stokes Seeds, Inc.
  W. J. Unwin, Ltd.
ARABIS
  W. Atlee Burpee Co.
  DeGiorgi Company, Inc.
  Joseph Harris Co., Inc.
  L. L. Olds Seed Company
  Stokes Seeds, Inc.
  W. J. Unwin, Ltd.
ARABIS, rock cress
  Geo. W. Park Seed Co., Inc.
ARALIA
  Geo. W. Park Seed Co., Inc.
ARALIA seiboldii
  W. J. Unwin, Ltd.
ARBORVITAE
  Carino Nurseries
  Henry Field Seed & Nursery
    Co.
  Girard Nurseries
  Gurney Seed & Nursery Co.
  Silver Falls Nursery
  Western Maine Forest Nursery

ARBUTUS
  Clyde Robin Seed Co., Inc.
ARCHONTOPHOENIX
  Clyde Robin Seed Co., Inc.
ARCTOMECON
  Clyde Robin Seed Co., Inc.
ARCTOSTAPHYLOS
  Clyde Robin Seed Co., Inc.
  F. W. Schumacher Co.
ARCTOTIS
  W. Atlee Burpee Co.
  DeGiorgi Company, Inc.
  L. L. Olds Seed Company
  Geo. W. Park Seed Co., Inc.
  W. J. Unwin, Ltd.
ARENARIA
  DeGiorgi Company, Inc.
  Geo. W. Park Seed Co., Inc.
ARENIA
  Clyde Robin Seed Co., Inc.
ARGEMONE
  Clyde Robin Seed Co., Inc.
ARISTOLOCHIA
  DeGiorgi Company, Inc.
  F. W. Schumacher Co.
ARMERIA
  DeGiorgi Company, Inc.
  L. L. Olds Seed Company
  Geo. W. Park Seed Co., Inc.
  Clyde Robin Seed Co., Inc.
  Stokes Seeds, Inc.
ARNICA
  Geo. W. Park Seed Co., Inc.
  Clyde Robin Seed Co., Inc.
ARONIA
  F. W. Schumacher Co.
ARTEMISIA
  Gurney Seed & Nursery Co.
  Inter-State Nurseries
  J. W. Jung Seed Co.
  Thomas B. Kyle, Jr. — Spring
    Hill Nurseries Co.
  Clyde Robin Seed Co., Inc.
ARTICHOKE
  Burgess Seed and Plant Co.
  DeGiorgi Company, Inc.
  Ferndale Gardens
  Gurney Seed & Nursery Co.

161

Thomas B. Kyle, Jr. — Spring
  Hill Nurseries Co.
Lakeland Nurseries Sales
Earl May Seed & Nursery Co.
R. H. Shumway Seedsman
W. J. Unwin, Ltd.
ARTIFICIAL soils
  Joseph Harris Co., Inc.
ARUNEUS
  Clyde Robin Seed Co., Inc.
ASCIEPIA
  DeGiorgi Company, Inc.
ASCLEPIAS
  Geo. W. Park Seed Co., Inc.
  Clyde Robin Seed Co., Inc.
ASH tree
  Henry Field Seed & Nursery Co.
  Gurney Seed & Nursery Co.
  Inter-State Nurseries
  J. W. Jung Seed Co.
  Thomas B. Kyle, Jr. — Spring
    Hill Nurseries Co.
ASIMINA
  F. W. Schumacher Co.
ASPARAGUS
  Brittingham Plant Farms
  Burgess Seed and Plant Co.
  W. Atlee Burpee Co.
  D. V. Burrell Seed Growers Co.
  DeGiorgi Company, Inc.
  Farmer Seed & Nursery Com-
    pany
  Ferndale Gardens
  Henry Field Seed & Nursery Co.
  Gurney Seed & Nursery Co.
  Inter-State Nurseries
  Jackson & Perkins Co.
  J. W. Jung Seed Co.
  Thomas B. Kyle, Jr. — Spring
    Hill Nurseries Co.
  Lakeland Nurseries Sales
  Earl May Seed & Nursery Co.
  L. L. Olds Seed Company
  Seedway, Inc.
  Stark Bro's Nurseries
  Stokes Seeds, Inc.
  W. J. Unwin, Ltd.
  Waynesboro Nurseries, Inc.

ASPARAGUS fern
  W. Atlee Burpee Co.
  Geo. W. Park Seed Co., Inc.
ASPARAGUS meyersii
  W. J. Unwin, Ltd.
ASPARAGUS, ornamental
  W. J. Unwin, Ltd.
ASPARAGUS plumosis
  W. J. Unwin, Ltd.
ASPARAGUS roots
  R. H. Shumway Seedsman
ASPARAGUS seeds
  Joseph Harris Co., Inc.
  R. H. Shumway Seedsman
ASPARAGUS sprengeri
  W. J. Unwin, Ltd.
ASPERULA
  DeGiorgi Company, Inc.
ASPHODELUS
  Geo. W. Park Seed Co., Inc.
ASTER, annual
  Geo. W. Park Seed Co., Inc.
ASTER, perennial
  Geo. W. Park Seed Co., Inc.
  W. J. Unwin, Ltd.
ASTER plants
  R. H. Shumway Seedsman
ASTERS
  W. Atlee Burpee Co.
  D. V. Burrell Seed Growers Co.
  DeGiorgi Company, Inc.
  Henry Field Seed & Nursery Co.
  Gurney Seed & Nursery Co.
  Joseph Harris Co., Inc.
  Inter-State Nurseries
  Jackson & Perkins Co.
  J. W. Jung Seed Co.
  Thomas B. Kyle, Jr. — Spring
    Hill Nurseries Co.
  Earl May Seed & Nursery Co.
  L. L. Olds Seed Company
  Clyde Robin Seed Co., Inc.
  Seedway, Inc.
  Stokes Seeds, Inc.
  Otis S. Twilley Seed Co.
  W. J. Unwin, Ltd.
ASTILBE
  W. Atlee Burpee Co.

Henry Field Seed & Nursery Co.
Thomas B. Kyle, Jr. — Spring
  Hill Nurseries Co.
Geo. W. Park Seed Co., Inc.
ATRIPLEX
  Clyde Robin Seed Co., Inc.
AUBERGINE
  W. J. Unwin, Ltd.
AUBRETIA
  Joseph Harris Co., Inc.
  Geo. W. Park Seed Co., Inc.
  W. J. Unwin, Ltd.
AUBRIETA
  W. Atlee Burpee Co.
  DeGiorgi Company, Inc.
  Seedway, Inc.
  Stokes Seeds, Inc.
AURICULA
  W. J. Unwin, Ltd.
AUSTRIAN pine
  DeGiorgi Company, Inc.
AUTUMN olive, cardinal
  J. W. Jung Seed Co.
AVENA
  Geo. W. Park Seed Co., Inc.
AZALEA mollis
  J. W. Jung Seed Co.
AZALEAS
  Burgess Seed and Plant Co.
  W. Atlee Burpee Co.
  Farmer Seed & Nursery Com-
    pany
  Ferndale Gardens
  Henry Field Seed & Nursery Co.
  Girard Nurseries
  Gurney Seed & Nursery Co.
  Inter-State Nurseries
  Thomas B. Kyle, Jr. — Spring
    Hill Nurseries Co.
  Lakeland Nurseries Sales
  Geo. W. Park Seed Co., Inc.
  F. W. Schumacher Co.
  Silver Falls Nursery
AZURE caryopteris (see Caryop-
  teris, azure)
BABTISTIA
  DeGiorgi Company, Inc.

BABY blue eyes
  W. Atlee Burpee Co.
  Geo. W. Park Seed Co., Inc.
  W. J. Unwin, Ltd.
BABY rose mini (see Mini, baby
  rose)
BABY'S breath
  W. Atlee Burpee Co.
  DeGiorgi Company, Inc.
  Ferndale Gardens
  Henry Field Seed & Nursery Co.
  Gurney Seed & Nursery Co.
  Joseph Harris Co., Inc.
  Jackson & Perkins Co.
  J. W. Jung Seed Co.
  Thomas B. Kyle, Jr. — Spring
    Hill Nurseries Co.
  Lakeland Nurseries Sales
  Geo. W. Park Seed Co., Inc.
  Seedway, Inc.
BABY evergreens and shrubs
  Girard Nurseries
BACCHARIUS
  Clyde Robin Seed Co., Inc.
BACHELOR'S button
  W. Atlee Burpee Co.
  DeGiorgi Company, Inc.
  Henry Field Seed & Nursery Co.
  Gurney Seed & Nursery Co.
  Joseph Harris Co., Inc.
  Jackson & Perkins Co.
  J. W. Jung Seed Co.
  L. L. Olds Seed Company
  Geo. W. Park Seed Co., Inc.
  Seedway, Inc.
  Stokes Seeds, Inc.
BAERIA
  Clyde Robin Seed Co., Inc.
BAILEYA
  Clyde Robin Seed Co., Inc.
BALM
  Burgess Seed and Plant Co.
  DeGiorgi Company, Inc.
  L. L. Olds Seed Company
  W. J. Unwin, Ltd.
BALLOON flower
  Henry Field Seed & Nursery Co.
  Gurney Seed & Nursery Co.

BALLOON vine
DeGiorgi Company, Inc.
BALSAM
W. Atlee Burpee Co.
D. V. Burrell Seed Growers Co.
DeGiorgi Company, Inc.
Henry Field Seed & Nursery Co.
Gurney Seed & Nursery Co.
Joseph Harris Co., Inc.
Jackson & Perkins Co.
J. W. Jung Seed Co.
L. L. Olds Seed Company
Geo. W. Park Seed Co., Inc.
Stokes Seeds, Inc.
Otis S. Twilley Seed Co.
W. J. Unwin, Ltd.
BALSAM fir
Western Maine Forest Nursery
BALSAM pear
DeGiorgi Company, Inc.
BAMBOO
Ferndale Gardens
Gurney Seed & Nursery Co.
Lakeland Nurseries Sales
BANANA tree
R. H. Shumway Seedsman
BAPTISIA
Geo. W. Park Seed Co., Inc.
BARBERRY
W. Atlee Burpee Co.
Henry Field Seed & Nursery Co.
Gurney Seed & Nursery Co.
Inter-State Nurseries
J. W. Jung Seed Co.
Thomas B. Kyle, Jr. – Spring
    Hill Nurseries Co.
L. L. Olds Seed Company
Silver Falls Nursery
BARBERTON transvaal daisy
W. J. Unwin, Ltd.
BARTONIA
DeGiorgi Company, Inc.
Geo. W. Park Seed Co., Inc.
BARTONIA aurea
W. J. Unwin, Ltd.
BASIL
DeGiorgi Company, Inc.
Joseph Harris Co., Inc.

J. W. Jung Seed Co.
L. L. Olds Seed Company
Geo. W. Park Seed Co., Inc.
W. J. Unwin, Ltd.
BASIL, ornamental
W. Atlee Burpee Co.
Joseph Harris Co., Inc.
Seedway, Inc.
Stokes Seeds, Inc.
W. J. Unwin, Ltd.
BASIL, sweet
Burgess Seed and Plant Co.
W. Atlee Burpee Co.
BASKETS of gold
Thomas B. Kyle, Jr. – Spring
    Hill Nurseries Co.
BAUHINIA
F. W. Schumacher Co.
BEANS, broad
W. J. Unwin, Ltd.
BEANS, dry
Burgess Seed and Plant Co.
W. Atlee Burpee Co.
DeGiorgi Company, Inc.
Farmer Seed & Nursery Com-
    pany
Henry Field Seed & Nursery Co.
Joseph Harris Co., Inc.
Johnny's Selected Seeds
J. W. Jung Seed Co.
Earl May Seed & Nursery Co.
Nichols Garden Nursery
L. L. Olds Seed Company
Seedway, Inc.
R. H. Shumway Seedsman
Stokes Seeds, Inc.
BEANS, dwarf french
W. J. Unwin, Ltd.
BEANS, fava
Joseph Harris Co., Inc.
BEANS, field
Joseph Harris Co., Inc.
BEANS, green
Burgess Seed and Plant Co.
W. Atlee Burpee Co.
D. V. Burrell Seed Growers Co.
DeGiorgi Company, Inc.

Farmer Seed & Nursery Company
Henry Field Seed & Nursery Co.
Gurney Seed & Nursery Co.
Joseph Harris Co., Inc.
Jackson & Perkins Co.
Johnny's Selected Seeds
J. W. Jung Seed Co.
Kitayawa Seed Company
Earl May Seed & Nursery Co.
Nichols Garden Nursery
L. L. Olds Seed Company
Seedway, Inc.
R. H. Shumway Seedsman
Spring Hill Farm
Stokes Seeds, Inc.
Otis S. Twilley Seed Co.
BEANS, runner
W. J. Unwin, Ltd.
BEARDED iris (see Iris, bearded)
BEAUTY bush
Gurney Seed & Nursery Co.
Inter-State Nurseries
J. W. Jung Seed Co.
BEE brushes
Diamond International Corp.
BEECH
Silver Falls Nursery
BEE escape boards
Diamond International Corp.
BEE escapes (see Escapes, bee)
BEE feeders (see Feeders, bee)
BEE hive paint
Diamond International Corp.
BEE hives (see Hives, bee)
BEEKEEPING supplies
Dadant & Sons, Inc.
Sunstream
BEE pins
The Walter T. Kelley Company
BEES and queens
Diamond International Corp.
The Walter T. Kelley Company
BEE smokers (see Smokers, bee)
BEE supplies
Leahy Manufacturing Co.
BEE veils
Diamond International Corp.

BEET plants
Evans Plant Company
BEETS
W. Atlee Burpee Co.
D. V. Burrell Seed Growers Co.
DeGiorgi Company, Inc.
Farmer Seed & Nursery Company
Henry Field Seed & Nursery Co.
Gurney Seed & Nursery Co.
Joseph Harris Co., Inc.
Jackson & Perkins Co.
Johnny's Selected Seeds
J. W. Jung Seed Co.
Earl May Seed & Nursery Co.
Nichols Garden Nursery
L. L. Olds Seed Company
Seedway, Inc.
R. H. Shumway Seedsman
Spring Hill Farm
Stokes Seeds, Inc.
Otis S. Twilley Seed Co.
W. J. Unwin, Ltd.
BEETS, novelty
Stokes Seeds, Inc.
BEGONIA
Burgess Seed and Plant Co.
W. Atlee Burpee Co.
DeGiorgi Company, Inc.
Farmer Seed & Nursery Company
Ferndale Gardens
Henry Field Seed & Nursery Co.
Gurney Seed & Nursery Co.
Joseph Harris Co., Inc.
Inter-State Nurseries
J. W. Jung Seed Co.
Thomas B. Kyle, Jr. — Spring Hill Nurseries Co.
Lakeland Nurseries Sales
Earl May Seed & Nursery Co.
L. L. Olds Seed Company
Geo. W. Park Seed Co., Inc.
Stokes Seeds, Inc.
W. J. Unwin, Ltd.
Van Bourgondien Brothers
Wilson Brothers Floral Co., Inc.

BEGONIA bulbs
  R. H. Shumway Seedsman
BEGONIA plants
  R. H. Shumway Seedsman
BEGONIA rex
  W. J. Unwin, Ltd.
BEGONIA seed
  Joseph Harris Co., Inc.
  J. W. Jung Seed Co.
BEGONIAS, fibrous
  Jackson & Perkins Co.
BELAMCANDA
  Geo. W. Park Seed Co., Inc.
  Clyde Robin Seed Co., Inc.
BELLFLOWER
  Thomas B. Kyle, Jr. — Spring
    Hill Nurseries Co.
  Geo. W. Park Seed Co., Inc.
  Stokes Seeds, Inc.
BELLIS
  DeGiorgi Company, Inc.
  Joseph Harris Co., Inc.
  Geo. W. Park Seed Co., Inc.
BELLIS monstrosum
  L. L. Olds Seed Company
BELLIS perennis
  W. Atlee Burpee Co.
  Stokes Seeds, Inc.
  W. J. Unwin, Ltd.
BELLOWS
  The Walter T. Kelley Company
BELLS of ireland
  W. Atlee Burpee Co.
  D. V. Burrell Seed Growers Co.
  DeGiorgi Company, Inc.
  Henry Field Seed & Nursery Co.
  Gurney Seed & Nursery Co.
  Joseph Harris Co., Inc.
  Jackson & Perkins Co.
  J. W. Jung Seed Co.
  L. L. Olds Seed Company
  Geo. W. Park Seed Co., Inc.
  Seedway, Inc.
  Stokes Seeds, Inc.
  W. J. Unwin, Ltd.
BENT grass
  DeGiorgi Company, Inc.
  L. L. Olds Seed Company

BENZALDEHYDE
  Diamond International Corp.
BERBERIS
  F. W. Schumacher Co.
BERGAMOT
  W. J. Unwin, Ltd.
BERGENIA
  Geo. W. Park Seed Co., Inc.
BERRIES
  Boatman Nursery & Seed Co.
  Jackson & Perkins Co.
BETULA
  Clyde Robin Seed Co., Inc.
  F. W. Schumacher Co.
BEVERLY bells
  Geo. W. Park Seed Co., Inc.
BIGNONIA
  W. Atlee Burpee Co.
  Geo. W. Park Seed Co., Inc.
BIRCH
  J. W. Jung Seed Co.
  Silver Falls Nursery
BIRCH trees
  Henry Field Seed & Nursery Co.
  Gurney Seed & Nursery Co.
  Inter-State Nurseries
  Thomas B. Kyle, Jr. — Spring
    Hill Nurseries Co.
  R. H. Shumway Seedsman
BIRD feeders
  Barzen of Minneapolis, Inc.
  W. Atlee Burpee Co.
BIRD food
  Barzen of Minneapolis, Inc.
BIRD houses
  Barzen of Minneapolis, Inc.
  W. Atlee Burpee Co.
BIRD of paradise
  DeGiorgi Company, Inc.
  Ferndale Gardens
  Gurney Seed & Nursery Co.
  Geo. W. Park Seed Co., Inc.
  Wilson Brothers Floral Co., Inc.
"BIRDS Off" mesh
  French Textiles Co., Inc.
BITTER melon (see Melon, bitter)
BITTERSWEET
  DeGiorgi Company, Inc.

166

Ferndale Gardens
Henry Field Seed & Nursery Co.
Gurney Seed & Nursery Co.
Inter-State Nurseries
Thomas B. Kyle, Jr. — Spring
   Hill Nurseries Co.
L. L. Olds Seed Company
Silver Falls Nursery
BITTERSWEET vine
   J. W. Jung Seed Co.
BLACKBERRY lily
   Geo. W. Park Seed Co., Inc.
BLACKBERRY plants
   Burgess Seed and Plant Co.
   W. Atlee Burpee Co.
   Ferndale Gardens
   Henry Field Seed & Nursery Co.
   Gurney Seed & Nursery Co.
   Inter-State Nurseries
   Thomas B. Kyle, Jr. — Spring
      Hill Nurseries Co.
   Lakeland Nurseries Sales
   New York State Fruit Testing
      Cooperative Association
   Stark Bro's Nurseries
   Waynesboro Nurseries, Inc.
BLACK-eyed cow peas
   W. Atlee Burpee Co.
BLACK-eyed peas
   L. L. Olds Seed Company
BLACK-eyed susan
   DeGiorgi Company, Inc.
   Thomas B. Kyle, Jr. — Spring
      Hill Nurseries Co.
BLACK-eyed susan vine
   W. Atlee Burpee Co.
BLANKET flowers
   Joseph Harris Co., Inc.
BLEEDING hearts
   W. Atlee Burpee Co.
   DeGiorgi Company, Inc.
   Farmer Seed & Nursery Company
   Henry Field Seed & Nursery Co.
   Gurney Seed & Nursery Co.
   Inter-State Nurseries
   J. W. Jung Seed Co.
   Thomas B. Kyle, Jr. — Spring
      Hill Nurseries Co.

Earl May Seed & Nursery Co.
Geo. W. Park Seed Co., Inc.
BLETILLA
   W. Atlee Burpee Co.
   Geo. W. Park Seed Co., Inc.
BLOOMERIA
   Clyde Robin Seed Co., Inc.
BLOW torch
   Diamond International Corp.
BLUEBELLS
   Gurney Seed & Nursery Co.
   Thomas B. Kyle, Jr. — Spring
      Hill Nurseries Co.
BLUEBERRY plants
   Alexander's Blueberry Nurseries
   Brittingham Plant Farms
   W. Atlee Burpee Co.
   Farmer Seed & Nursery Com-
      pany
   Ferndale Gardens
   Henry Field Seed & Nursery Co.
   Inter-State Nurseries
   J. W. Jung Seed Co.
   Thomas B. Kyle, Jr. — Spring
      Hill Nurseries Co.
   Henry Leuthardt Nurseries, Inc.
   New York State Fruit Testing
      Cooperative Association
   R. H. Shumway Seedsman
   Waynesboro Nurseries, Inc.
BLUEBERRY tree
   Lakeland Nurseries Sales
BLUE bird flower
   J. W. Jung Seed Co.
BLUE bonnet
   DeGiorgi Company, Inc.
BLUE bottle
   DeGiorgi Company, Inc.
BLUE cup flower
   W. Atlee Burpee Co.
BLUE flax
   Henry Field Seed & Nursery Co.
   Joseph Harris Co., Inc.
BLUE grass
   DeGiorgi Company, Inc.
   Farmer Seed & Nursery Com-
      pany
   L. L. Olds Seed Company

BLUE lace flower
  W. Atlee Burpee Co.
  DeGiorgi Company, Inc.
  J. W. Jung Seed Co.
BLUE moon flowers
  Thomas B. Kyle, Jr. — Spring
    Hill Nurseries Co.
BLUE salvia
  W. Atlee Burpee Co.
  Joseph Harris Co., Inc.
BLUE stokesia
  Ferndale Gardens
BOILERS
  The Walter T. Kelley Company
BOLUSANTHUS
  Clyde Robin Seed Co., Inc.
BONE meal
  Gurney Seed & Nursery Co.
  Earl May Seed & Nursery Co.
  L. L. Olds Seed Company
BONSAI
  Thomas B. Kyle, Jr. — Spring
    Hill Nurseries Co.
BONSAI trees
  Girard Nurseries
BONSAL
  Gurney Seed & Nursery Co.
BORAGE
  W. Atlee Burpee Co.
  DeGiorgi Company, Inc.
  Joseph Harris Co., Inc.
  L. L. Olds Seed Company
  W. J. Unwin, Ltd.
BORECALE
  Joseph Harris Co., Inc.
  J. W. Jung Seed Co.
  W. J. Unwin, Ltd.
BOSTON ivy
  DeGiorgi Company, Inc.
  Gurney Seed & Nursery Co.
BOTTOM boards
  The Walter T. Kelley Company
BOTTOMS, hive
  Diamond International Corp.
BOUGAINVILLEA
  Geo. W. Park Seed Co., Inc.
  Wilson Brothers Floral Co., Inc.

BOUVARDIA
  Geo. W. Park Seed Co., Inc.
BOXWOOD
  Gurney Seed & Nursery Co.
  Thomas B. Kyle, Jr. — Spring
    Hill Nurseries Co.
BOXWOOD, korean
  Inter-State Nurseries
BOYSENBERRY plants
  Burgess Seed & Plant Co.
  W. Atlee Burpee Co.
  Henry Field Seed & Nursery Co.
  Gurney Seed & Nursery Co.
  Inter-State Nurseries
  Thomas B. Kyle, Jr. — Spring
    Hill Nurseries Co.
  R. H. Shumway Seedsman
  Waynesboro Nurseries, Inc.
BRACHYCHITON
  Clyde Robin Seed Co., Inc.
BRACHYCOME
  W. Atlee Burpee Co.
  DeGiorgi Company, Inc.
  L. L. Olds Seed Company
  Geo. W. Park Seed Co., Inc.
  Stokes Seeds, Inc.
BRADFORD pear trees
  Henry Field Seed & Nursery Co.
BRAND capping melter
  Diamond International Corp.
BRANDING irons
  Diamond International Corp.
  The Walter T. Kelley Company
BRIDAL wreath
  Inter-State Nurseries
  L. L. Olds Seed Company
  Silver Falls Nursery
BRIZA
  DeGiorgi Company, Inc.
  Geo. W. Park Seed Co., Inc.
BRIZA maxima
  W. Atlee Burpee Co.
BROADLEAF evergreens
  Girard Nurseries
  Musser Forests, Inc.
BROCCOLI
  Burgess Seed and Plant Co.
  W. Atlee Burpee Co.

D. V. Burrell Seed Growers Co.
DeGiorgi Company, Inc.
Farmer Seed & Nursery Company
Henry Field Seed & Nursery Co.
Gurney Seed & Nursery Co.
Joseph Harris Co., Inc.
Jackson & Perkins Co.
Johnny's Selected Seeds
J. W. Jung Seed Co.
Earl May Seed & Nursery Co.
Nichols Garden Nursery
L. L. Olds Seed Company
Seedway, Inc.
Spring Hill Farm
Stokes Seeds, Inc.
Otis S. Twilley Seed Co.
W. J. Unwin, Ltd.
BROCCOLI plants
Evans Plant Company
R. H. Shumway Seedsman
Steele Plant Co.
BROCCOLI raab
DeGiorgi Company, Inc.
BROCCOLI seeds
R. H. Shumway Seedsman
BRODIAEA
Clyde Robin Seed Co., Inc.
BROOD chamber, slide out
Diamond International Corp.
BROOD and honey frames (see
Frames, brood and honey)
BROOM corn seeds
Rabbit Hop Nursery
BROOMS
Silver Falls Nursery
W. J. Unwin, Ltd.
BROUSSONETIA
F. W. Schumacher Co.
BROWALLA
W. Atlee Burpee Co.
DeGiorgi Company, Inc.
L. L. Olds Seed Company
Geo. W. Park Seed Co., Inc.
Stokes Seeds, Inc.
BRUSHES
Diamond International Corp.
The Walter T. Kelley Company

BRUSSELS sprouts
Burgess Seed and Plant Co.
W. Atlee Burpee Co.
D. V. Burrell Seed Growers Co.
DeGiorgi Company, Inc.
Farmer Seed & Nursery Company
Henry Field Seed & Nursery Co.
Gurney Seed & Nursery Co.
Joseph Harris Co., Inc.
Jackson & Perkins Co.
Johnny's Selected Seeds
J. W. Jung Seed Co.
Earl May Seed & Nursery Co.
Nichols Garden Nursery
L. L. Olds Seed Company
Seedway, Inc.
Spring Hill Farm
Steele Plant Co.
Stokes Seeds, Inc.
W. J. Unwin, Ltd.
BRUSSELS sprouts plants
Evans Plant Company
R. H. Shumway Seedsman
BRUSSELS sprouts seeds
R. H. Shumway Seedsman
BUCKEYE tree
Lakeland Nurseries Sales
BUCKWHEAT
Farmer Seed & Nursery Company
BUDDLEIA
Inter-State Nurseries
Geo. W. Park Seed Co., Inc.
F. W. Schumacher Co.
BUFFALO berries
Gurney Seed & Nursery Co.
BULBS
Boatman Nursery & Seed Co.
Farmer Seed & Nursery Company
Jackson & Perkins Co.
L. L. Olds Seed Company
Waynesboro Nurseries, Inc.
BUPTHALMUM
Geo. W. Park Seed Co., Inc.
BURDOCK
Johnny's Selected Seeds
Kitayawa Seed Company

BURNET
W. J. Unwin, Ltd.
BURNING bush
W. Atlee Burpee Co.
Henry Field Seed & Nursery Co.
Gurney Seed & Nursery Co.
Joseph Harris Co., Inc.
Inter-State Nurseries
J. W. Jung Seed Co.
Thomas B. Kyle, Jr. – Spring
Hill Nurseries Co.
L. L. Olds Seed Company
Stokes Seeds, Inc.
W. J. Unwin, Ltd.
BUSH apricot
Ferndale Gardens
Lakeland Nurseries Sales
BUSH bittersweet
J. W. Jung Seed Co.
BUSH cherries
Ferndale Gardens
Henry Field Seed & Nursery Co.
Gurney Seed & Nursery Co.
J. W. Jung Seed Co.
Lakeland Nurseries Sales
BUTEA
F. W. Schumacher Co.
BUTTERCUP
Henry Field Seed & Nursery Co.
Gurney Seed & Nursery Co.
BUTTER daisy
Geo. W. Park Seed Co., Inc.
BUTTERFLY bush
Henry Field Seed & Nursery Co.
Gurney Seed & Nursery Co.
J. W. Jung Seed Co.
BUTTERFLY flower
W. Atlee Burpee Co.
BUTTERFLY lily
Geo. W. Park Seed Co., Inc.
BUTTERFLY plant
J. W. Jung Seed Co.
BUTTERNUT trees
Burgess Seed and Plant Co.
Gurney Seed & Nursery Co.
Lakeland Nurseries Sales
BUXUX
F. W. Schumacher Co.

CABBAGE
Burgess Seed and Plant Co.
W. Atlee Burpee Co.
D. V. Burrell Seed Growers Co.
DeGiorgi Company, Inc.
Farmer Seed & Nursery Company
Henry Field Seed & Nursery Co.
Gurney Seed & Nursery Co.
Joseph Harris Co., Inc.
Jackson & Perkins Co.
Johnny's Selected Seeds
J. W. Jung Seed Co.
Nichols Garden Nursery
L. L. Olds Seed Company
Seedway, Inc.
Spring Hill Farm
Stokes Seeds, Inc.
Otis S. Twilley Seed Co.
W. J. Unwin, Ltd.
CABBAGE, flowering
Geo. W. Park Seed Co., Inc.
CABBAGE plants
Evans Plant Company
Farmer Seed & Nursery Company
L. L. Olds Seed Company
R. H. Shumway Seedsman
Steele Plant Co.
CABBAGE, savoy
Seedway, Inc.
CABBAGE seeds
R. H. Shumway Seedsman
CACALIA
W. J. Unwin, Ltd.
CACTUS
Burgess Seed and Plant Co.
W. Atlee Burpee Co.
DeGiorgi Company, Inc.
Desert Plant Co.
Ferndale Gardens
Henry Field Seed & Nursery Co.
Gurney Seed & Nursery Co.
Ben Haines Company
Jackson & Perkins Co.
J. W. Jung Seed Co.
Lakeland Nurseries Sales
L. L. Olds Seed Company

Geo. W. Park Seed Co., Inc.
R. H. Shumway Seedsman
Stokes Seeds, Inc.
W. J. Unwin, Ltd.
Wilson Brothers Floral Co., Inc.

CAGE, queen
Diamond International Corp.

CAGES
The Walter T. Kelley Company

CALABRESE
W. J. Unwin, Ltd.

CALADIUM
W. Atlee Burpee Co.
Henry Field Seed & Nursery Co.
Inter-State Nurseries
J. W. Jung Seed Co.
Thomas B. Kyle, Jr. — Spring
    Hill Nurseries Co.
Lakeland Nurseries Sales
Earl May Seed & Nursery Co.
L. L. Olds Seed Company
Geo. W. Park Seed Co., Inc.
Van Bourgondien Brothers

CALADIUM bulbs
R. H. Shumway Seedsman

CALANDRINIA
Geo. W. Park Seed Co., Inc.

CALCEOLLARIA
W. Atlee Burpee Co.
DeGiorgi Company, Inc.
Geo. W. Park Seed Co., Inc.
Stokes Seeds, Inc.
W. J. Unwin, Ltd.

CALCIUM cyanide
Diamond International Corp.

CALENDULA
W. Atlee Burpee Co.
D. V. Burrell Seed Growers Co.
DeGiorgi Company, Inc.
Joseph Harris Co., Inc.
Jackson & Perkins Co.
J. W. Jung Seed Co.
L. L. Olds Seed Company
Geo. W. Park Seed Co., Inc.
Seedway, Inc.
Stokes Seeds, Inc.
Otis S. Twilley Seed Co.

CALENDULA officinalis
W. J. Unwin, Ltd.

CALIFORNIA poppy
W. Atlee Burpee Co.
DeGiorgi Company, Inc.
Joseph Harris Co., Inc.
J. W. Jung Seed Co.
L. L. Olds Seed Company

CALLA lilies
W. Atlee Burpee Co.
Henry Field Seed & Nursery Co.
Gurney Seed & Nursery Co.
Inter-State Nurseries
J. W. Jung Seed Co.
Earl May Seed & Nursery Co.
L. L. Olds Seed Company
Geo. W. Park Seed Co., Inc.
R. H. Shumway Seedsman

CALLICARPA
F. W. Schumacher Co.

CALLIOPSIS
W. Atlee Burpee Co.
DeGiorgi Company, Inc.
L. L. Olds Seed Company
Geo. W. Park Seed Co., Inc.
Stokes Seeds, Inc.

CALLIRHOE
Clyde Robin Seed Co., Inc.

CALLISTEMON
Clyde Robin Seed Co., Inc.

CALLITRIS
Clyde Robin Seed Co., Inc.

CALLUNA
F. W. Schumacher Co.

CALOCHORTUS
Clyde Robin Seed Co., Inc.

CALODENDRUM
Clyde Robin Seed Co., Inc.

CALYCANTHUS
Clyde Robin Seed Co., Inc.
F. W. Schumacher Co.

CALYPTRIDUM
Clyde Robin Seed Co., Inc.

CAMASSIA
Clyde Robin Seed Co., Inc.

CAMELLIAS
Ferndale Gardens
Lakeland Nurseries Sales
Geo. W. Park Seed Co., Inc.
Clyde Robin Seed Co., Inc.
F. W. Schumacher Co.

171

CAMPANULA
W. Atlee Burpee Co.
DeGiorgi Company, Inc.
Thomas B. Kyle, Jr. — Spring
   Hill Nurseries Co.
Geo. W. Park Seed Co., Inc.
Clyde Robin Seed Co., Inc.
Stokes Seeds, Inc.
W. J. Unwin, Ltd.
CAMPION lychnis (see Lychnis,
   campion)
CAMPSIS
Clyde Robin Seed Co., Inc.
F. W. Schumacher Co.
CANADIAN hemlock
Carino Nurseries
Girard Nurseries
CANARY bird vine
DeGiorgi Company, Inc.
J. W. Jung Seed Co.
CANARY creeper
W. Atlee Burpee Co.
W. J. Unwin, Ltd.
CANDYTUFT
W. Atlee Burpee Co.
D. V. Burrell Seed Growers Co.
DeGiorgi Company, Inc.
Henry Field Seed & Nursery Co.
Gurney Seed & Nursery Co.
Joseph Harris Co., Inc.
Inter-State Nurseries
Jackson & Perkins Co.
J. W. Jung Seed Co.
Thomas B. Kyle, Jr. — Spring
   Hill Nurseries Co.
L. L. Olds Seed Company
Geo. W. Park Seed Co., Inc.
Stokes Seeds, Inc.
W. J. Unwin, Ltd.
CANNA
W. Atlee Burpee Co.
DeGiorgi Company, Inc.
Farmer Seed & Nursery Com-
   pany
Henry Field Seed & Nursery Co.
Gurney Seed & Nursery Co.
Inter-State Nurseries
J. W. Jung Seed Co.

Thomas B. Kyle, Jr. — Spring
   Hill Nurseries Co.
Lakeland Nurseries Sales
Earl May Seed & Nursery Co.
L. L. Olds Seed Company
Geo. W. Park Seed Co., Inc.
W. J. Unwin, Ltd.
Van Bourgondien Brothers
Waynesboro Nurseries, Inc.
CANNA bulbs
R. H. Shumway Seedsman
CANS, honey
Diamond International Corp.
CANTELOUPE
Burgess Seed and Plant Co.
W. Atlee Burpee Co.
DeGiorgi Company, Inc.
Joseph Harris Co., Inc.
Nichols Garden Nursery
Stokes Seeds, Inc.
Otis S. Twilley Seed Co.
CANTERBURY bells
W. Atlee Burpee Co.
D. V. Burrell Seed Growers Co.
Henry Field Seed & Nursery Co.
Gurney Seed & Nursery Co.
Joseph Harris Co., Inc.
Inter-State Nurseries
J. W. Jung Seed Co.
L. L. Olds Seed Company
Geo. W. Park Seed Co., Inc.
Seedway, Inc.
W. J. Unwin, Ltd.
CAPE daisy
W. Atlee Burpee Co.
CAPE marigold
Joseph Harris Co., Inc.
CAPPINGS drier
Diamond International Corp.
CAPPINGS melter
Diamond International Corp.
The Walter T. Kelley Company
CAPPING scratcher
Diamond International Corp.
The Walter T. Kelley Company
CAP remover
Diamond International Corp.

CAPISCUM
    Joseph Harris Co., Inc.
    Geo. W. Park Seed Co., Inc.
    W. J. Unwin, Ltd.
CAPTAN
    Joseph Harris Co., Inc.
    L. L. Olds Seed Company
CARAGANA
    DeGiorgi Company, Inc.
    Clyde Robin Seed Co., Inc.
CARAWAY
    Burgess Seed and Plant Co.
    W. Atlee Burpee Co.
    DeGiorgi Company, Inc.
    Gurney Seed & Nursery Co.
    L. L. Olds Seed Company
    W. J. Unwin, Ltd.
CARBOLIC acid crystals
    Diamond International Corp.
CARBOLIC covers
    Diamond International Corp.
CARDINAL climber
    W. Atlee Burpee Co.
    DeGiorgi Company, Inc.
    J. W. Jung Seed Co.
CARDINAL flower
    Thomas B. Kyle, Jr. – Spring
      Hill Nurseries Co.
CARDINAL shrub
    Inter-State Nurseries
    J. W. Jung Seed Co.
CARDOON
    DeGiorgi Company, Inc.
CARGANA
    F. W. Schumacher Co.
CARNATION
    W. Atlee Burpee Co.
    D. V. Burrell Seed Growers Co.
    DeGiorgi Company, Inc.
    Ferndale Gardens
    Henry Field Seed & Nursery Co.
    Gurney Seed & Nursery Co.
    Joseph Harris Co., Inc.
    Jackson & Perkins Co.
    J. W. Jung Seed Co.
    Thomas B. Kyle, Jr. – Spring
      Hill Nurseries Co.
    Lakeland Nurseries Sales

Earl May Seed & Nursery Co.
L. L. Olds Seed Company
Geo. W. Park Seed Co., Inc.
Seedway, Inc.
Stokes Seeds, Inc.
Otis S. Twilley Seed Co.
W. J. Unwin, Ltd.
Wilson Brothers Floral Co., Inc.
CARNATIONS, hardy
    Inter-State Nurseries
CARNATION plants
    R. H. Shumway Seedsman
CARNIVOROUS plants
    Armstrong Associates
CARPATHIAN walnut tree
    Lakeland Nurseries Sales
CARPINUS
    F. W. Schumacher Co.
CARRISA
    F. W. Schumacher Co.
CARROTS
    Burgess Seed and Plant Co.
    W. Atlee Burpee Co.
    D. V. Burrell Seed Growers Co.
    DeGiorgi Company, Inc.
    Farmer Seed & Nursery Com-
      pany
    Henry Field Seed & Nursery Co.
    Gurney Seed & Nursery Co.
    Joseph Harris Co., Inc.
    Jackson & Perkins Co.
    Johnny's Selected Seeds
    J. W. Jung Seed Co.
    Earl May Seed & Nursery Co.
    Nichols Garden Nursery
    L. L. Olds Seed Company
    Seedway, Inc.
    R. H. Shumway Seedsman
    Spring Hill Farm
    Stokes Seeds, Inc.
    Otis S. Twilley Seed Co.
    W. J. Unwin, Ltd.
CARTHAMUS
    Clyde Robin Seed Co., Inc.
CARYA
    F. W. Schumacher Co.
CARYOPTERIS, azure
    Inter-State Nurseries

CASSES
  F. W. Schumacher Co.
CASSIA
  DeGiorgi Company, Inc.
  Geo. W. Park Seed Co., Inc.
  Clyde Robin Seed Co., Inc.
CASTILLIJA
  Clyde Robin Seed Co., Inc.
CASTINGS/worm manure
  Clear Creek Farms, Inc.
CASTOR oil bean
  DeGiorgi Company, Inc.
  Henry Field Seed & Nursery Co.
  Joseph Harris Co., Inc.
  J. W. Jung Seed Co.
  L. L. Olds Seed Company
  Geo. W. Park Seed Co., Inc.
CASTOR oil plant
  Stokes Seeds, Inc.
  W. J. Unwin, Ltd.
CATALPA
  F. W. Schumacher Co.
CATANANCHE
  DeGiorgi Company, Inc.
  Geo. W. Park Seed Co., Inc.
CATMINT
  W. Atlee Burpee Co.
  W. J. Unwin, Ltd.
CATMINT nepeta (see Nepeta,
  catmint)
CATNIP
  W. Atlee Burpee Co.
  DeGiorgi Company, Inc.
  Gurney Seed & Nursery Co.
  L. L. Olds Seed Company
CAULIFLOWER
  Burgess Seed and Plant Co.
  W. Atlee Burpee Co.
  D. V. Burrell Seed Growers Co.
  DeGiorgi Company, Inc.
  Farmer Seed & Nursery Com-
    pany
  Henry Field Seed & Nursery Co.
  Gurney Seed & Nursery Co.
  Joseph Harris Co., Inc.
  Jackson & Perkins Co.
  Johnny's Selected Seeds
  J. W. Jung Seed Co.

Earl May Seed & Nursery Co.
Nichols Garden Nursery
L. L. Olds Seed Company
Seedway, Inc.
Spring Hill Farm
Stokes Seeds, Inc.
Otis S. Twilley Seed Co.
W. J. Unwin, Ltd.
CAULIFLOWER plants
  Evans Plant Company
  R. H. Shumway Seedsman
  Steele Plant Co.
CAULIFLOWER seeds
  R. H. Shumway Seedsman
CEANOTHUS
  Clyde Robin Seed Co., Inc.
  F. W. Schumacher Co.
CEDARS
  Silver Falls Nursery
CEDRUS
  Clyde Robin Seed Co., Inc.
  F. W. Schumacher Co.
CELASTRUS
  Clyde Robin Seed Co., Inc.
  F. W. Schumacher Co.
CELASTRUS scandens
  DeGiorgi Company, Inc.
CELERIAC
  W. Atlee Burpee Co.
  DeGiorgi Company, Inc.
  Gurney Seed & Nursery Co.
  Joseph Harris Co., Inc.
  L. L. Olds Seed Company
  R. H. Shumway Seedsman
  Stokes Seeds, Inc.
  W. J. Unwin, Ltd.
CELERY
  Burgess Seed and Plant Co.
  W. Atlee Burpee Co.
  D. V. Burrell Seed Growers Co.
  DeGiorgi Company, Inc.
  Farmer Seed & Nursery Com-
    pany
  Henry Field Seed & Nursery Co.
  Gurney Seed & Nursery Co.
  Joseph Harris Co., Inc.
  Jackson & Perkins Co.
  J. W. Jung Seed Co.

Earl May Seed & Nursery Co.
L. L. Olds Seed Company
Seedway, Inc.
R. H. Shumway Seedsman
Stokes Seeds Inc.
Otis S. Twilley Seed Co.
W. J. Unwin, Ltd.
CELERY cabbage
 W. Atlee Burpee Co.
 J. W. Jung Seed Co.
CELL protectors
 Diamond International Corp.
CELOSIA
 W. Atlee Burpee Co.
 DeGiorgi Company, Inc.
 Gurney Seed & Nursery Co.
 Joseph Harris Co., Inc.
 Jackson & Perkins Co.
 J. W. Jung Seed Co.
 L. L. Olds Seed Company
 Geo. W. Park Seed Co., Inc.
 Stokes Seeds, Inc.
 Otis S. Twilley Seed Co.
 W. J. Unwin, Ltd.
CELSIA
 Geo. W. Park Seed Co., Inc.
CELTIS
 F. W. Schumacher Co.
CELTUCE
 W. Atlee Burpee Co.
 Stokes Seeds, Inc.
CENTAUREA
 W. Atlee Burpee Co.
 D. V. Burrell Seed Growers Co.
 DeGiorgi Company, Inc.
 Joseph Harris Co., Inc.
 J. W. Jung Seed Co.
 L. L. Olds Seed Company
 Geo. W. Park Seed Co., Inc.
 Stokes Seeds, Inc.
 Otis S. Twilley Seed Co.
CENTAUREA cyanus
 W. J. Unwin, Ltd.
CENTAUREA imperalis
 W. J. Unwin, Ltd.
CENTRATHERUM
 Geo. W. Park Seed Co., Inc.

CEPHALOTAXUS
 F. W. Schumacher Co.
CERASTIUM
 W. Atlee Burpee Co.
 DeGiorgi Company, Inc.
 Geo. W. Park Seed Co., Inc.
 Stokes Seeds, Inc.
CERATONIA
 F. W. Schumacher Co.
CERCIDIPHYLLUM
 F. W. Schumacher Co.
CERCIDIUM
 Clyde Robin Seed Co., Inc.
CERCIS
 Clyde Robin Seed Co., Inc.
 F. W. Schumacher
CEROCARPUA
 Clyde Robin Seed Co., Inc.
CHAENOMELES
 F. W. Schumacher Co.
CHAIN tree
 Ferndale Gardens
 Lakeland Nurseries Sales
CHAMAECYPARIS
 Clyde Robin Seed Co., Inc.
 F. W. Schumacher Co.
CHAMAEROPS
 F. W. Schumacher Co.
CHAMONILE
 DeGiorgi Company, Inc.
CHARD
 W. J. Unwin, Ltd.
CHARTREUSE shrub
 Thomas B. Kyle, Jr. — Spring
  Hill Nurseries Co.
CHEILANTHES
 Clyde Robin Seed Co., Inc.
CHEIRANTHUS
 W. Atlee Burpee Co.
 Geo. W. Park Seed Co., Inc.
 Clyde Robin Seed Co., Inc.
 Stokes Seeds, Inc.
 W. J. Unwin, Ltd.
CHEIRANTHUS allioni
 DeGiorgi Company, Inc.
CHELONE
 DeGiorgi Company, Inc.
 Geo. W. Park Seed Co., Inc.
 W. J. Unwin, Ltd.

CHENILLE plants
Wilson Brothers Floral Co., Inc.
CHERRY, bush
Thomas B. Kyle, Jr. — Spring
Hill Nurseries Co.
CHERRY, flowering
Thomas B. Kyle, Jr. — Spring
Hill Nurseries Co.
Silver Falls Nursery
CHERRY, jerusalem
DeGiorgi Company, Inc.
CHERRY, kwanzan flowering
Inter-State Nurseries
CHERRY pie
W. J. Unwin, Ltd.
CHERRY trees
Armstrong Nurseries, Inc.
Farmer Seed & Nursery Company
Henry Field Seed & Nursery Co.
Gurney Seed & Nursery Co.
Inter-State Nurseries
J. W. Jung Seed Co.
Thomas B. Kyle, Jr. — Spring
Hill Nurseries Co.
Lakeland Nurseries Sales
Henry Leuthardt Nurseries, Inc.
Earl May Seed & Nursery Co.
J. E. Miller Nurseries, Inc.
New York State Fruit Testing
Cooperative Association
L. L. Olds Seed Company
R. H. Shumway Seedsman
Stark Bro's Nurseries
Waynesboro Nurseries, Inc.
CHERVIL
DeGiorgi Company, Inc.
L. L. Olds Seed Company
W. J. Unwin, Ltd.
CHESTNUT, chinese
Inter-State Nurseries
CHESTNUT trees
Burgess Seed and Plant Co.
Ferndale Gardens
Gurney Seed & Nursery Co.
Stark Bro's Nurseries
CHICKENS
Gurney Seed & Nursery Co.

CHICORY
W. Atlee Burpee Co.
DeGiorgi Company, Inc.
Gurney Seed & Nursery Co.
Joseph Harris Co., Inc.
L. L. Olds Seed Company
R. H. Shumway Seedsman
Stokes Seeds, Inc.
W. J. Unwin, Ltd.
CHILOPSIS
Clyde Robin Seed Co., Inc.
CHIMAPHILA
Clyde Robin Seed Co., Inc.
CHIMONANTHUS
F. W. Schumacher Co.
CHINA bells
Wilson Brothers Floral Co., Inc.
CHINA rose tree
J. W. Jung Seed Co.
CHINCHERINCHEE
Lakeland Nurseries Sales
CHINESE cabbage
W. Atlee Burpee Co.
D. V. Burrell Seed Growers Co.
Joseph Harris Co., Inc.
Johnny's Selected Seeds
Kitayawa Seed Company
Seedway, Inc.
Spring Hill Farm
Stokes Seeds, Inc.
CHINESE chestnut
J. W. Jung Seed Co.
CHINESE elm (see Elm,
chinese)
CHINESE forget-me-not
W. Atlee Burpee Co.
D. V. Burrell Seed Growers Co.
Joseph Harris Co., Inc.
CHINESE lantern
W. Attlee Burpee Co.
DeGiorgi Company, Inc.
Henry Field Seed & Nursery Co.
J. W. Jung Seed Co.
Thomas B. Kyle, Jr. — Spring
Hill Nurseries Co.
L. L. Olds Seed Company
W. J. Unwin, Ltd.

CHINESE tree wisteria
  Lakeland Nurseries Sales
CHIONANTHUS
  F. W. Schumacher Co.
CHIVES
  Burgess Seed and Plant Co.
  W. Atlee Burpee Co.
  DeGiorgi Company, Inc.
  Henry Field Seed & Nursery Co.
  Gurney Seed & Nursery Co.
  J. W. Jung Seed Co.
  Earl May Seed & Nursery Co.
  L. L. Olds Seed Company
  R. H. Shumway Seedsman
  W. J. Unwin, Ltd.
CHLORDANE dust
  Diamond International Corp.
CHLOROGALUM
  Clyde Robin Seed Co., Inc.
CHOKE cherries
  Gurney Seed & Nursery Co.
CHOP suey
  DeGiorgi Company, Inc.
CHORIZANHE
  Clyde Robin Seed Co., Inc.
CHRISTMAS cactus
  Wilson Brothers Floral Co., Inc.
CHRISTMAS cherry
  W. Atlee Burpee Co.
  DeGiorgi Company, Inc.
  Stokes Seeds, Inc.
CHRISTMAS pepper
  W. Atlee Burpee Co.
  DeGiorgi Company, Inc.
  Stokes Seeds, Inc.
CHRISTMAS rose
  DeGiorgi Company, Inc.
  Ferndale Gardens
  Thomas B. Kyle, Jr. – Spring
    Hill Nurseries Co.
  Lakeland Nurseries Sales
CHRISTMAS trees
  Carino Nurseries
CHRYSANTHEMUM
  W. Atlee Burpee Co.
  D. V. Burrell Seed Growers Co.
  DeGiorgi Company, Inc.
  Farmer Seed & Nursery Company

Henry Field Seed & Nursery Co.
Gurney Seed & Nursery Co.
Joseph Harris Co., Inc.
Inter-State Nurseries
J. W. Jung Seed Co.
Thomas B. Kyle, Jr. – Spring
  Hill Nurseries Co.
L. L. Olds Seed Company
Geo. W. Park Seed Co., Inc.
Clyde Robin Seed Co., Inc.
Stokes Seeds, Inc.
Thon's Garden Mums
W. J. Unwin, Ltd.
Waynesboro Nurseries, Inc.
CHRYSANTHEMUM plants
  R. H. Shumway Seedsman
CHRYSANTHEMUM seed
  J. W. Jung Seed Co.
CHRYSOTHAMNUS
  Clyde Robin Seed Co., Inc.
CIMICIFUGA
  Clyde Robin Seed Co., Inc.
CINERARIA
  W. Atlee Burpee Co.
  DeGiorgi Company, Inc.
  L. L. Olds Seed Company
  Geo. W. Park Seed Co., Inc.
  Stokes Seeds, Inc.
  W. J. Unwin, Ltd.
CINNAMOMUM
  F. W. Schumacher Co.
CINNAMON vine
  DeGiorgi Company, Inc.
CIRSIUM
  Clyde Robin Seed Co., Inc.
CIRSUIM japonecuni
  DeGiorgi Company, Inc.
CISTUS
  Clyde Robin Seed Co., Inc.
  W. J. Unwin, Ltd.
CITRON
  Henry Field Seed & Nursery Co.
  Gurney Seed & Nursery Co.
  J. W. Jung Seed Co.
  L. L. Olds Seed Company
  R. H. Shumway Seedsman
  Stokes Seeds, Inc.

CITRUS
  F. W. Schumacher Co.
CITRUS plants
  Gurney Seed & Nursery Co.
  Thomas B. Kyle, Jr. — Spring
    Hill Nurseries Co.
CLADANTHUS
  Geo. W. Park Seed Co., Inc.
CLADRASTIS
  F. W. Schumacher Co.
CLAMPS, hose
  Diamond International Corp.
CLARKIA
  W. Atlee Burpee Co.
  D. V. Burrell Seed Growers Co.
  DeGiorgi Company, Inc.
  Gurney Seed & Nursery Co.
  J. W. Jung Seed Co.
  L. L. Olds Seed Company
  Geo. W. Park Seed Co., Inc.
  Clyde Robin Seed Co., Inc.
  Stokes Seeds, Inc.
  W. J. Unwin, Ltd.
CLARY
  Geo. W. Park Seed Co., Inc.
  W. J. Unwin, Ltd.
CLEATS
  Diamond International Corp.
CLEMATIS
  W. Atlee Burpee Co.
  DeGiorgi Company, Inc.
  Farmer Seed & Nursery Com-
    pany
  Henry Field Seed & Nursery Co.
  Gurney Seed & Nursery Co.
  Inter-State Nurseries
  J. W. Jung Seed Co.
  Thomas B. Kyle, Jr. — Spring
    Hill Nurseries Co.
  Earl May Seed & Nursery Co.
  Geo. W. Park Seed Co., Inc.
  Clyde Robin Seed Co., Inc.
  F. W. Schumacher Co.
  Van Bourgondien Brothers
CLEOME
  W. Atlee Burpee Co.
  DeGiorgi Company, Inc.
  Joseph Harris Co., Inc.

Jackson & Perkins Co.
J. W. Jung Seed Co.
L. L. Olds Seed Company
Geo. W. Park Seed Co., Inc.
Stokes Seeds, Inc.
W. J. Unwin, Ltd.
CLERODENDRON
  F. W. Schumacher Co.
CLETHRA
  F. W. Schumacher Co.
CLEYERA
  F. W. Schumacher Co.
CLIANTHUS
  Geo. W. Park Seed Co., Inc.
CLIMBING flowers
  W. Atlee Burpee Co.
CLIMBING lily (see Lily, climbing)
CLIMBING snapdragon (see Snap-
  dragon, climbing)
CLIMBING strawberry vines
  Dean Foster Nurseries
CLITORIA butterfly
  Geo. W. Park Seed Co., Inc.
CLIVIA
  Geo. W. Park Seed Co., Inc.
CLOCK vine
  Joseph Harris Co., Inc.
CLOVE pinks
  J. W. Jung Seed Co.
CLOVER
  Farmer Seed & Nursery Company
  J. W. Jung Seed Co.
  L. L. Olds Seed Company
  R. H. Shumway Seedsman
CLOVER, white
  W. Atlee Burpee Co.
  Joseph Harris Co., Inc.
COBAEA
  W. Atlee Burpee Co.
  Geo. W. Park Seed Co., Inc.
  Stokes Seeds, Inc.
COBEA
  DeGiorgi Company, Inc.
COBEA scandens
  L. L. Olds Seed Company
  W. J. Unwin, Ltd.
COBRA lily
  Lakeland Nurseries Sales

178

COBRA orchid
  Geo. W. Park Seed Co., Inc.
COCKSCOMB
  W. Atlee Burpee Co.
  DeGiorgi Company, Inc.
  Henry Field Seed & Nursery Co.
  Gurney Seed & Nursery Co.
  Joseph Harris Co., Inc.
  J. W. Jung Seed Co.
  Earl May Seed & Nursery Co.
  L. L. Olds Seed Company
  Geo. W. Park Seed Co., Inc.
  Seedway, Inc.
  W. J. Unwin, Ltd.
COFFEA
  Geo. W. Park Seed Co., Inc.
COFFEA arabica
  W. J. Unwin, Ltd.
COFFEE tree
  Ferndale Gardens
  Lakeland Nurseries Sales
COLEUS
  W. Atlee Burpee Co.
  D. V. Burrell Seed Growers Co.
  DeGiorgi Company, Inc.
  Henry Field Seed & Nursery Co.
  Gurney Seed & Nursery Co.
  Joseph Harris Co., Inc.
  Jackson & Perkins Co.
  J. W. Jung Seed Co.
  L. L. Olds Seed Company
  Geo. W. Park Seed Co., Inc.
  Seedway, Inc.
  Stokes Seeds, Inc.
  Otis S. Twilley Seed Co.
  W. J. Unwin, Ltd.
  Wilson Brothers Floral Co., Inc.
COLEUS plants
  R. H. Shumway Seedsman
COLLARD plants
  Evans Plant Company
COLLARDS
  W. Atlee Burpee Co.
  DeGiorgi Company, Inc.
  Henry Field Seed & Nursery Co.
  Gurney Seed & Nursery Co.
  Joseph Harris Co., Inc.
  Jackson & Perkins Co.

L. L. Olds Seed Company
R. H. Shumway Seedsman
Stokes Seeds, Inc.
Otis S. Twilley Seed Co.
COLLECTIONS of vegetable seeds
  W. J. Unwin, Ltd.
COLLINSIA
  Clyde Robin Seed Co., Inc.
COLORADO blue spruce
  DeGiorgi Company, Inc.
COLUMBINE
  W. Atlee Burpee Co.
  DeGiorgi Company, Inc.
  Henry Field Seed & Nursery Co.
  Gurney Seed & Nursery Co.
  Joseph Harris Co., Inc.
  Inter-State Nurseries
  Thomas B. Kyle, Jr. – Spring
    Hill Nurseries Co.
  Earl May Seed & Nursery Co.
  Geo. W. Park Seed Co., Inc.
  Seedway, Inc.
  Stokes Seeds, Inc.
  W. J. Unwin, Ltd.
COLUMNEA
  Wilson Brothers Floral Co., Inc.
COLUTEA
  F. W. Schumacher Co.
COLVILLEA
  Clyde Robin Seed Co., Inc.
COLX
  DeGiorgi Company, Inc.
COMARSTAPHYLIS
  Clyde Robin Seed Co., Inc.
COMB foundation
  The Walter T. Kelley Company
COMB honey cutter
  The Walter T. Kelley Company
COMB honey equipment
  Diamond International Corp.
COMFREY
  Gurney Seed & Nursery Co.
  Hamman
COMPOST bin
  Earl May Seed & Nursery Co.
COMPOSTEES
  Various Designs

179

COMPOST KITS
  Gurney Seed & Nursery Co.
  R. H. Shumway Seedsman
COMPOST shredder
  Amerind-MacKissic, Inc.
CONVALLARIA
  Geo. W. Park Seed Co., Inc.
CONVOLVULUS
  W. J. Unwin, Ltd.
COOLING exhaust fans
  Redwood Domes
CORAL bells
  DeGiorgi Company, Inc.
  Henry Field Seed & Nursery Co.
  Gurney Seed & Nursery Co.
  Thomas B. Kyle, Jr. – Spring
    Hill Nurseries Co.
  L. L. Olds Seed Company
  Geo. W. Park Seed Co., Inc.
CORDYLINE
  Geo. W. Park Seed Co., Inc.
  F. W. Schumacher Co.
  W. J. Unwin, Ltd.
COREOPSIS
  D. V. Burrell Seed Growers Co.
  DeGiorgi Company, Inc.
  Henry Field Seed & Nursery Co.
  Gurney Seed & Nursery Co.
  Joseph Harris Co., Inc.
  L. L. Olds Seed Company
  Geo. W. Park Seed Co., Inc.
  Clyde Robin Seed Co., Inc.
  Stokes Seeds, Inc.
  W. J. Unwin, Ltd.
CORETHROGYNE
  Clyde Robin Seed Co., Inc.
CORIANDER
  Burgess Seed and Plant Co.
  DeGiorgi Company, Inc.
  L. L. Olds Seed Company
  W. J. Unwin, Ltd.
CORN
  Burgess Seed and Plant Co.
  J. W. Jung Seed Co.
  Nichols Garden Nursery
CORN cutter
  Earl May Seed & Nursery Co.

CORN, drying
  Johnny's Selected Seeds
CORN, field
  Gurney Seed & Nursery Co.
  R. H. Shumway Seedsman
CORNFLOWER
  W. Atlee Burpee Co.
  DeGiorgi Company, Inc.
  Gurney Seed & Nursery Co.
  Joseph Harris Co., Inc.
  Jackson & Perkins Co.
  Geo. W. Park Seed Co., Inc.
  Stokes Seeds, Inc.
  W. J. Unwin, Ltd.
CORN, hybrid
  R. H. Shumway Seedsman
CORN knives
  DeGiorgi Company, Inc.
CORN, ornamental
  W. Atlee Burpee Co.
  Geo. W. Park Seed Co., Inc.
  Seedway, Inc.
  Stokes Seeds, Inc.
  Otis S. Twilley Seed Co.
CORN salad
  DeGiorgi Company, Inc.
  Joseph Harris Co., Inc.
  R. H. Shumway Seedsman
  Stokes Seeds, Inc.
  W. J. Unwin, Ltd.
CORN, sweet
  W. Atlee Burpee Co.
  D. V. Burrell Seed Growers Co.
  DeGiorgi Company, Inc.
  Farmer Seed & Nursery Company
  Henry Field Seed & Nursery Co.
  Gurney Seed & Nursery Co.
  Joseph Harris Co., Inc.
  Jackson & Perkins Co.
  Johnny's Selected Seeds
  Earl May Seed & Nursery Co.
  L. L. Olds Seed Company
  Seedway, Inc.
  R. H. Shumway Seedsman
  Spring Hill Farm
  Stokes Seeds, Inc.
  Otis S. Twilley Seed Co.
  W. J. Unwin, Ltd.

CORNUS
DeGiorgi Company, Inc.
Clyde Robin Seed Co., Inc.
F. W. Schumacher Co.
CORONILLA
Ferndale Gardens
Lakeland Nurseries Sales
Geo. W. Park Seed Co., Inc.
CORYDALIS
Geo. W. Park Seed Co., Inc.
CORYLUS
F. W. Schumacher Co.
CORYNOCARPUS
Geo. W. Park Seed Co., Inc.
COS lettuce
Joseph Harris Co., Inc.
COSMEA
W. J. Unwin, Ltd.
COSMOS
W. Atlee Burpee Co.
D. V. Burrell Seed Growers Co.
DeGiorgi Company, Inc.
Henry Field Seed & Nursery Co.
Gurney Seed & Nursery Co.
Joseph Harris Co., Inc.
Jackson & Perkins Co.
J. W. Jung Seed Co.
Earl May Seed & Nursery Co.
L. L. Olds Seed Company
Geo. W. Park Seed Co., Inc.
Seedway, Inc.
Stokes Seeds, Inc.
Otis S. Twilley Seed Co.
COTINUS
F. W. Schumacher Co.
COTONEASTER
J. W. Jung Seed Co.
Thomas B. Kyle, Jr. – Spring
Hill Nurseries Co.
Clyde Robin Seed Co., Inc.
F. W. Schumacher Co.
Silver Falls Nursery
COTTON
Gurney Seed & Nursery Co.
COTTON, ornamental
Geo. W. Park Seed Co., Inc.
COTTONWOOD
J. W. Jung Seed Co.

COTTONWOOD trees
Henry Field Seed & Nursery Co.
COTULA
DeGiorgi Company, Inc.
COTYLEDON
DeGiorgi Company, Inc.
Geo. W. Park Seed Co., Inc.
COURGETTE
W. J. Unwin, Ltd.
COVERALLS and bee suits
Diamond International Corp.
COVERS, hive
Diamond International Corp.
COWANIA
Clyde Robin Seed Co., Inc.
F. W. Schumacher Co.
COWPEAS
W. Atlee Burpee Co.
DeGiorgi Company, Inc.
R. H. Shumway Seedsman
COWSLIP
DeGiorgi Company, Inc.
CRABAPPLE trees
Henry Field Seed & Nursery Co.
Gurney Seed & Nursery Co.
Henry Leuthardt Nurseries, Inc.
New York State Fruit Testing
Cooperative Association
Silver Falls Nursery
Stark Bro's Nurseries
CRAB, flowering
Inter-State Nurseries
Thomas B. Kyle, Jr. – Spring
Hill Nurseries Co.
CRANBERRY, dwarf
J. W. Jung Seed Co.
CRANBERRY, high bush
J. W. Jung Seed Co.
CRAPE myrtle
Burgess Seed and Plant Co.
Henry Field Seed & Nursery Co.
Inter-State Nurseries
Geo. W. Park Seed Co., Inc.
CRATAEGUS
F. W. Schumacher Co.
CRAYON
Diamond International Corp.

CRAYON holder
  Diamond International Corp.
CREEPING zinnia
  Joseph Harris Co., Inc.
  Stokes Seeds, Inc.
CREPE myrtle
  Thomas B. Kyle, Jr. — Spring
    Hill Nurseries Co.
CRESS
  W. Atlee Burpee Co.
  DeGiorgi Company, Inc.
  Gurney Seed & Nursery Co.
  Joseph Harris Co., Inc.
  J. W. Jung Seed Co.
  L. L. Olds Seed Company
  Seedway, Inc.
  R. H. Shumway Seedsman
  Stokes Seeds, Inc.
  W. J. Unwin, Ltd.
CROCIDIUM
  Clyde Robin Seed Co., Inc.
CROCUS
  Farmer Seed & Nursery Com-
    pany
  J. W. Jung Seed Co.
  L. L. Olds Seed Company
CROSSANDRA
  Geo. W. Park Seed Co., Inc.
  Stokes Seeds, Inc.
  Wilson Brothers Floral Co., Inc.
CROTALARIA
  Geo. W. Park Seed Co., Inc.
CROTON
  Geo. W. Park Seed Co., Inc.
CROWDER peas
  Gurney Seed & Nursery Co.
  R. H. Shumway Seedsman
CROWNVETCH
  Burgess Seed and Plant Co.
  W. Atlee Burpee Co.
  Henry Field Seed & Nursery Co.
  Gurney Seed & Nursery Co.
  Joseph Harris Co., Inc.
  Inter-State Nurseries
  J. W. Jung Seed Co.
  Geo. W. Park Seed Co., Inc.
CRUCIANELLA
  DeGiorgi Company, Inc.

CRYPTOMERIA
  Clyde Robin Seed Co., Inc.
  F. W. Schumacher Co.
CUCUMBERS
  Burgess Seed and Plant Co.
  W. Atlee Burpee Co.
  D. V. Burrell Seed Growers Co.
  DeGiorgi Company, Inc.
  Farmer Seed & Nursery Company
  Henry Field Seed & Nursery Co.
  Gurney Seed & Nursery Co.
  Joseph Harris Co., Inc.
  Johnny's Selected Seeds
  J. W. Jung Seed Co.
  Kitayawa Seed Company
  Earl May Seed & Nursery Co.
  Nichols Garden Nursery
  L. L. Olds Seed Company
  R. H. Shumway Seedsman
  Stokes Seeds, Inc.
  Otis S. Twilley Seed Co.
  W. J. Unwin, Ltd.
CULINARY peas
  W. J. Unwin, Ltd.
CUNONIA
  Geo. W. Park Seed Co., Inc.
CUP and saucer
  DeGiorgi Company, Inc.
CUPHEA
  DeGiorgi Company, Inc.
  L. L. Olds Seed Company
  Geo. W. Park Seed Co., Inc.
CUPRESSUS
  Clyde Robin Seed Co., Inc.
  F. W. Schumacher Co.
CURLY cress
  W. Atlee Burpee Co.
CURRANTS
  Farmer Seed & Nursery Com-
    pany
  Henry Field Seed & Nursery Co.
  Gurney Seed & Nursery Co.
  Inter-State Nurseries
  J. W. Jung Seed Co.
  Henry Leuthardt Nurseries, Inc.
  Earl May Seed & Nursery Co.
  L. L. Olds Seed Company
  R. H. Shumway Seedsman

182

CUT flowers
World Gardens
CYANOGAS
Diamond International Corp.
CYCLAMEN
W. Atlee Burpee Co.
DeGiorgi Company, Inc.
Ferndale Gardens
Thomas B. Kyle, Jr. — Spring
Hill Nurseries Co.
Lakeland Nurseries Sales
Geo. W. Park Seed Co., Inc.
Stokes Seeds, Inc.
W. J. Unwin, Ltd.
CYCLONE seeder
Countryside General Store
CYDONIA
F. W. Schumacher Co.
CYNARA
Clyde Robin Seed Co., Inc.
CYNOGLOSUM
W. Atlee Burpee Co.
DeGiorgi Company, Inc.
Joseph Harris Co., Inc.
Geo. W. Park Seed Co., Inc.
Clyde Robin Seed Co., Inc.
Stokes Seeds, Inc.
CYPERUS
DeGiorgi Company, Inc.
Geo. W. Park Seed Co., Inc.
Stokes Seeds, Inc.
W. J. Unwin, Ltd.
CYPRESS
Girard Nurseries
Silver Falls Nursery
CYPRESS kochia (see Kochia,
cypress)
CYPRESS vine
W. Atlee Burpee Co.
DeGiorgi Company, Inc.
Geo. W. Park Seed Co., Inc.
CYPHOMANDRA
Geo. W. Park Seed Co., Inc.
CYPRIPEDIUM
Clyde Robin Seed Co., Inc.
CYTISUS broom
Geo. W. Park Seed Co., Inc.
Clyde Robin Seed Co., Inc.
F. W. Schumacher Co.

DAFFODILS
Farmer Seed & Nursery Com-
pany
DAHLBORG daisy
Geo. W. Park Seed Co., Inc.
DAHLIA
Burgess Seed and Plant Co.
W. Atlee Burpee Co.
D. V. Burrell Seed Growers Co.
DeGiorgi Company, Inc.
Farmer Seed & Nursery Com-
pany
Henry Field Seed & Nursery Co.
Gurney Seed & Nursery Co.
Joseph Harris Co., Inc.
Inter-State Nurseries
Jackson & Perkins Co.
J. W. Jung Seed Co.
Thomas B. Kyle, Jr. — Spring
Hill Nurseries Co.
Earl May Seed & Nursery Co.
L. L. Olds Seed Company
Geo. W. Park Seed Co., Inc.
Seedway, Inc.
R. H. Shumway Seedsman
Stokes Seeds, Inc.
Otis S. Twilley Seed Co.
W. J. Unwin, Ltd.
Van Bourgondien Brothers
DAIS
Clyde Robin Seed Co., Inc.
DAISIES
Henry Field Seed & Nursery Co.
Gurney Seed & Nursery Co.
J. W. Jung Seed Co.
Thomas B. Kyle, Jr. — Spring
Hill Nurseries Co.
L. L. Olds Seed Company
W. J. Unwin, Ltd.
DAISY, african
DeGiorgi Company, Inc.
Joseph Harris Co., Inc.
Jackson & Perkins Co.
Stokes Seeds, Inc.
DAISY, english
W. Atlee Burpee Co.
DeGiorgi Company, Inc.
Joseph Harris Co., Inc

183

L. L. Olds Seed Company
Geo. W. Park Seed Co., Inc.
Seedway, Inc.
Stokes Seeds, Inc.
DAISY, gloriosa
W. Atlee Burpee Co.
Joseph Harris Co., Inc.
DAISY, painted
W. Atlee Burpee Co.
DeGiorgi Company, Inc.
Joseph Harris Co., Inc.
Geo. W. Park Seed Co., Inc.
Seedway, Inc.
Stokes Seeds, Inc.
DAISY, pyrethrum
DeGiorgi Company, Inc.
DAISY, rudbeckia
Seedway, Inc.
DAISY, shasta
W. Atlee Burpee Co.
DeGiorgi Company, Inc.
Joseph Harris Co., Inc.
Inter-State Nurseries
Seedway, Inc.
DAISY, tahoka
W. Atlee Burpee Co.
DALEA
Clyde Robin Seed Co., Inc.
DANDELION
W. Atlee Burpee Co.
Johnny's Selected Seeds
R. H. Shumway Seedsman
Stokes Seeds, Inc.
DAPHNE
Burgess Seed and Plant Co.
Geo. W. Park Seed Co., Inc.
DARLINGTONIA
Geo. W. Park Seed Co., Inc.
Clyde Robin Seed Co., Inc.
DATE trees
R. H. Shumway Seedsman
DATURA
DeGiorgi Company, Inc.
J. W. Jung Seed Co.
L. L. Olds Seed Company
Geo. W. Park Seed Co., Inc.
Clyde Robin Seed Co., Inc.
Stokes Seeds, Inc.

DAUBENTONIA
Clyde Robin Seed Co., Inc.
DAVIDIA
F. W. Schumacher Co.
DAWN redwood
Ferndale Gardens
Henry Field Seed & Nursery Co.
Lakeland Nurseries Sales
DAY lilies
Alexander's Blueberry Nurseries
W. Atlee Burpee Co.
Gurney Seed & Nursery Co.
Inter-State Nurseries
J. W. Jung Seed Co.
Thomas B. Kyle, Jr. — Spring
Hill Nurseries Co.
Geo. W. Park Seed Co., Inc.
DELONIX
F. W. Schumacher Co.
DELPHINIUM
W. Atlee Burpee Co.
D. V. Burrell Seed Growers Co.
DeGiorgi Company, Inc.
Henry Field Seed & Nursery Co.
Gurney Seed & Nursery Co.
Inter-State Nurseries
Jackson & Perkins Co.
J. W. Jung Seed Co.
Thomas B. Kyle, Jr. — Spring
Hill Nurseries Co.
Earl May Seed & Nursery Co.
L. L. Olds Seed Company
Geo. W. Park Seed Co., Inc.
Clyde Robin Seed Co., Inc.
Seedway, Inc.
Stokes Seeds, Inc.
Otis S. Twilley Seed Co.
W. J. Unwin, Ltd.
DELPHINIUM, annual
Joseph Harris Co., Inc.
DELPHINIUM, hardy
Joseph Harris Co., Inc.
DENDROMECON
Clyde Robin Seed Co., Inc.
DEUTZIA gracillis
Henry Field Seed & Nursery Co.
DEVIL in the bush
DeGiorgi Company, Inc.

DEWBERRIES
    Burgess Seed and Plant Co.
    Henry Field Seed & Nursery Co.
    Gurney Seed & Nursery Co.
    Thomas B. Kyle, Jr. — Spring
        Hill Nurseries Co.
    Waynesboro Nurseries, Inc.
DIANTHUS
    W. Atlee Burpee Co.
    D. V. Burrell Seed Growers Co.
    DeGiorgi Company, Inc.
    Ferndale Gardens
    Henry Field Seed & Nursery Co.
    Joseph Harris Co., Inc.
    Inter-State Nurseries
    Jackson & Perkins Co.
    L. L. Olds Seed Company
    Geo. W. Park Seed Co., Inc.
    Stokes Seeds, Inc.
    Otis S. Twilley Seed Co.
    W. J. Unwin, Ltd.
DIASCIA
    DeGiorgi Company, Inc.
    W. J. Unwin, Ltd.
DIATOMACEOUS earth insecti-
        cides
    J. Mullin, Nursery
DIAZINON
    Joseph Harris Co., Inc.
    L. L. Olds Seed Company
DICENTRA
    DeGiorgi Company, Inc.
    Geo. W. Park Seed Co., Inc.
    Clyde Robin Seed Co., Inc.
DICHONDRA
    Geo. W. Park Seed Co., Inc.
DICTAMNUS
    DeGiorgi Company, Inc.
    L. L. Olds Seed Company
    Geo. W. Park Seed Co., Inc.
DIDISCUS
    W. Atlee Burpee Co.
    DeGiorgi Company, Inc.
    L. L. Olds Seed Company
    Geo. W. Park Seed Co., Inc.
DIGITATA schefflers (see Scheff-
    lera, digitata)

DIGITALIS
    W. Atlee Burpee Co.
    D. V. Burrell Seed Growers Co.
    DeGiorgi Company, Inc.
    Joseph Harris Co., Inc.
    L. L. Olds Seed Company
    Geo. W. Park Seed Co., Inc.
    Clyde Robin Seed Co., Inc.
    Stokes Seeds, Inc.
    W. J. Unwin, Ltd.
DILL
    Burgess Seed and Plant Co.
    W. Atlee Burpee Co.
    D. V. Burrell Seed Growers Co.
    DeGiorgi Company, Inc.
    Farmer Seed & Nursery Com-
        pany
    Henry Field Seed & Nursery Co.
    Gurney Seed & Nursery Co.
    Joseph Harris Co., Inc.
    J. W. Jung Seed Co.
    Earl May Seed & Nursery Co.
    L. L. Olds Seed Company
    W. J. Unwin, Ltd.
DIMORPHOTHECA
    W. Atlee Burpee Co.
    DeGiorgi Company, Inc.
    Joseph Harris Co., Inc.
    Jackson & Perkins Co.
    Geo. W. Park Seed Co., Inc.
    Clyde Robin Seed Co., Inc.
    Stokes Seeds, Inc.
    W. J. Unwin, Ltd.

DIOSPYROS
    F. W. Schumacher Co.
DIPEL biological insecticide
    Galt Research Incorporated
DISANTHUS
    F. W. Schumacher Co.
DIVISION boards
    Diamond International Corp.
DODECATHEON
    Geo. W. Park Seed Co., Inc.
    Clyde Robin Seed Co., Inc.
DOG tooth violet
    DeGiorgi Company, Inc.
DOGWOOD
    Ferndale Gardens

Henry Field Seed & Nursery Co.
Gurney Seed & Nursery Co.
Inter-State Nurseries
J. W. Jung Seed Co.
Thomas B. Kyle, Jr. — Spring
  Hill Nurseries Co.
Lakeland Nurseries Sales
Silver Falls Nursery
DOGWOOD, red twig
  Henry Field Seed & Nursery Co.
DOLICHOS
  L. L. Olds Seed Company
  F. W. Schumacher Co.
DOMBEYA
  Geo. W. Park Seed Co., Inc.
DOMESTIC rye grass (see Rye
grass, domestic)
DORONICUM
  DeGiorgi Company, Inc.
  Joseph Harris Co., Inc.
  L. L. Olds Seed Company
  Geo. W. Park Seed Co., Inc.
  Stokes Seeds. Inc.

DOUBLE daisy
  W. J. Unwin, Ltd.
DOWPON
  L. L. Olds Seed Co.
DRACANEA
  DeGiorgi Company, Inc.
  Stokes Seeds, Inc.
DRACEANA indivisa
  W. J. Unwin, Ltd.
DRIED blood
  Gurney Seed & Nursery Co.
DRIED herbs and spices
  Nichols Garden Nursery
DRYAS
  Geo. W. Park Seed Co., Inc.
DRY brow
  Diamond International Corp.
DRYING corn (see Corn, drying)
DUDLEYA
  Clyde Robin Seed Co., Inc.
DUSTY miller
  W. Atlee Burpee Co.
  DeGiorgi Company, Inc.
  Gurney Seed & Nursery Co.
  Joseph Harris Co., Inc.

Jackson & Perkins Co.
Geo. W. Park Seed Co., Inc.
Stokes Seeds, Inc.
DUTCHMAN'S pipe vine
  Lakeland Nurseries Sales
DWARF apple trees
  Farmer Seed & Nursery Com-
    pany
DWARF citrus trees
  Armstrong Nurseries, Inc.
DWARF cranberry (see Cranberry,
  dwarf)
DWARF fruit trees (see Fruit
  trees, dwarf)
DWARF iris
  Ferndale Gardens
DWARF lace plant
  Henry Field Seed & Nursery Co.
DWARF maple
  Ferndale Gardens
  Lakeland Nurseries Sales
DWARF pear tree
  Lakeland Nurseries Sales
DYSSODIA
  Clyde Robin Seed Co., Inc.
EARTHWORM books
  Shield's Publications
EARTHWORMS
  Bronwood Worm Farms
  Ferndale Gardens
  Lakeland Nurseries Sales
  Connie Mahan's Annelid Acres
ECCREMOCARPUS
  W. J. Unwin, Ltd.
ECHEVERIA
  DeGiorgi Company, Inc.
  Geo. W. Park Seed Co., Inc.
ECHINACEA
  Clyde Robin Seed Co., Inc.
ECHINOCACTUS
  Clyde Robin Seed Co., Inc.
ECHINOPS
  DeGiorgi Company, Inc.
  Geo. W. Park Seed Co., Inc.
ECHIUM
  DeGiorgi Company, Inc.
  Geo. W. Park Seed Co., Inc.
  W. J. Unwin, Ltd.

EDELWEISS
  DeGiorgi Company, Inc.
  Lakeland Nurseries Sales
EDIBLE soybeans (see Soybeans, edible)
EGGPLANT
  Burgess Seed and Plant Co.
  W. Atlee Burpee Co.
  D. V. Burrell Seed Growers Co.
  DeGiorgi Company, Inc.
  Farmer Seed & Nursery Company
  Henry Field Seed & Nursery Co.
  Gurney Seed & Nursery Co.
  Joseph Harris Co., Inc.
  Jackson & Perkins Co.
  Johnny's Selected Seeds
  J. W. Jung Seed Co.
  Kitayawa Seed Company
  Earl May Seed & Nursery Co.
  Nichols Garden Nursery
  L. L. Olds Seed Company
  Seedway, Inc.
  R. H. Shumway Seedsman
  Stokes Seeds, Inc.
  Otis S. Twilley Seed Co.
EGGPLANT, ornamental
  Geo. W. Park Seed Co., Inc.
EGGPLANT plants
  Evans Plant Company
ELAEAGNUS
  Clyde Robin Seed Co., Inc.
  F. W. Schumacher
ELDERBERRIES
  W. Atlee Burpee Co.
  Ferndale Gardens
  Henry Field Seed & Nursery Co.
  Gurney Seed & Nursery Co.
  Thomas B. Kyle, Jr. — Spring Hill Nurseries Co.
  New York State Fruit Testing Cooperative Association
ELECTRIC knives
  The Walter T. Kelley Company
ELECTRIC smoke house
  Various Designs
ELECTRIC uncapping knives
  Diamond International Corp.

ELEPHANT garlic
  Quality Seed Garlic
ELEPHANT ears
  W. Atlee Burpee Co.
  Lakeland Nurseries Sales
  R. H. Shumway Seedsman
ELIMINATION of moles, gophers & ground squirrels
  Danhaven Farms
ELM, chinese
  Henry Field Seed & Nursery Co.
  Inter-State Nurseries
ELM, hamburg
  Inter-State Nurseries
ELM trees
  Henry Field Seed & Nursery Co.
  Gurney Seed & Nursery Co.
  Thomas B. Kyle, Jr. — Spring Hill Nurseries Co.
  Earl May Seed & Nursery Co.
  R. H. Shumway Seedsman
EMBEDDER, wire
  Diamond International Corp.
EMILIA
  Geo. W. Park Seed Co., Inc.
EMMENANTHE
  Clyde Robin Seed Co., Inc.
EMPRESS tree
  Ferndale Gardens
ENCELIA
  Clyde Robin Seed Co., Inc.
ENDIVE
  Burgess Seed and Plant Co.
  W. Atlee Burpee Co.
  DeGiorgi Company, Inc.
  Gurney Seed & Nursery Co.
  Joseph Harris Co., Inc.
  Jackson & Perkins Co.
  Johnny's Selected Seeds
  J. W. Jung Seed Co.
  Earl May Seed & Nursery Co.
  L. L. Olds Seed Company
  Seedway, Inc.
  R. H. Shumway Seedsman
  Stokes Seeds, Inc.
  Otis S. Twilley Seed Co.
  W. J. Unwin, Ltd.
ENGLISH daisy (see Daisy, english)

ENKIANTHUS
F. W. Schumacher Co.
ENTRANCE guard
Diamond International Corp.
ENVIRONMENTAL calendars
Concern, Inc.
EPHEDRA
Clyde Robin Seed Co., Inc.
EPILOBIUM
Clyde Robin Seed Co., Inc.
EPISCIA
Geo. W. Park Seed Co., Inc.
Wilson Brothers Floral Co., Inc.
ERANTHIS
Geo. W. Park Seed Co., Inc.
EREMOCARPUS
Clyde Robin Seed Co., Inc.
EREMURUS
DeGiorgi Company, Inc.
Geo. W. Park Seed Co., Inc.
ERIGERON
DeGiorgi Company, Inc.
Geo. W. Park Seed Co., Inc.
Clyde Robin Seed Co., Inc.
W. J. Unwin, Ltd.
ERINUS
DeGiorgi Company, Inc.
Geo. W. Park Seed Co., Inc.
ERIODICTYON
Clyde Robin Seed Co., Inc.
ERIOGONUM
Clyde Robin Seed Co., Inc.
ERIOPHYLLUM
Clyde Robin Seed Co., Inc.
ERYNIGIUM
DeGiorgi Company, Inc.
Geo. W. Park Seed Co., Inc.
W. J. Unwin, Ltd.
ERYSIMUM
Clyde Robin Seed Co., Inc.
ERYTHRINA
Geo. W. Park Seed Co., Inc.
F. W. Schumacher Co.
DeGiorgi Company, Inc.
ERYTHRONIUM
DeGiorgi Company, Inc.
Geo. W. Park Seed Co., Inc.
Clyde Robin Seed Co., Inc.

ERSIMUM
DeGiorgi Company, Inc.
ESCAPES, bee
Diamond International Corp.
The Walter T. Kelley Company
ESCAROLE
DeGiorgi Company, Inc.
Gurney Seed & Nursery Co.
Stokes Seeds, Inc.
ESCHSCHOLTZIA
W. Atlee Burpee Co.
D. V. Burrell Seed Growers Co.
DeGiorgi Company, Inc.
Joseph Harris Co., Inc.
Geo. W. Park Seed Co., Inc.
Stokes Seeds, Inc.
W, J, Unwin, Ltd.
ESCHSCHOLZIA
Clyde Robin Seed Co., Inc.
ESPALIER apple trees
Henry Leuthardt Nurseries, Inc.
ESPALIER flowering crabapple
trees
Henry Leuthardt Nurseries, Inc.
ESPALIER peach trees
Henry Leuthardt Nurseries, Inc.
ESPALIER pear trees
Henry Leuthardt Nurseries, Inc.
EUCALPTUS
DeGiorgi Company, Inc.
Geo. W. Park Seed Co., Inc.
Clyde Robin Seed Co., Inc.
F. W. Schumacher Co.
EUCALYPTUS
W. J. Unwin, Ltd.
EUCHARIS
Geo. W. Park Seed Co., Inc.
EUCOMIS
Geo. W. Park Seed Co., Inc.
EUONYMUS
Inter-State Nurseries
Thomas B. Kyle, Jr. — Spring
Hill Nurseries Co.
Clyde Robin Seed Co., Inc.
F. W. Schumacher Co.
EUONYMUS shrubs
Henry Field Seed & Nursery Co.

EUPATORIUM
Geo. W. Park Seed Co., Inc.
EUPHORBIA
W. Atlee Burpee Co.
DeGiorgi Company, Inc.
Joseph Harris Co., Inc.
Geo. W. Park Seed Co., Inc.
Stokes Seeds, Inc.
W. J. Unwin, Ltd.
EUSTOMA
Clyde Robin Seed Co., Inc.
EUTOCA
Geo. W. Park Seed Co., Inc.
EVERGREEN bittersweet
J. W. Jung Seed Co.
EVERGREEN holly
Ferndale Gardens
Lakeland Nurseries Sales
EVERGREENS
Boatman Nursery & Seed Co.
W. Atlee Burpee Co.
Farmer Seed & Nursery Company
Henry Field Seed & Nursery Co.
Gurney Seed & Nursery Co.
Inter-State Nurseries
J. W. Jung Seed Co.
Thomas B. Kyle, Jr. – Spring Hill Nurseries Co.
Earl May Seed & Nursery Co.
R. H. Shumway Seedsman
EVERGREEN seedlings
Musser Forests, Inc.
EVERGREEN seeds
Girard Nurseries
EVERGREEN shrubs (see Shrubs, evergreen)
EVERGREEN transplants
Musser Forests, Inc.
EVERGREENS, broadleaved
Waynesboro Nurseries, Inc.
EVERGREENS, coniferous
Waynesboro Nurseries, Inc.
EVERLASTING pea (see Pea, everlasting)
EVERLASTINGS
W. Atlee Burpee Co.
DeGiorgi Company, Inc.

Gurney Seed & Nursery Co.
J. W. Jung Seed Co.
Nichols Garden Nursery
L. L. Olds Seed Company
Geo. W. Park Seed Co., Inc.
Stokes Seeds, Inc.
Otis S. Twilley Seed Co.
EVODIA
F. W. Schumacher Co.
EXACUM
Geo. W. Park Seed Co., Inc.
W. J. Unwin, Ltd.
EXCLUDERS
Diamond International Corp.
EXHAUST fan
McGregor Greenhouses
EXOCHORDA
F. W. Schumacher Co.
EXTRACTORS
The Walter T. Kelley Company
EXTRACTORS, honey
Diamond International Corp.
EXTRACTORS, wax
Diamond International Corp.
EYELETS, metal
Diamond International Corp.
EYELET tool
Diamond International Corp.
FAGUS
F. W. Schumacher Co.
FALL bulbs
Farmer Seed & Nursery Company
FALLUGIA
Clyde Robin Seed Co., Inc.
FANTAIL willow (see Willow, fantail)
FATSIA, aralia
Geo. W. Park Seed Co., Inc.
F. W. Schumacher Co.
FAVA beans
W. Atlee Burpee Co.
Joseph Harris Co., Inc.
FEATHERED cockscomb
W. J. Unwin, Ltd.
FEEDERS, bee
Diamond International Corp.

189

FEIJOA
  F. W. Schumacher Co.
FELICIA
  DeGiorgi Company, Inc.
  Geo. W. Park Seed Co., Inc.
  Clyde Robin Seed Co., Inc.
FENNEL
  W. Atlee Burpee Co.
  DeGiorgi Company, Inc.
  Gurney Seed & Nursery Co.
  Joseph Harris Co., Inc.
  W. J. Unwin, Ltd.
FERNS
  W. Atlee Burpee Co.
  DeGiorgi Company, Inc.
  Ferndale Gardens
  Henry Field Seed & Nursery Co.
  Gurney Seed & Nursery Co.
  Ben Haines Company
  Inter-State Nurseries
  J. W. Jung Seed Co.
  Thomas B. Kyle, Jr. — Spring
    Hill Nurseries Co.
  Lakeland Nurseries Sales
  Earl May Seed & Nursery Co.
  Geo. W. Park Seed Co., Inc.
  R. H. Shumway Seedsman
  Silver Falls Nursery
  Stokes Seeds, Inc.
  Wilson Brothers Floral Co.
FEROCACTUS
  Clyde Robin Seed Co., Inc.
FERTILIZERS
  Barzen of Minneapolis, Inc.
  W. Atlee Burpee Co.
  Farmer Seed & Nursery Company
  Gurney Seed & Nursery Co.
  Joseph Harris Co., Inc.
  Earl May Seed & Nursery Co.
  L. L. Olds Seed Company
  R. H. Shumway Seedsman
  Sudbury Laboratory, Inc.
FESCUES
  L. L. Olds Seed Company
  R. H. Shumway Seedsman
FESTUCA glauca
  J. W. Jung Seed Co.

FEVERFEW
  W. Atlee Burpee Co.
  DeGiorgi Company, Inc.
  Thomas B. Kyle, Jr. — Spring
    Hill Nurseries Co.
  Stokes Seeds, Inc.
FICUS
  Geo. W. Park Seed Co., Inc.
FICUS bengalensis
  W. J. Unwin, Ltd.
FIELD beans
  Joseph Harris Co., Inc.
  J. W. Jung Seed Co.
FIELD corn (see Corn, field)
FIELD seeds
  Gurney Seed & Nursery Co.
  R. H. Shumway Seedsman
FIG trees
  Armstrong Nurseries, Inc.
  Burgess Seed and Plant Co.
  Ferndale Gardens
  Henry Field Seed & Nursery Co.
  Gurney Seed & Nursery Co.
  Thomas B. Kyle, Jr. — Spring
    Hill Nurseries Co.
  Lakeland Nurseries Sales
  R. H. Shumway Seedsman
  Waynesboro Nurseries, Inc.
FILBERT trees
  Burgess Seed and Plant Co.
  Henry Leuthardt Nurseries, Inc.
FINOCCHIO
  W. Atlee Burpee Co.
  Joseph Harris Co., Inc.
FIR
  Carino Nurseries
  Girard Nurseries
  Silver Falls Nursery
  Western Maine Forest Nursery
FIREBUSH
  Thomas B. Kyle, Jr. — Spring
    Hill Nurseries Co.
  Seedway, Inc.
FIRETHORN
  Inter-State Nurseries
FIRMIANA
  F. W. Schumacher Co.
FLAG iris (see Iris, flag)

FLAG of spain
  Geo. W. Park Seed Co., Inc.
FLAME flower
  DeGiorgi Company, Inc.
FLAMINGO flower
  Lakeland Nurseries Sales
  Wilson Brothers Floral Co., Inc.
FLAT tins (see Tins, flat)
FLAX
  W. Atlee Burpee Co.
  Gurney Seed & Nursery Co.
  W. J. Unwin, Ltd.
FLAX, linum
  Geo. W. Park Seed Co., Inc.
FLORENCE fennel
  L. L. Olds Seed Company
FLOSS flower
  Stokes Seeds, Inc.
FLOWER plants
  W. Atlee Burpee Co.
FLOWER seeds
  Jardin du Gourmet
  Nichols Garden Nursery
  R. H. Shumway Seedsman
FLOWERING almond (see
  Almond, flowering)
FLOWERING cabbage
  Joseph Harris Co., Inc.
FLOWERING cherry (see Cherry,
  flowering)
FLOWERING crab (see Crab,
  flowering)
FLOWERING crab apple
  Farmer Seed & Nursery Com-
    pany
  Ferndale Gardens
  J. W. Jung Seed Co.
  Lakeland Nurseries Sales
  L. L. Olds Seed Company
FLOWERING kale (see Kale,
  flowering)
FLOWERING plants
  Carino Nurseries
FLOWERING quince (see Quince,
  flowering)
FLOWERING shrubs (see Shrubs,
  flowering)

FLOWERING tobacco (see
  Tobacco, flowering)
FLOWERING trees (see Trees,
  flowering)
FLOWERING vines
  Carino Nurseries
FLY parasites
  California Green Lacewings
FLY trap plant
  R. H. Shumway Seedsman
  Wilson Brothers Floral Co., Inc.
FOENICULUM
  Clyde Robin Seed Co., Inc.
FOLIAGE
  Stokes Seeds, Inc.
FOLLOWER boards
  Diamond International Corp.
FORDHOOK spinach
  W. Atlee Burpee Co.
FOREST trees
  Carino Nurseries
FORGET me not
  W. Atlee Burpee Co.
  DeGiorgi Company, Inc.
  Henry Field Seed & Nursery Co.
  Gurney Seed & Nursery Co.
  Joseph Harris Co., Inc.
  Thomas B. Kyle, Jr. — Spring
    Hill Nurseries Co.
  L. L. Olds Seed Company
  Geo. W. Park Seed Co., Inc.
  Stokes Seeds, Inc.
  W. J. Unwin, Ltd.
FORGET me not, chinese
  W. Atlee Burpee Co.
FORGET me not, summer
  W. Atlee Burpee Co.
FORSYTHIA
  Henry Field Seed & Nursery Co.
  Gurney Seed & Nursery Co.
  Inter-State Nurseries
  J. W. Jung Seed Co.
  Thomas B. Kyle, Jr. — Spring
    Hill Nurseries Co.
  L. L. Olds Seed Company
FOUNDATION, bee comb
  Diamond International Corp.

191

FOUNDATION fasteners
  Diamond International Corp.
FOUGUIERIA
  Clyde Robin Seed Co., Inc.
FOUR o'clock
  W. Atlee Burpee Co.
  DeGiorgi Company, Inc.
  Henry Field Seed & Nursery Co.
  Gurney Seed & Nursery Co.
  Joseph Harris Co., Inc.
  J. W. Jung Seed Co.
  L. L. Olds Seed Company
  Geo. W. Park Seed Co., Inc.
  Seedway, Inc.
  Stokes Seeds, Inc.
FOXGLOVE
  W. Atlee Burpee Co.
  DeGiorgi Company, Inc.
  Gurney Seed & Nursery Co.
  Joseph Harris Co., Inc.
  Thomas B. Kyle, Jr. — Spring
    Hill Nurseries Co.
  L. L. Olds Seed Company
  Geo. W. Park Seed Co., Inc.
  Stokes Seeds, Inc.
  W. J. Unwin, Ltd.
FRAGARIA
  Clyde Robin Seed Co., Inc.
FRAMES, brood and honey
  Diamond International Corp.
FRAME cleaner
  The Walter T. Kelley Company
FRAME grips
  Diamond International Corp.
FRAMES, nailed, fndan. fixed
  Diamond International Corp.
FRAME nailing device
  The Walter T. Kelley Company
FRAME parts
  Diamond International Corp.
FRAME rests, flat tins
  Diamond International Corp.
FRAME spacers (see Spacers, frame)
FRAME wire
  Diamond International Corp.
FRANKLINIA
  Geo. W. Park Seed Co., Inc.
  F. W. Schumacher Co.

FRANSERIA
  Clyde Robin Seed Co., Inc.
FRAXINUS
  Clyde Robin Seed Co., Inc.
  F. W. Schumacher Co.
FREESIAS
  Ferndale Gardens
  Geo. W. Park Seed Co., Inc.
  Stokes Seeds, Inc.
  W. J. Unwin, Ltd.
FREMONTIA
  Clyde Robin Seed Co., Inc.
FREMONTODENDRON
  Clyde Robin Seed Co., Inc.
FRENCH endive
  W. Atlee Burpee Co.
  Joseph Harris Co., Inc.
FRENCH hybrid lilacs
  Girard Nurseries
FRENCH marigold
  Joseph Harris Co., Inc.
FRITILLARIA
  Clyde Robin Seed Co., Inc.
FRUIT trees
  Boatman Nursery & Seed Co.
  W. Atlee Burpee Co.
  Henry Field Seed & Nursery Co.
  Inter-State Nurseries
  Jackson & Perkins Co.
  L. L. Olds Seed Company
FRUIT trees, dwarf
  Henry Field Seed & Nursery Co.
  Gurney Seed & Nursery Co.
  Thomas B. Kyle, Jr. — Spring
    Hill Nurseries Co.
  Earl May Seed & Nursery Co.
  J. E. Miller Nurseries, Inc.
  R. H. Shumway Seedsman
  Waynesboro Nurseries, Inc.
FUCHSIAS
  Burgess Seed and Plant Co.
  Gurney Seed & Nursery Co.
  Thomas B. Kyle, Jr. — Spring
    Hill Nurseries Co.
  Geo. W. Park Seed Co., Inc.
  R. H. Shumway Seedsman
  Stokes Seeds Inc.
  W. J. Unwin, Ltd.

Wilson Brothers Floral Co., Inc.
FUMIGANTS
Diamond International Corp.
FUNGICIDES
Earl May Seed & Nursery Co.
FUNKA-lily
DeGiorgi Company, Inc.
FUNKIA, hosta
Geo. W. Park Seed Co., Inc.
GAILLARDIA
W. Atlee Burpee Co.
D. V. Burrell Seed Growers Co.
DeGiorgi Company, Inc.
Henry Field Seed & Nursery Co.
Gurney Seed & Nursery Co.
Joseph Harris Co., Inc.
J. W. Jung Seed Co.
Thomas B. Kyle, Jr. – Spring
Hill Nurseries Co.
L. L. Olds Seed Company
Geo. W. Park Seed Co., Inc.
Clyde Robin Seed Co., Inc.
Stokes Seeds, Inc.
W. J. Unwin, Ltd.
GALTONIA
Geo. W. Park Seed Co., Inc.
GALVEZIA
Clyde Robin Seed Co., Inc.
GARDEN aids
W. Atlee Burpee Co.
Jardin du Gourmet
J. E. Miller Nurseries, Inc.
GARDEN cart
Garden Way Research
GARDEN cultivator
Mother's General Store
GARDEN huckleberry
Burgess Seed and Plant Co.
R. H. Shumway Seedsman
Stokes Seeds, Inc.
GARDEN mixtures
Geo. W. Park Seed Co., Inc.
GARDEN pink (see Pink, garden)
GARDEN tillers
Amerind-MacKissic, Inc.
GARDENIA
Ferndale Gardens

Gurney Seed & Nursery Co.
Lakeland Nurseries Sales
Wilson Brothers Floral Co., Inc.
"GARDEN Straddler, The"
C. W. Michaels Co.
GARLIC
W. Atlee Burpee Co.
Burgess Seed and Plant Co.
DeGiorgi Company, Inc.
Farmer Seed & Nursery Com-
pany
Henry Field Seed & Nursery Co.
Gallants Herb Products, Inc.
Gurney Seed & Nursery Co.
Joseph Harris Co., Inc.
J. W. Jung Seed Co.
Earl May Seed & Nursery Co.
Nichols Garden Nursery
L. L. Olds Seed Company
R. H. Shumway Seedsman
GARLIC ointment
Gallants Herb Products, Inc.
GARRYA
Clyde Robin Seed Co., Inc.
GARZANIA
W. J. Unwin, Ltd.
GAS plant
J. W. Jung Seed Co.
Lakeland Nurseries Sales
GATES, honey
Diamond International Corp.
GAULTHERIA
Clyde Robin Seed Co.
F. W. Schumacher Co.
GAYFEATHER liatrus (see
Liatrus, gayfeather)
GAZANIA
W. Atlee Burpee Co.
Joseph Harris Co., Inc.
Jackson & Perkins Co.
Geo. W. Park Seed Co., Inc.
Stokes Seeds, Inc.
GENERATOR, steam
Diamond International Corp.
GENISTA
F. W. Schumacher Co.

GENTIAN
Geo. W. Park Seed Co., Inc.
GENTIANA
DeGiorgi Company, Inc.
Clyde Robin Seed Co., Inc.
GERANIUM
Burgess Seed and Plant Co.
W. Atlee Burpee Co.
D. V. Burrell Seed Growers Co.
DeGiorgi Company, Inc.
Farmer Seed & Nursery Company
Ferndale Gardens
Henry Field Seed & Nursery Co.
Gurney Seed & Nursery Co.
Joseph Harris Co., Inc.
Jackson & Perkins Co.
Thomas B. Kyle, Jr. — Spring Hill Nurseries Co.
Lakeland Nurseries Sales
Earl May Seed & Nursery Co.
L. L. Olds Seed Company
Geo. W. Park Seed Co., Inc.
R. H. Shumway Seedsman
Stokes Seeds, Inc.
Otis S. Twilley Seed Co.
W. J. Unwin, Ltd.
Wilson Brothers Floral Co., Inc.
GERANIUM alpinum
Inter-State Nurseries
GERANIUM food
Earl May Seed & Nursery Co.
GERANIUM seed
J. W. Jung Seed Co.
GERBERA
W. Atlee Burpee Co.
DeGiorgi Company, Inc.
Henry Field Seed & Nursery Co.
Gurney Seed & Nursery Co.
Inter-State Nurseries
Geo. W. Park Seed Co., Inc.
Stokes Seeds, Inc.
W. J. Unwin, Ltd.
GERMAN iris
Van Bourgondien Brothers
GESNERIA
Geo. W. Park Seed Co., Inc.
W. J. Unwin, Ltd.

GESNERIADS
DeGiorgi Company, Inc.
Fischer Greenhouses
Geo. W. Park Seed Co., Inc.
GEUM
W. Atlee Burpee Co.
DeGiorgi Company, Inc.
L. L. Olds Seed Company
Stokes Seeds, Inc.
W. J. Unwin, Ltd.
GEUM, avens
Geo. W. Park Seed Co., Inc.
GIANT reed (see Reed, giant)
GILIA
DeGiorgi Company, Inc.
Geo. W. Park Seed Co., Inc.
GILLIFLOWER stocks (see Stocks, gilliflower)
GILLIUM
Clyde Robin Seed Co., Inc.
GINKGO
Thomas B. Kyle, Jr. — Spring Hill Nurseries Co.
Clyde Robin Seed Co., Inc.
F. W. Schumacher Co.
GINKGO tree
Henry Field Seed & Nursery Co.
GINSENG capsules
Heise's Wausau Farms
GINSENG powder
Heise's Wausau Farms
GINSENG roots
The American Ginseng Gardens
Ferndale Gardens
The Fmali Co.
Gurney Seed & Nursery Co.
Heise's Wausau Farms
Lakeland Nurseries Sales
Nichols Garden Nursery
L. L. Olds Seed Company
GINSENG seeds
The American Ginseng Gardens
The Fmali Co.
Johnny's Selected Seeds
GLADIOLUS
Burgess Seed and Plant Co.
W. Atlee Burpee Co.

DeGiorgi Company, Inc.
Farmer Seed & Nursery Company
Ferndale Gardens
Henry Field Seed & Nursery Co.
Gurney Seed & Nursery Co.
Joseph Harris Co., Inc.
Inter-State Nurseries
J. W. Jung Seed Co.
Thomas B. Kyle, Jr. — Spring Hill Nurseries Co.
Lakeland Nurseries Sales
Earl May Seed & Nursery Co.
L. L. Olds Seed Company
Geo. W. Park Seed Co., Inc.
Seedway, Inc.
R. H. Shumway Seedsman
Otis S. Twilley Seedsman
Van Bourgondien Brothers
Waynesboro Nurseries, Inc.

GLEDITSIA
F. W. Schumacher Co.

GLIRICIDIA
Clyde Robin Seed Co., Inc.

GLOBE amaranth
W. Atlee Burpee Co.
DeGiorgi Company, Inc.

GLOBULARIA
Geo. W. Park Seed Co., Inc.

GLORIOSA daisy
W. Atlee Burpee Co.
D. V. Burrell Seed Growers Co.
DeGiorgi Company, Inc.
Joseph Harris Co., Inc.
Jackson & Perkins Co.
J. W. Jung Seed Co.
Geo. W. Park Seed Co., Inc.
Stokes Seeds, Inc.
Otis S. Twilley Seed Co.

GLORIOSA lily
W. Atlee Burpee Co.
Geo. W. Park Seed Co., Inc.

GLORY flower
Geo. W. Park Seed Co., Inc.

GLOVES, bee
Diamond International Corp.
The Walter T. Kelley Company

GLOVE sleeves
Diamond International Corp.

GLOXINIA
W. Atlee Burpee Co.
DeGiorgi Company, Inc.
Gurney Seed & Nursery Co.
J. W. Jung Seed Co.
Lakeland Nurseries Sales
L. L. Olds Seed Company
Geo. W. Park Seed Co., Inc.
R. H. Shumway Seedsman
Stokes Seeds, Inc.
W. J. Unwin, Ltd.

GODETIA
W. Atlee Burpee Co.
DeGiorgi Company, Inc.
Gurney Seed & Nursery Co.
L. L. Olds Seed Company
Stokes Seeds, Inc.
W. J. Unwin, Ltd.

GODETIA, satinflower
Geo. W. Park Seed Co., Inc.

GOLDEN elder
Henry Field Seed & Nursery Co.

GOLDEN rain tree
Henry Field Seed & Nursery Co.

GOLDENROD
W. J. Unwin, Ltd.

GOLDENSEAL roots
The American Ginseng Gardens
The Fmali Co.

GOLDENSEAL seed
The American Ginseng Gardens

GOLDFISH
William Tricker, Inc.

GOLDFISH plant
Wilson Brothers Floral Co., Inc.

GOMPHOCARPUS
Geo. W. Park Seed Co., Inc.

GOMPHOLOBIUM
Clyde Robin Seed Co., Inc.

GOMPHRENA
W. Atlee Burpee Co.
DeGiorgi Company, Inc.
Joseph Harris Co., Inc.
L. L. Olds Seed Company
Geo. W. Park Seed Co., Inc.
Stokes Seeds, Inc.

GOOSEBERRIES
Farmer Seed & Nursery Company
Henry Field Seed & Nursery Co.
Gurney Seed & Nursery Co.
Inter-State Nurseries
J. W. Jung Seed Co.
Henry Leuthardt Nurseries, Inc.
R. H. Shumway Seedsman

GOSSYPIUM
W. J. Unwin, Ltd.

GOURDS
DeGiorgi Company, Inc.
Farmer Seed & Nursery Company
Henry Field Seed & Nursery Co.
Gurney Seed & Nursery Co.
Joseph Harris Co., Inc.
Jackson & Perkins Co.
J. W. Jung Seed Co.
L. L. Olds Seed Company
Geo. W. Park Seed Co., Inc.
Seedway, Inc.
R. H. Shumway Seedsman
Stokes Seeds, Inc.
W. J. Unwin, Ltd.

GOURDS, ornamental
W. Atlee Burpee Co.

GRAFTING tool, automatic
Diamond International Corp.

GRAPE vines
Armstrong Nurseries, Inc.
Boatman Nursery & Seed Co.
Brittingham Plant Farms
Burgess Seed and Plant Co.
W. Atlee Burpee Co.
Farmer Seed & Nursery Company
Henry Field Seed & Nursery Co.
Gurney Seed & Nursery Co.
Inter-State Nurseries
Jackson & Perkins Co.
J. W. Jung Seed Co.
Thomas B. Kyle, Jr. — Spring Hill Nurseries Co.
Henry Leuthardt Nurseries, Inc.
Earl May Seed & Nursery Co.
J. E. Miller Nurseries, Inc.

New York State Fruit Testing Cooperative Association
L. L. Olds Seed Company
R. H. Shumway Seedsman
Stark Bro's Nurseries
Waynesboro Nurseries, Inc.

GRASSES
DeGiorgi Company, Inc.
W. J. Unwin, Ltd.

GRASS, fountain
Inter-State Nurseries

GRASS hook
DeGiorgi Company, Inc.

GRASS, lawn
W. Atlee Burpee Co.
Joseph Harris Co., Inc.
Geo. W. Park Seed Co., Inc.
W. J. Unwin, Ltd.

GRASS, ornamental
W. Atlee Burpee Co.
DeGiorgi Company, Inc.
Gurney Seed & Nursery Co.
Geo. W. Park Seed Co., Inc.

GRASS seed
Farmer Seed & Nursery Company
Gurney Seed & Nursery Co.
J. W. Jung Seed Co.
L. L. Olds Seed Company

GREENHOUSE accessories
Gro-More Greenhouses

GREENHOUSE coolers
Pacific Coast Greenhouse Mfg. Co.

GREENHOUSE fans
Pacific Coast Greenhouse Mfg. Co.

GREENHOUSE heaters
Aluminum Greenhouses, Inc.
McGregor Greenhouses
Pacific Coast Greenhouse Mfg. Co.
Redwood Domes

GREENHOUSE heating cable
Aluminum Greenhouses, Inc.

GREENHOUSE humidifier
Pacific Coast Greenhouse Mfg. Co.

Redwood Domes
GREENHOUSE supplies
   Fischer Greenhouses
   The Houseplant Corner, Ltd.
GREENHOUSE thermostat
   McGregor Greenhouses
GREENHOUSE vents
   Aluminum Greenhouses, Inc.
GREENHOUSE watering systems
   Aluminum Greenhouses, Inc.
GREENHOUSES
   Aluminum Greenhouses, Inc.
   Environmental Dynamics
   Gro-More Greenhouses
   McGregor Greenhouses
   Pacific Coast Greenhouse
     Mfg. Co.
   Redwood Domes
   R. H. Shumway Seedsman
   Various Designs
GREENS
   Johnny's Selected Seeds
GREVILLEA
   DeGiorgi Company, Inc.
   L. L. Olds Seed Company
   Geo. W. Park Seed Co., Inc.
   F. W. Schumacher Co.
   Stokes Seeds, Inc.
GREVILLEA robusta
   W. J. Unwin, Ltd.
GRINDER/shredder
   W-W Grinder Corporation
GROUND cherry
   Burgess Seed and Plant Co.
   Farmer Seed & Nursery Company
   Henry Field Seed & Nursery Co.
   Joseph Harris Co., Inc.
   J. W. Jung Seed Co.
   L. L. Olds Seed Company
   Stokes Seeds, Inc.
GROUND covers
   Boatman Nursery & Seed Co.
   Burgess Seed and Plant Co.
   W. Atlee Burpee Co.
   Carino Nurseries
   Farmer Seed & Nursery Company
   Henry Field Seed & Nursery Co.

Gurney Seed & Nursery Co.
Inter-State Nurseries
J. W. Jung Seed Co.
J. E. Miller Nurseries, Inc.
Musser Forests, Inc.
R. H. Shumway Seedsman
Van Bourgondien Brothers
Waynesboro Nurseries, Inc.
GROWING benches
   Redwood Domes
GUARD, entrance
   Diamond International Corp.
GUMBO
   DeGiorgi Company, Inc.
   Joseph Harris Co., Inc.
GYMNOCLADUS
   F. W. Schumacher Co.
GYSOPHILA
   W. Atlee Burpee Co.
   D. V. Burrell Seed Growers Co.
   DeGiorgi Company, Inc.
   Gurner Seed & Nursery Co.
   Joseph Harris Co., Inc.
   Inter-State Nurseries
   Jackson & Perkins Co.
   L. L. Olds Seed Company
   Geo. W. Park Seed Co., Inc.
   Stokes Seeds, Inc.
   Otis S. Twilley Seed Co.
   W. J. Unwin, Ltd.
HACKBERRIES
   Henry Field Seed & Nursery Co.
HALESIA
   F. W. Schumacher Co.
HAMAMELIS
   F. W. Schumacher Co.
HAMBURG elm (see Elm,
   hamburg)
HAND baler
   Various Designs
HANGING basket pots (see Pots,
   hanging basket)
HANGING baskets
   Gurney Seed & Nursery Co.
HANGING plants
   Gurney Seed & Nursery Co.
HAPLOPAPPUS
   Clyde Robin Seed Co., Inc.

HARDWOOD seedlings
Musser Forests, Inc.
HARDWOOD shrubs
Musser Forests, Inc.
HARDY carnations (see Carnations,
hardy)
HARDY larkspur (see Larkspur,
hardy)
HARDY lily (see Lily, hardy)
HARDY linum (see Linum, hardy)
HARDY lupines (see Lupines, hardy)
HARDY orchids (see Orchids,
hardy)
HARDY perennials
Van Bourgondien Brothers
HARDY phlox
DeGiorgi Company, Inc.
HARDY sweet peas (see Sweet peas,
hardy)
HARPEPHYLLUM
Geo. W. Park Seed Co., Inc.
HAWAIIAN perfumes
World Gardens
HAZELNUT trees
Burgess Seed and Plant Co.
Gurney Seed & Nursery Co.
Lakeland Nurseries Sales
HEARTEASE pansy (see Pansy,
heartease)
HEATH
Ferndale Gardens
Lakeland Nurseries Sales
Silver Falls Nursery
HEATHER
Geo. W. Park Seed Co., Inc.
Silver Falls Nursery
HEDGE plants
Farmer Seed & Nursery Com-
pany
L. L. Olds Seed Company
HEDGES
Boatman Nursery & Seed Co.
W. Atlee Burpee Co.
Carino Nurseries
Henry Field Seed & Nursery Co.
Gurney Seed & Nursery Co.
Inter-State Nurseries
J. W. Jung Seed Co.

Thomas B. Kyle, Jr. — Spring
Hill Nurseries Co.
Earl May Seed & Nursery Co.
Musser Forests, Inc.
R. H. Shumway Seedsman
Stark Bro's Nurseries
Waynesboro Nurseries, Inc.
HEDYCHIUM
Geo. W. Park Seed Co., Inc.
HELENIUM
DeGiorgi Company, Inc.
Joseph Harris Co., Inc.
Inter-State Nurseries
Geo. W. Park Seed Co., Inc.
Clyde Robin Seed Co., Inc.
W. J. Unwin, Ltd.
HELIANTHEMUM
W. Atlee Burpee Co.
DeGiorgi Company, Inc.
Geo. W. Park Seed Co., Inc.
Clyde Robin Seed Co., Inc.
Stokes Seeds, Inc.
HELIANTHUS
W. Atlee Burpee Co.
DeGiorgi Company, Inc.
Jackson & Perkins Co.
L. L. Olds Seed Company
Geo. W. Park Seed Co., Inc.
Clyde Robin Seed Co., Inc.
Stokes Seeds, Inc.
HELICHRYSUM
W. Atlee Burpee Co.
DeGiorgi Company, Inc.
Joseph Harris Co., Inc.
L. L. Olds Seed Company
Geo. W. Park Seed Co., Inc.
W. J. Unwin, Ltd.
HELICHRYSUM montrosum
Stokes Seeds, Inc.
HELIOPSIS
DeGiorgi Company, Inc.
Geo. W. Park Seed Co., Inc.
W. J. Unwin, Ltd.
HELIOTROPE
W. Atlee Burpee Co.
Joseph Harris Co., Inc.
L. L. Olds Seed Company
Geo. W. Park Seed Co., Inc.

Stokes Seeds, Inc.
W. J. Unwin, Ltd.
HELIPTERUM
W. Atlee Burpee Co.
Geo. W. Park Seed Co., Inc.
HELLEBORUS
Geo. W. Park Seed Co., Inc.
Clyde Robin Seed Co., Inc.
HELMET
Diamond International Corp.
The Walter T. Kelley Company
HEMEROCALLIS
W. Atlee Burpee Co.
Henry Field Seed & Nursery Co.
Gurney Seed & Nursery Co.
Geo. W. Park Seed Co., Inc.
Stokes Seeds, Inc.
W. J. Unwin, Ltd.
HEMLOCK
Silver Falls Nursery
Western Maine Forest Nursery
HEN & chickens plants
Henry Field Seed & Nursery Co.
Thomas B. Kyle, Jr. — Spring
Hill Nurseries Co.
HERACLEUM
Clyde Robin Seed Co., Inc.
HERB plants
Nichols Garden Nursery
HERBS
Burgess Seed and Plant Co.
W. Atlee Burpee Co.
DeGiorgi Company, Inc.
Farmer Seed & Nursery Company
Henry Field Seed & Nursery Co.
Gurney Seed & Nursery Co.
Joseph Harris Co., Inc.
Jackson & Perkins Co.
Johnny's Selected Seeds
J. W. Jung Seed Co.
Lakeland Nurseries Sales
Earl May Seed & Nursery Co.
L. L. Olds Seed Company
Geo. W. Park Seed Co., Inc.
Seedway, Inc.
R. H. Shumway Seedsman
Stokes Seeds, Inc.

Otis S. Twilley Seed Co.
W. J. Unwin, Ltd.
HERNIARIA
Geo. W. Park Seed Co., Inc.
HESPERIS
DeGiorgi Company, Inc.
Geo. W. Park Seed Co., Inc.
HETEROMELES
Clyde Robin Seed Co., Inc.
HEUCHERA
W. Atlee Burpee Co.
Inter-State Nurseries
J. W. Jung Seed Co.
L. L. Olds Seed Company
Geo. W. Park Seed Co., Inc.
Clyde Robin Seed Co., Inc.
Stokes Seeds, Inc.
W. J. Unwin, Ltd.
HIBISCUS
W. Atlee Burpee Co.
DeGiorgi Company, Inc.
Henry Field Seed & Nursery Co.
Joseph Harris Co., Inc.
Inter-State Nurseries
J. W. Jung Seed Co.
Thomas B. Kyle, Jr. — Spring
Hill Nurseries Co.
Lakeland Nurseries Sales
L. L. Olds Seed Company
Geo. W. Park Seed Co., Inc.
Clyde Robin Seed Co., Inc.
F. W. Schumacher Co.
Stokes Seeds, Inc.
Otis S. Twilley Seed Co.
W. J. Unwin, Ltd.
Wilson Brothers Floral Co., Inc.
HICKORY
Gurney Seed & Nursery Co.
Stark Bro's Nurseries
HIERACIUM
DeGiorgi Company, Inc.
HIGH bush cranberry
Henry Field Seed & Nursery Co.
HIGH hedge
J. W. Jung Seed Co.
HIMALAYAN cherry
Burgess Seed and Plant Co.

HINDU rope
  Wilson Brothers Floral Co., Inc.
HIPPOPHAE
  F. W. Schumacher Co.
HIVE bodies (super)
  Diamond International Corp.
HIVES, bee
  Diamond International Corp.
  The Walter T. Kelley Company
HIVE bomb
  Diamond International Corp.
HIVE bottoms
  Diamond International Corp.
HIVE covers (see Covers, hive)
HIVE paint
  Diamond International Corp.
HIVE scrapers
  Diamond International Corp.
HIVE staples
  Diamond International Corp.
HIVE tools (see Tools, hive)
HOLLY
  Burgess Seed and Plant Co.
  Gurney Seed & Nursery Co.
  Thomas B. Kyle, Jr. – Spring
    Hill Nurseries Co.
  Silver Falls Nursery
HOLLYHOCK
  W. Atlee Burpee Co.
  D. V. Burrell Seed Growers Co.
  DeGiorgi Company, Inc.
  Henry Field Seed & Nursery Co.
  Gurney Seed & Nursery Co.
  Joseph Harris Co., Inc.
  Inter-State Nurseries
  Jackson & Perkins Co.
  J. W. Jung Seed Co.
  Thomas B. Kyle, Jr. – Spring
    Hill Nurseries Co.
  L. L. Olds Seeds Company
  Seedway, Inc.
  Stokes Seeds, Inc.
  Otis S. Twilley Seed Co.
  W. J. Unwin, Ltd.
HOLLYHOCK, althea
  Geo. W. Park Seed Co., Inc.
HOLODISCUS
  Clyde Robin Seed Co., Inc.

HOMINY corn
  Earl May Seed & Nursery Co.
HONESTY
  W. Atlee Burpee Co.
  Joseph Harris Co., Inc.
  W. J. Unwin, Ltd.
HONEY bear
  Diamond International Corp.
HONEY gate
  Diamond International Corp.
  The Walter T. Kelley Company
HONEY jars
  Diamond International Corp.
HONEY labels (see Labels, honey)
HONEY pump (see Pump, honey)
HONEY strainers and material
  Diamond International Corp.
HONEYSUCKLE
  Henry Field Seed & Nursery Co.
  Gurney Seed & Nursery Co.
  Inter-State Nurseries
  J. W. Jung Seed Co.
  Thomas B. Kyle, Jr. – Spring
    Hill Nurseries Co.
  Earl May Seed & Nursery Co.
  L. L. Olds Seed Company
HOP
  Geo. W. Park Seed Co., Inc.
HOREHOUND
  W. Atlee Burpee Co.
  Gurney Seed & Nursery Co.
  L. L. Olds Seed Company
HORKELIA
  Clyde Robin Seed Co., Inc.
HORMINUM salvia (see Salvia,
  horminum)
HORSERADISH
  Burgess Seed and Plant Co.
  DeGiorgi Company, Inc.
  Farmer Seed & Nursery Com-
    pany
  Henry Field Seed & Nursery Co.
  Gurney Seed & Nursery Co.
  Inter-State Nurseries
  J. W. Jung Seed Co.
  Thomas B. Kyle, Jr. – Spring
    Hill Nurseries Co.
    Lakeland Nurseries Sales

200

Earl May Seed & Nursery Co.
Seedway, Inc.
HORSERADISH roots
W. Atlee Burpee Co.
R. H. Shumway Seedsman
HOSE, steam
Diamond International Corp.
HOSTA
Henry Field Seed & Nursery Co.
Inter-State Nurseries
Thomas B. Kyle, Jr. — Spring
Hill Nurseries Co.
Geo. W. Park Seed Co., Inc.
HOTKAPS
Farmer Seed & Nursery Com-
pany
Gurney Seed & Nursery Co.
Joseph Harris Co., Inc.
L. L. Olds Seed Company
R. H. Shumway Seedsman
HOUCHERA
DeGiorgi Company, Inc.
HOUSEPLANT seed
J. W. Jung Seed Co.
HOUSEPLANTS
Burgess Seed and Plant Co.
W. Atlee Burpee Co.
Gurney Seed & Nursery Co.
The Houseplant Corner, Ltd.
Thomas B. Kyle, Jr. — Spring
Hill Nurseries Co.
Earl May Seed & Nursery Co.
R. H. Shumway Seedsman
W. J. Unwin, Ltd.
Van Bourgondien Brothers
HOVENIA
Clyde Robin Seed Co., Inc.
F. W. Schumacher Co.
HOYA
Geo. W. Park Seed Co., Inc.
Wilson Brothers Floral Co., Inc.
HUCKLEBERRIES
Farmer Seed & Nursery Com-
pany
Henry Field Seed & Nursery Co.
Gurney Seed & Nursery Co.
J. W. Jung Seed Co.
L. L. Olds Seed Company

HUMIDIFIER
McGregor Greenhouses
HUNNEMANIA
DeGiorgi Company, Inc.
Geo. W. Park Seed Co., Inc.
Clyde Robin Seed Co., Inc.
HYACINTH bean
DeGiorgi Company, Inc.
HYACINTHS
Farmer Seed & Nursery Com-
pany
J. W. Jung Seed Co.
L. L. Olds Seed Company
Geo. W. Park Seed Co., Inc.
HYBRID corn (see Corn, hybrid)
HYBRID elm
Henry Field Seed & Nursery Co.
HYBRID lilies
Van Bourgondien Brothers
HYDRANGEA
Henry Field Seed & Nursery Co.
Gurney Seed & Nursery Co.
Inter-State Nurseries
J. W. Jung Seed Co.
Thomas B. Kyle, Jr. — Spring
Hill Nurseries Co.
L. L. Olds Seed Company
F. W. Schumacher Co.
HYDRANGEA tree
Burgess Seed and Plant Co.
HYDROPONIC information
Hydroponic Society of America
HYDROPONIC units
Environmental Dynamics
HYPERICUM
DeGiorgi Company, Inc.
Inter-State Nurseries
Thomas B. Kyle, Jr. — Spring
Hill Nurseries Co.
Geo. W. Park Seed Co., Inc.
Clyde Robin Seed Co., Inc.
F. W. Schumacher Co.
HYPOESTES
Geo. W. Park Seed Co., Inc.
HYSSOP
W. J. Unwin, Ltd.
IBERIS
W. Atlee Burpee Co.

DeGiorgi Company, Inc.
Joseph Harris Co., Inc.
Inter-State Nurseries
L. L. Olds Seed Company
Geo. W. Park Seed Co., Inc.
Stokes Seeds, Inc.
IBERIS sempervirens
W. J. Unwin, Ltd.
ICELAND poppy (see Poppy, iceland)
ICE plant
DeGiorgi Company, Inc.
Geo. W. Park Seed Co., Inc.
Stokes Seeds, Inc.
ILEX
Clyde Robin Seed Co., Inc.
F. W. Schumacher Co.
IMMORTELLE
DeGiorgi Company, Inc.
IMPATIENS
W. Atlee Burpee Co.
DeGiorgi Company, Inc.
Henry Fields Seed & Nursery Co.
Gurney Seed & Nursery Co.
Joseph Harris Co., Inc.
Jackson & Perkins Co.
J. W. Jung Seed Co.
L. L. Olds Seed Company
Geo. W. Park Seed Co., Inc.
Stokes Seeds, Inc.
Otis S. Twilley Seed Co.
W. J. Unwin, Ltd.
INCARVILLEA
Geo. W. Park Seed Co., Inc.
W. J. Unwin, Ltd.
INDIAN corn
DeGiorgi Company, Inc.
INDIAN pink
DeGiorgi Company, Inc.
INFLATABLE greenhouses
Terra-Phernalia, Earth Oriented Imports
INNER covers
Diamond International Corp.
INTRODUCING cage, sureway
Diamond International Corp.
INULA
DeGiorgi Company, Inc.

W. J. Unwin, Ltd.
IPOMEA
DeGiorgi Company, Inc.
Joseph Harris Co., Inc.
L. L. Olds Seed Company
Geo. W. Park Seed Co., Inc.
Clyde Robin Seed Co., Inc.
Stokes Seeds, Inc.
W. J. Unwin, Ltd.
IRIS
DeGiorgi Company, Inc.
Farmer Seed & Nursery Company
Henry Field Seed & Nursery Co.
Gurney Seed & Nursery Co.
Inter-State Nurseries
J. W. Jung Seed Co.
Thomas B. Kyle, Jr. — Spring Hill Nurseries Co.
Earl May Seed & Nursery Co.
Clyde Robin Seed Co., Inc.
Stokes Seeds, Inc.
Waynesboro Nurseries, Inc.
IRIS, bearded
W. Atlee Burpee Co.
IRIS, flag
Geo. W. Park Seed Co., Inc.
IRISH lace
DeGiorgi Company, Inc.
ISMENE
W. Atlee Burpee Co.
Geo. W. Park Seed Co., Inc.
ISMENE calathina
L. L. Olds Seed Company
ISOMERIS
Clyde Robin Seed Co., Inc.
IVY
W. Atlee Burpee Co.
Farmer Seed & Nursery Company
Henry Field Seed & Nursery Co.
Gurney Seed & Nursery Co.
Inter-State Nurseries
J. W. Jung Seed Co.
Thomas B. Kyle, Jr. — Spring Hill Nurseries Co.
R. H. Shumway Seedsman

JACARANDA
DeGiorgi Company, Inc.
Geo. W. Park Seed Co., Inc.
Clyde Robin Seed Co., Inc.
W. J. Unwin, Ltd.
JACOBEA
DeGiorgi Company, Inc.
W. J. Unwin, Ltd.
JACOBINIA
Geo. W. Park Seed Co., Inc.
JACK in the pulpit
DeGiorgi Company, Inc.
JAPANESE greens
Kitayawa Seed Company
JAPANESE pagoda tree
Henry Field Seed & Nursery Co.
JAPANESE radish (see Radish,
japanese)
JARS
Diamond International Corp.
JASIONE
Geo. W. Park Seed Co., Inc.
W. J. Unwin, Ltd.
JASMINE, yellow
Geo. W. Park Seed Co., Inc.
JATROPHA
Clyde Robin Seed Co., Inc.
JELLY spoon
Diamond International Corp.
JERUSALEM cherry
DeGiorgi Company, Inc.
JEWELS of opar
Joseph Harris Co., Inc.
Geo. W. Park Seed Co., Inc.
JOB'S tears
W. Atlee Burpee Co.
DeGiorgi Company, Inc.
L. L. Olds Seed Company
Geo. W. Park Seed Co., Inc.
Rabbit Hop Nursery
JOSEPH'S coat
DeGiorgi Company, Inc.
JUGLANS
F. W. Schumacher Co.
JUJUBE trees
Armstrong Nurseries, Inc.
JUNCUS
Clyde Robin Seed Co., Inc.

JUNEBERRIES
Thomas B. Kyle, Jr. — Spring
Hill Nurseries Co.
JUNIPERS
Ferndale Gardens
Girard Nurseries
Gurney Seed & Nursery Co.
Spring Falls Nursery
JUNIPERUS
Clyde Robin Seed Co., Inc.
F. W. Schumacher Co.
KALANCHOE
DeGiorgi Company, Inc.
Geo. W. Park Seed Co., Inc.
Stokes Seeds, Inc.
W. J. Unwin, Ltd.
KALE
Burgess Seed and Plant Co.
W. Atlee Burpee Co.
DeGiorgi Company, Inc.
Farmer Seed & Nursery Com-
pany
Henry Field Seed & Nursery Co.
Gurney Seed & Nursery Co.
Joseph Harris Co., Inc.
Jackson & Perkins Co.
Johnny's Selected Seeds
Earl May Seed & Nursery Co.
L. L. Olds Seed Company
Seedway, Inc.
R. H. Shumway Seedsman
Stokes Seeds, Inc.
Otis S. Twilley Seed Co.
W. J. Unwin, Ltd.
KALE, flowering
J. W. Jung Seed Co.
Geo. W. Park Seed Co., Inc.
KALMIA
Clyde Robin Seed Co., Inc.
F. W. Schumacher Co.
KAZAN pyracantha (see Pyracan-
tha, kazan)
KENTUCKY blue grass
DeGiorgi Company, Inc.
KERRIA
F. W. Schumacher Co.
KIDNEY beans
Joseph Harris Co., Inc.

KITCHEN aids
  W. Atlee Burpee Co.
KNIPHOFIA
  W. Atlee Burpee Co.
  W. J. Unwin, Ltd.
KNIVES, uncapping
  Diamond International Corp.
  The Walter T. Kelley Company
KOCHIA
  W. Atlee Burpee Co.
  DeGiorgi Company, Inc.
  Joseph Harris Co., Inc.
  J. W. Jung Seed Co.
  L. L. Olds Seed Company
  Stokes Seeds, Inc.
  W. J. Unwin, Ltd.
KOCHIA, cypress
  Geo. W. Park Seed Co., Inc.
KOELREUTERIA
  Clyde Robin Seed Co., Inc.
  F. W. Schumacher Co.
KOHLRABI
  Burgess Seed and Plant Co.
  W. Atlee Burpee Co.
  DeGiorgi Company, Inc.
  Farmer Seed & Nursery Company
  Henry Field Seed & Nursery Co.
  Gurney Seed & Nursery Co.
  Joseph Harris Co., Inc.
  Jackson & Perkins Co.
  J. W. Jung Seed Co.
  Earl May Seed & Nursery Co.
  L. L. Olds Seed Company
  Seedway, Inc.
  R. H. Shumway Seedsman
  Stokes Seeds, Inc.
  Otis S. Twilley Seed Co.
  W. J. Unwin, Ltd.
KOLKWITZIA
  F. W. Schumacher Co.
KOREAN boxwood
  Henry Field Seed & Nursery Co.
KUDZU vine
  DeGiorgi Company, Inc.
  Geo. W. Park Seed Co., Inc.
KWANZAN flowering cherry (see
  Cherry, kwanzan flowering)

LABELS, honey
  Diamond International Corp.
LABEL paste
  Diamond International Corp.
LABURNUM
  Geo. W. Park Seed Co., Inc.
  F. W. Schumacher Co.
LACE flower
  DeGiorgi Company, Inc.
LACEWINGS
  California Green Lacewings
LADYBUGS
  Bio-Control Co.
  Countryside General Store
  Ferndale Gardens
  Lakeland Nurseries Sales
LADY slipper
  DeGiorgi Company, Inc.
  Joseph Harris Co., Inc.
  Thomas B. Kyle, Jr. — Spring
    Hill Nurseries Co.
  Stokes Seeds, Inc.
LAGERSTROEMIA
  Clyde Robin Seed Co., Inc.
  F. W. Schumacher Co.
  W. J. Unwin, Ltd.
LAGURUS
  DeGiorgi Company, Inc.
  Clyde Robin Seed Co., Inc.
LANDSCAPE evergreens
  Musser Forests, Inc.
LANDSCAPE ornamentals
  Musser Forests, Inc.
LANTANA
  DeGiorgi Company, Inc.
  L. L. Olds Seed Company
  Geo. W. Park Seed Co., Inc.
  Wilson Brothers Floral Co., Inc.
LARCH
  Carino Nurseries
  Silver Falls Nursery
LARIX
  F. W. Schumacher Co.
LARKSPUR
  W. Atlee Burpee Co.
  D. V. Burrell Seed Growers Co.
  DeGiorgi Company, Inc.
  Henry Field Seed & Nursery Co.

Gurney Seed & Nursery Co.
Jackson & Perkins Co.
J. W. Jung Seed Co.
Earl May Seed & Nursery Co.
L. L. Olds Seed Company
Geo. W. Park Seed Co., Inc.
Stokes Seeds, Inc.
Joseph Harris Co., Inc.

LARKSPUR, annual
Joseph Harris Co., Inc.

LARKSPUR, hardy
Joseph Harris Co., Inc.

LARKSPUR, regal
Seedway, Inc.

LATANIA
Geo. W. Park Seed Co., Inc.

LATHYRUS
W. Atlee Burpee Co.
DeGiorgi Company, Inc.
Joseph Harris Co., Inc.
L. L. Olds Seed Company
Geo. W. Park Seed Co., Inc.
Clyde Robin Seed Co., Inc.
Stokes Seeds, Inc.

LAURUS
Clyde Robin Seed Co., Inc.
F. W. Schumacher Co.

LAVANDULA
Clyde Robin Seed Co., Inc.
Stokes Seeds, Inc.

LAVATERA
DeGiorgi Company, Inc.
Joseph Harris Co., Inc.
Geo. W. Park Seed Co., Inc.
Clyde Robin Seed Co., Inc.
Stokes Seeds, Inc.
W. J. Unwin, Ltd.

LAVATERS
J. W. Jung Seed Co.

LAVENDER
Burgess Seed and Plant Co.
W. Atlee Burpee Co.
DeGiorgi Company, Inc.
Ferndale Gardens
Henry Field Seed & Nursery Co.
Gurney Seed & Nursery Co.
Joseph Harris Co., Inc.
L. L. Olds Seed Company

Geo. W. Park Seed Co., Inc.
Stokes Seeds, Inc.
W. J. Unwin, Ltd.

LAVENDER shrub
Thomas B. Kyle, Jr. — Spring
Hill Nurseries Co.

LAWN care items
Barzen of Minneapolis, Inc.

LAWN grass
W. Atlee Burpee Co.
DeGiorgi Company, Inc.
Farmer Seed & Nursery Company
Joseph Harris Co., Inc.
J. W. Jung Seed Co.

LAWN seed
Barzen of Minneapolis, Inc.
Henry Field Seed & Nursery Co.
Gurney Seed & Nursery Co.
Earl May Seed & Nursery Co.
L. L. Olds Seed Company

LAYIA
DeGiorgi Company, Inc.
Geo. W. Park Seed Co., Inc.
Clyde Robin Seed Co., Inc.
W. J. Unwin, Ltd.

LAZY daisy
Geo. W. Park Seed Co., Inc.

LEEK
Burgess Seed and Plant Co.
W. Atlee Burpee Co.
DeGiorgi Company, Inc.
Henry Field Seed & Nursery Co.
Gurney Seed & Nursery Co.
Joseph Harris Co., Inc.
Johnny's Selected Seeds
J. W. Jung Seed Co.
Earl May Seed & Nursery Co.
L. L. Olds Seed Company
Stokes Seeds, Inc.
W. J. Unwin, Ltd.

LEMON fluff
Thomas B. Kyle, Jr. — Spring
Hill Nurseries Co.

LEMON tree
Burgess Seed and Plant Co.
Ferndale Gardens
Lakeland Nurseries Sales

Wilson Brothers Floral Co., Inc.

LEONTOPODIUM
Geo. W. Park Seed Co., Inc.
Clyde Robin Seed Co., Inc.

LEONTOPODIUM alpinum
W. J. Unwin, Ltd.

LEOPARD'S bane
Joseph Harris Co., Inc.

LEPECHINIA
Clyde Robin Seed Co., Inc.

LEPTOSIPHON
DeGiorgi Company, Inc.
W. J. Unwin, Ltd.

LESPEDEZA
Clyde Robin Seed Co., Inc.
F. W. Schumacher Co.
R. H. Shumway Seedsman

LETTUCE
Burgess Seed and Plant Co.
W. Atlee Burpee Co.
D. V. Burrell Seed Growers Co.
DeGiorgi Company, Inc.
Farmer Seed & Nursery Company
Henry Field Seed & Nursery Co.
Gurney Seed & Nursery Co.
Joseph Harris Co., Inc.
Jackson & Perkins Co.
Johnny's Selected Seeds
J. W. Jung Seed Co.
Earl May Seed & Nursery Co.
Nichols Garden Nursery
L. L. Olds Seed Company
Seedway, Inc.
R. H. Shumway Seedsman
Spring Hill Farm
Stokes Seeds, Inc.
Otis S. Twilley Seed Co.
W. J. Unwin, Ltd.

LETTUCE plants
Evans Plant Company

LEUCADENDRON
Clyde Robin Seed Co., Inc.

LEUCAENA
Clyde Robin Seed Co.

LEUCANTHEMUM
Geo. W. Park Seed Co., Inc.

LEUCOSPERMUM
Clyde Robin Seed Co., Inc.

LEUCOTHOE
Clyde Robin Seed Co., Inc.
F. W. Schumacher Co.

LEWISIA
Geo. W. Park Seed Co., Inc.
Clyde Robin Seed Co., Inc.

LIATRIS
DeGiorgi Company, Inc.
J. W. Jung Seed Co.
L. L. Olds Seed Company
Clyde Robin Seed Co., Inc.
W. J. Unwin, Ltd.

LIATRIS, gayfeather
Geo. W. Park Seed Co., Inc.

LIBOCEDRUS
Clyde Robin Seed Co., Inc.
F. W. Schumacher Co.

LIGUSTRUM
F. W. Schumacher Co.

LILACS
Alexander's Blueberry Nurseries
W. Atlee Burpee Co.
Farmer Seed & Nursery Company
Henry Field Seed & Nursery Co.
Gurney Seed & Nursery Co.
Inter-State Nurseries
J. W. Jung Seed Co.
Thomas B. Kyle, Jr. — Spring Hill Nurseries Co.
L. L. Olds Seed Company

LILIES
W. Atlee Burpee Co.
Henry Field Seed & Nursery Co.
Gurney Seed & Nursery Co.
Inter-State Nurseries
J. W. Jung Seed Co.
Thomas B. Kyle, Jr. — Spring Hill Nurseries Co.
Lakeland Nurseries Sales
Earl May Seed & Nursery Co.
L. L. Olds Seed Company
R. H. Shumway Seedsman

LILLIUM
DeGiorgi Company, Inc.
W. J. Unwin, Ltd.

LILIUM, lily
  Geo. W. Park Seed Co., Inc.
  Clyde Robin Seed Co., Inc.
LILY, climbing
  Lakeland Nurseries Sales
LILY, hardy
  R. H. Shumway Seedsman
LILY, lilium (see Lilium, lily)
LILY of the nile
  Gurney Seed & Nursery Co.
LILY of the valley
  W. Atlee Burpee Co.
  Ferndale Gardens
  Henry Field Seed & Nursery Co.
  Gurney Seed & Nursery Co.
  Inter-State Nurseries
  J. W. Jung Seed Co.
  Thomas B. Kyle, Jr. — Spring
    Hill Nurseries Co.
  Lakeland Nurseries Sales
  Geo. W. Park Seed Co., Inc.
  R. H. Shumway Seedsman
  Van Bourgondien Brothers
LILY seed
  J. W. Jung Seed Co.
  R. H. Shumway Seedsman
LIMA beans
  W. Atlee Burpee Co.
  Joseph Harris Co., Inc.
LIME tree
  Burgess Seed and Plant Co.
  Ferndale Gardens
  Lakeland Nurseries Sales
LIMNANTHES
  Clyde Robin Seed Co., Inc.
LIMONIUM
  W. Atlee Burpee Co.
LINARIA
  W. Atlee Burpee Co.
  DeGiorgi Company, Inc.
  L. L. Olds Seed Company
  Clyde Robin Seed Co., Inc.
  Stokes Seeds, Inc.
  W. J. Unwin, Ltd.
LINARIA, toadflax
  Geo. W. Park Seed Co., Inc.
LINDEN
  Henry Field Seed & Nursery Co.

Inter-State Nurseries
Thomas B. Kyle, Jr. — Spring
  Hill Nurseries Co.
LINUM
  W. Atlee Burpee Co.
  DeGiorgi Company, Inc.
  L. L. Olds Seed Company
  Clyde Robin Seed Co., Inc.
  Stokes Seeds, Inc.
  W. J. Unwin, Ltd.
LINUM, hardy
  Joseph Harris Co., Inc.
LIPSTICK vine
  Wilson Brothers Floral Co., Inc.
LIQUIDAMBAR
  Clyde Robin Seed Co., Inc.
  F. W. Schumacher Co.
LIRIODENDRON
  Clyde Robin Seed Co., Inc.
  F. W. Schumacher Co.
LIRIOPE
  Geo. W. Park Seed Co., Inc.
LIVE forever
  Thomas B. Kyle, Jr. — Spring
    Hill Nurseries Co.
LIVING stones
  Geo. W. Park Seed Co., Inc.
LIVINGSTONE daisy
  W. J. Unwin, Ltd.
LOBELIA
  W. Atlee Burpee Co.
  D. V. Burrell Seed Growers Co.
  DeGiorgi Company, Inc.
  Gurney Seed & Nursery Co.
  Joseph Harris Co., Inc.
  Jackson & Perkins Co.
  L. L. Olds Seed Company
  Geo. W. Park Seed Co., Inc.
  Clyde Robin Seed Co., Inc.
  Stokes Seeds, Inc.
  W. J. Unwin, Ltd.
LOCUST
  Gurney Seed & Nursery Co.
  Inter-State Nurseries
  J. W. Jung Seed Co.
  Thomas B. Kyle, Jr. — Spring
    Hill Nurseries Co.

LOFUS
Geo. W. Park Seed Co., Inc.
LOGANBERRIES
Gurney Seed & Nursery Co.
LOG chippers
Amerind-MacKissic, Inc.
LONGBERRIES
Lakeland Nurseries Sales
LONICERA
Clyde Robin Seed Co., Inc.
F. W. Schumacher Co.
LOOSESTRIFE
Henry Field Seed & Nursery Co.
Gurney Seed & Nursery Co.
LOVE in a mist
W. Atlee Burpee Co.
J. W. Jung Seed Co.
W. J. Unwin, Ltd.
LOVE-lies-bleeding
W. J. Unwin, Ltd.
LUETKEA
Clyde Robin Seed Co., Inc.
LUFFA sponge
Gurney Seed & Nursery Co.
LUNARIA
W. Atlee Burpee Co.
DeGiorgi Company, Inc.
Joseph Harris Co., Inc.
J. W. Jung Seed Co.
L. L. Olds Seed Company
Geo. W. Park Seed Co., Inc.
Clyde Robin Seed Co., Inc.
Stokes Seeds, Inc.
LUPINES
W. Atlee Burpee Co.
Henry Field Seed & Nursery Co.
Gurney Seed & Nursery Co.
J. W. Jung Seed Co.
Thomas B. Kyle, Jr. — Spring
Hill Nurseries Co.
Geo. W. Park Seed Co., Inc.
Seedway, Inc.
Stokes Seeds, Inc.
LUPINES, hardy
Joseph Harris Co., Inc.
LUPINUS
DeGiorgi Company, Inc.
L. L. Olds Seed Company

Clyde Robin Seed Co., Inc.
W. J. Unwin, Ltd.
LYCHNIS
W. Atlee Burpee Co.
DeGiorgi Company, Inc.
J. W. Jung Seed Co.
W. J. Unwin, Ltd.
LYCHNIS, campion
Geo. W. Park Seed Co., Inc.
LYCORIS
Geo. W. Park Seed Co., Inc.
LYSIMACHIA
W. J. Unwin, Ltd.
LYTHRUM
DeGiorgi Company, Inc.
Ferndale Gardens
Henry Field Seed & Nursery Co.
Inter-State Nurseries
J. W. Jung Seed Co.
Thomas B. Kyle, Jr. — Spring
Hill Nurseries Co.
L. L. Olds Seed Company
Geo. W. Park Seed Co., Inc.
W. J. Unwin, Ltd.
MAACKIA
F. W. Schumacher Co.
MACADAMIA
F. W. Schumacher Co.
MACHAERANTHERA
Geo. W. Park Seed Co., Inc.
MACLURA
F. W. Schumacher Co.
MADEIRA vines
Ferndale Gardens
Geo. W. Park Seed Co., Inc.
R. H. Shumway Seedsman
MADIA
Clyde Robin Seed Co., Inc.
MAD wort
DeGiorgi Company, Inc.
MAGIC flower
Thomas B. Kyle, Jr. — Spring
Hill Nurseries Co.
MAGIC lily
W. Atlee Burpee Co.
MAGNOLIA
Henry Field Seed & Nursery Co.

Gurney Seed & Nursery Co.
Inter-State Nurseries
Thomas B. Kyle, Jr. — Spring
Hill Nurseries Co.
Earl May Seed & Nursery Co.
F. W. Schumacher Co.
R. H. Shumway Seedsman
MAHONIA
Clyde Robin Seed Co., Inc.
F. W. Schumacher Co.
Silver Falls Nursery
MAIZE
W. J. Unwin, Ltd.
MALABAR spinach
W. Atlee Burpee Co.
MALLOW
Joseph Harris Co., Inc.
W. J. Unwin, Ltd.
MALLOW malvia (see Malvia,
mallow)
MALTESE cross
W. Atlee Burpee Co.
Thomas B. Kyle, Jr. — Spring
Hill Nurseries Co.
Geo. W. Park Seed Co., Inc.
MALUS
F. W. Schumacher Co.
MALVA, mallow
Geo. W. Park Seed Co., Inc.
MANAOS beauty
Geo. W. Park Seed Co., Inc.
MANDEVILLEA
Geo. W. Park Seed Co., Inc.
MANGELS
W. Atlee Burpee Co.
Farmer Seed & Nursery Com-
pany
Gurney Seed & Nursery Co.
J. W. Jung Seed Co.
L. L. Olds Seed Company
R. H. Shumway Seedsman
MANGO melon
R. H. Shumway Seedsman
MANZATE
Joseph Harris Co., Inc.
MAPLE trees
Burgess Seed and Plant Co.
Henry Field Seed & Nursery Co.

Gurney Seed & Nursery Co.
Inter-State Nurseries
J. W. Jung Seed Co.
Thomas B. Kyle. Jr. — Spring
Hill Nurseries Co.
Earl May Seed & Nursery Co.
R. H. Shumway Seedsman
Silver Falls Nursery
MARBLE vine
Geo. W. Park Seed Co., Inc.
MARGUERITE
DeGiorgi Company, Inc.
Geo. W. Park Seed Co., Inc.
MARIGOLD
W. Atlee Burpee Co.
D. V. Burrell Seed Growers Co.
DeGiorgi Company, Inc.
Henry Field Seed & Nursery Co.
Gurney Seed & Nursery Co.
Joseph Harris Co., Inc.
Jackson & Perkins Co.
J. W. Jung Seed Co.
Earl May Seed & Nursery Co.
L. L. Olds Seed Company
Seedway, Inc.
Stokes Seeds, Inc.
Otis S. Twilley Seed Co.
W. J. Unwin, Ltd.
MARIGOLD, tagetes
Geo. W. Park Seed Co., Inc.
MARJORAM
Farmer Seed & Nursery Com-
pany
Joseph Harris Co., Inc.
L. L. Olds Seed Company
W. J. Unwin, Ltd.
MARJORAN
DeGiorgi Company, Inc.
MARKING crayon
Diamond International Corp.
MARROW
W. J. Unwin, Ltd.
MARRUBIUM
Clyde Robin Seed Co., Inc.
MARTYNIA
Geo. W. Park Seed Co., Inc.
MARTYNIA proboscidea
DeGiorgi Company, Inc.

MARVEL of peru
  W. Atlee Burpee Co.
  D. V. Burrell Seed Growers Co.
  DeGiorgi Company, Inc.
  Joseph Harris Co., Inc.
  Stokes Seeds, Inc.
MATHIOLA
  W. Atlee Burpee Co.
  L. L. Olds Seed Company
  Geo. W. Park Seed Co., Inc.
MATHIOLA bicornis
  DeGiorgi Company, Inc.
MATRICARIA
  W. Atlee Burpee Co.
  DeGiorgi Company, Inc.
  Geo. W. Park Seed Co., Inc.
  Stokes Seeds, Inc.
  W. J. Unwin, Ltd.
MATTHIOLA
  Stokes Seeds, Inc.
  W. J. Unwin, Ltd.
MAURANDIA
  DeGiorgi Company, Inc.
  Geo. W. Park Seed Co., Inc.
MEADOW rue
  DeGiorgi Company, Inc.
MECONOPSIS
  Geo. W. Park Seed Co., Inc.
MECONOPSIS baileyi
  W. J. Unwin, Ltd.
MELIA
  Clyde Robin Seed Co., Inc.
MELON, bitter
  Kitayawa Seed Company
MELONS
  W. Atlee Burpee Co.
  D. V. Burrell Seed Growers Co.
  Joseph Harris Co., Inc.
  Jackson & Perkins Co.
  Johnny's Selected Seeds
  R. H. Shumway Seedsman
  Spring Hill Farm
  W. J. Unwin, Ltd.
MELON zucca
  Stokes Seeds, Inc.
MENTZELIA
  Clyde Robin Seed Co., Inc.

MERION blue grass
  Geo. W. Park Seed Co., Inc.
MERYTA sinclair
  Geo. W. Park Seed Co., Inc.
MESEMBRYANTHEMUM
  DeGiorgi Company, Inc.
  Geo. W. Park Seed Co., Inc.
  Stokes Seeds, Inc.
  W. J. Unwin, Ltd.
MESPILUS
  Clyde Robin Seed Co., Inc.
  F. W. Schumacher Co.
METAL eyelets
  Diamond International Corp.
MEXICAN heather
  Burgess Seed and Plant Co.
MEXICAN lily
  J. W. Jung Seed Co.
MEXICAN sunflower
  W. Atlee Burpee Co.
  W. J. Unwin, Ltd.
MICHAELMUM daisy
  DeGiorgi Company, Inc.
  Geo. W. Park Seed Co., Inc.
  W. J. Unwin, Ltd.
MICHIGAN banana
  Burgess Seed and Plant Co.
MICROSPERMA
  Geo. W. Park Seed Co., Inc.
MIDGET vegetables
  Farmer Seed & Nursery Company
  Henry Field Seed & Nursery Co.
MIGNONETTE
  W. Atlee Burpee Co.
  DeGiorgi Company, Inc.
  Gurney Seed & Nursery Co.
  Joseph Harris Co., Inc.
  J. W. Jung Seed Co.
  L. L. Olds Seed Company
  Geo. W. Park Seed Co., Inc.
  Stokes Seeds, Inc.
  W. J. Unwin, Ltd.
MILIA
  F. W. Schumacher Co.
MILLETS
  R. H. Shumway Seedsman

MILO maize
R. H. Shumway Seedsman
MIMOSA
W. Atlee Burpee Co.
DeGiorgi Company, Inc.
Henry Field Seed & Nursery Co.
Thomas B. Kyle, Jr. – Spring
Hill Nurseries Co.
L. L. Olds Seed Company
Geo. W. Park Seed Co., Inc.
Stokes Seeds, Inc.
MIMOSA, acacia
W. J. Unwin, Ltd.
MIMOSA, pudicia
W. J. Unwin, Ltd.
MIMULUS
DeGiorgi Company, Inc.
Geo. W. Park Seed Co., Inc.
Clyde Robin Seed Co., Inc.
Stokes Seeds, Inc.
W. J. Unwin, Ltd.
MINA
DeGiorgi Company, Inc.
MINA lobata
W. J. Unwin, Ltd.
MINIATURE roses
Gurney Seed & Nursery Co.
Lakeland Nurseries Sales
MINI, baby rose
DeGiorgi Company, Inc.
MINI vegetables
Burgess Seed and Plant Co.
MINTS
Burgess Seed and Plant Co.
Henry Field Seed & Nursery Co.
Gurney Seed & Nursery Co.
L. L. Olds Seed Company
W. J. Unwin, Ltd.
MIRABILIS
Geo. W. Park Seed Co., Inc.
Clyde Robin Seed Co., Inc.
W. J. Unwin, Ltd.
MISSOURI primrose (see Primrose,
missouri)
MOCK orange
Henry Field Seed & Nursery Co.
Gurney Seed & Nursery Co.
Inter-State Nurseries

J. W. Jung Seed Co.
Thomas B. Kyle, Jr. – Spring
Hill Nurseries Co.
MOLE killer
Earl May Seed & Nursery Co.
R. H. Shumway Seedsman
MOLUCELLA
Joseph Harris Co., Inc.
W. J. Unwin, Ltd.
MOMORDICA
Geo. W. Park Seed Co., Inc.
MONARDA
DeGiorgi Company, Inc.
Henry Field Seed & Nursery Co.
Geo. W. Park Seed Co., Inc.
W. J. Unwin, Ltd.
MONARDELLA
Clyde Robin Seed Co., Inc.
MONEY plant
Henry Field Seed & Nursery Co.
Stokes Seeds, Inc.
MONKEY flower
DeGiorgi Company, Inc.
MONKSHOOD
DeGiorgi Company, Inc.
MONTBRETIA
W. Atlee Burpee Co.
Geo. W. Park Seed Co., Inc.
MOON flower
W. Atlee Burpee Co.
DeGiorgi Company, Inc.
Joseph Harris Co., Inc.
J. W. Jung Seed Co.
L. L. Olds Seed Company
Stokes Seeds, Inc.
MORNING glory
DeGiorgi Company, Inc.
Henry Field Seed & Nursery Co.
Gurney Seed & Nursery Co.
Joseph Harris Co., Inc.
J. W. Jung Seed Co.
Earl May Seed & Nursery Co.
L. L. Olds Seed Company
Geo. W. Park Seed Co., Inc.
Seedway, Inc.
Stokes Seeds, Inc.
Otis S. Twilley Seed Co.
W. J. Unwin, Ltd.

MORUS
Clyde Robin Seed Co., Inc.
F. W. Schumacher Co.
MOSS rose
Joseph Harris Co., Inc.
L. L. Olds Seed Company
MOURNING bride
DeGiorgi Company, Inc.
MULBERRIES
Gurney Seed & Nursery Co.
Thomas B. Kyle, Jr. — Spring
Hill Nurseries Co.
MULBERRY trees
Burgess Seed and Plant Co.
MULCH
Earl May Seed & Nursery Co.
MULCH Away Adapter
Better Life Enterprises, Inc.
MULLEIN pink
DeGiorgi Company, Inc.
MULTIFLORA rose (see Rose,
multiflora)
MULTIFLORA hedge
Thomas B. Kyle, Jr. — Spring
Hill Nurseries Co.
MUNG bean
DeGiorgi Company, Inc.
Henry Field Seed & Nursery Co.
MUSA banana
Geo. W. Park Seed Co., Inc.
MUSHROOMS/mushroom spawn
W. Atlee Burpee Co.
DeGiorgi Company, Inc.
Henry Field Seed & Nursery Co.
Gurney Seed & Nursery Co.
Joseph Harris Co., Inc.
Nichols Garden Nursery
R. H. Shumway Seedsman
Stokes Seeds, Inc.
W. J. Unwin, Ltd.
MUSKMELONS
Burgess Seed and Plant Co.
W. Atlee Burpee Co.
D. V. Burrell Seed Growers Co.
DeGiorgi Company, Inc.
Farmer Seed & Nursery Com-
pany
Gurney Seed & Nursery Co.

Joseph Harris Co., Inc.
J. W. Jung Seed Co.
Earl May Seed & Nursery Co.
L. L. Olds Seed Company
Seedway, Inc.
Stokes Seeds, Inc.
MUSTARD
Burgess Seed and Plant Co.
D. V. Burrell Seed Growers Co.
DeGiorgi Company, Inc.
Farmer Seed & Nursery Com-
pany
Henry Field Seed & Nursery Co.
Joseph Harris Co., Inc.
J. W. Jung Seed Co.
Kitayawa Seed Company
Earl May Seed & Nursery Co.
L. L. Olds Seed Company
R. H. Shumway Seedsman
Otis S. Twilley Seed Co.
W. J. Unwin, Ltd.
MUSTARD greens
W. Atlee Burpee Co.
Jackson & Perkins Co.
MUSTARD spinach
R. H. Shumway Seedsman
MYOSOTIS
W. Atlee Burpee Co.
DeGiorgi Company, Inc.
Joseph Harris Co., Inc.
Geo. W. Park Seed Co., Inc.
Stokes Seeds, Inc.
W. J. Unwin, Ltd.
MYRICA
Clyde Robin Seed Co., Inc.
F. W. Schumacher Co.
MYSTERY lily
J. W. Jung Seed Co.
NAEGELIA
DeGiorgi Company, Inc.
Geo. W. Park Seed Co., Inc.
W. J. Unwin, Ltd.
NAILS
Diamond International Corp.
The Walter T. Kelley Company
NANDINA
Clyde Robin Seed Co., Inc.
F. W. Schumacher Co.

NARCISSUS
  Farmer Seed & Nursery Company
  L. L. Olds Seed Company
NARTHECIUM
  Clyde Robin Seed Co., Inc.
NASTURTIUM
  W. Atlee Burpee Co.
  D. V. Burrell Seed Growers Co.
  DeGiorgi Company, Inc.
  Henry Field Seed & Nursery Co.
  Gurney Seed & Nursery Co.
  Joseph Harris Co., Inc.
  Jackson & Perkins Co.
  J. W. Jung Seed Co.
  Earl May Seed & Nursery Co.
  L. L. Olds Seed Company
  Geo. W. Park Seed Co., Inc.
  Seedway, Inc.
  Stokes Seeds, Inc.
  Otis S. Twilley Seed Co.
  W. J. Unwin, Ltd.
NECTARINE trees
  Armstrong Nurseries, Inc.
  Burgess Seed and Plant Co.
  Ferndale Gardens
  Henry Field Seed & Nursery Co.
  Inter-State Nurseries
  Thomas B. Kyle, Jr. — Spring
    Hill Nurseries Co.
  Lakeland Nurseries Sales
  Henry Leuthardt Nurseries, Inc.
  New York State Fruit Testing
    Cooperative Association
  R. H. Shumway Seedsman
  Stark Bro's Nurseries
  Waynesboro Nurseries, Inc.
NEEDLES, transferring
  Diamond International Corp.
NEMESIA
  W. Atlee Burpee Co.
  DeGiorgi Company, Inc.
  L. L. Olds Seed Company
  Geo. W. Park Seed Co., Inc.
  Stokes Seeds, Inc.
  W. J. Unwin, Ltd.
NEMOPHILA
  W. Atlee Burpee Co.

DeGiorgi Company, Inc.
Geo. W. Park Seed Co., Inc.
Clyde Robin Seed Co., Inc.
Stokes Seeds, Inc.
W. J. Unwin, Ltd.
NEPETA
  W. Atlee Burpee Co.
  DeGiorgi Company, Inc.
  W. J. Unwin, Ltd.
NEPETA, catmint
  Geo. W. Park Seed Co., Inc.
NERTERA
  Geo. W. Park Seed Co., Inc.
NETTING
  Earl May Seed & Nursery Co.
NEW guinea vine
  Burgess Seed and Plant Co.
NICANDRA
  Geo. W. Park Seed Co., Inc.
NICOTIANA
  W. Atlee Burpee Co.
  DeGiorgi Company, Inc.
  Gurney Seed & Nursery Co.
  Joseph Harris Co., Inc.
  J. W. Jung Seed Co.
  L. L. Olds Seed Company
  Geo. W. Park Seed Co., Inc.
  Clyde Robin Seed Co., Inc.
  Stokes Seeds, Inc.
  W. J. Unwin, Ltd.
NIEREMBERGIA
  W. Atlee Burpee Co.
  DeGiorgi Company, Inc.
  Geo. W. Park Seed Co., Inc.
  Stokes Seeds, Inc.
NIGELLA
  W. Atlee Burpee Co.
  DeGiorgi Company, Inc.
  J. W. Jung Seed Co.
  L. L. Olds Seed Company
  Geo. W. Park Seed Co., Inc.
  Clyde Robin Seed Co., Inc.
  Stokes Seeds, Inc.
  W. J. Unwin, Ltd.
NIGHT-scented stocks (see Stocks,
  night-scented)
NINEBARK
  J. W. Jung Seed Co.

213

NITRAGIN
  Henry Field Seed & Nursery Co.
  Gurney Seed & Nursery Co.
  Inter-State Nurseries
  L. L. Olds Seed Company
  R. H. Shumway Seedsman
NOLINA
  Clyde Robin Seed Co., Inc.
NORFOLK island pine
  Ferndale Gardens
  Lakeland Nurseries Sales
  Wilson Brothers Floral Co., Inc.
NORSE fire plant
  Wilson Brothers Floral Co., Inc.
NOVELTY vegetables
  Nichols Garden Nursery
NULOMOLINE
  Diamond International Corp.
NURSERY stock
  L. L. Olds Seed Company
NUT trees (see Trees, nut)
NYSSA
  F. W. Schumacher Co.
OAK trees
  Gurney Seed & Nursery Co.
  Inter-State Nurseries
  Thomas B. Kyle, Jr. – Spring
    Hill Nurseries Co.
  R. H. Shumway Seedsman
  Silver Falls Nursery
OBSERVATION hive
  Diamond International Corp.
  The Walter T. Kelley Company
  Herman Kolb, Bee Hobbyist
OENOTHERA
  DeGiorgi Company, Inc.
  Geo. W. Park Seed Co., Inc.
  Clyde Robin Seed Co., Inc.
OKRA
  Burgess Seed and Plant Co.
  W. Atlee Burpee Co.
  D. V. Burrell Seed Growers Co.
  DeGiorgi Company, Inc.
  Henry Field Seed & Nursery Co.
  Gurney Seed & Nursery Co.
  Joseph Harris Co., Inc.
  Jackson & Perkins Co.
  J. W. Jung Seed Co.

  Earl May Seed & Nursery Co.
  L. L. Olds Seed Company
  Seedway, Inc.
  R. H. Shumway Seedsman
  Otis S. Twilley Seed Co.
OKRA, vine
  R. H. Shumway Seedsman
OLEA
  F. W. Schumacher Co.
OLIVE, russian
  Henry Field Seed & Nursery Co.
  Inter-State Nurseries
  J. W. Jung Seed Co.
  L. L. Olds Seed Company
OLIVE trees
  Thomas B. Kyle, Jr. – Spring
    Hill Nurseries Co.
ONION plants
  Evans Plant Company
  Joseph Harris Co., Inc.
  Seedway, Inc.
  R. H. Shumway Seedsman
  Steele Plant Co.
ONIONS
  Burgess Seed and Plant Co.
  W. Atlee Burpee Co.
  D. V. Burrell Seed Growers Co.
  DeGiorgi Company, Inc.
  Henry Field Seed & Nursery Co.
  Gurney Seed & Nursery Co.
  Joseph Harris Co., Inc.
  Jackson & Perkins Co.
  Johnny's Selected Seeds
  J. W. Jung Seed Co.
  Earl May Seed & Nursery Co.
  Nichols Garden Nursery
  L. L. Olds Seed Company
  Spring Hill Farm
  Otis S. Twilley Seed Co.
  W. J. Unwin, Ltd.
ONION seeds
  Farmer Seed & Nursery Com-
    pany
  Seedway, Inc.
  R. H. Shumway Seedsman
  Stokes Seeds, Inc.
ONION sets
  Farmer Seed & Nursery Company

Joseph Harris Co., Inc.
Lakeland Nurseries Sales
Seedway, Inc.
R. H. Shumway Seedsman
Stokes Seeds, Inc.
W. J. Unwin, Ltd.
OPUNTIA
Geo. W. Park Seed Co., Inc.
ORANGE glory flower
Thomas B. Kyle, Jr. — Spring
Hill Nurseries Co.
ORANGE tree
Burgess Seed and Plant Co.
Ferndale Gardens
Lakeland Nurseries Sales
Wilson Brothers Floral Co., Inc.
ORCHID, hardy
Thomas B. Kyle, Jr. — Spring
Hill Nurseries Co.
ORCHID lily
Lakeland Nurseries Sales
ORCHID orchis (see Orchis, orchard)
ORCHIDS
Gurney Seed & Nursery Co.
Lakeland Nurseries Sales
Clyde Robin Seed Co., Inc.
Wilson Brothers Floral Co., Inc.
ORCHIS, orchid
Geo. W. Park Seed Co., Inc.
OREGANO
L. L. Olds Seed Company
DeGiorgi Company, Inc.
OREGON grape
Silver Falls Nursery
ORGANIC hybro-tite (potassium)
Fertile Hills Organic Farms
ORGANIC plant protectant
Countryside General Store
ORGANIC rock phosphate
Fertile Hills Organic Farms
ORIENTAL poppy (see Poppy,
oriental)
ORIENTAL quince (see quince,
oriental)
ORIENTAL vegetables
Gurney Seed & Nursery Co.
L. L. Olds Seed Company

ORNAMENTAL apple trees
New York State Fruit Testing
Cooperative Association
ORNAMENTAL basil
Joseph Harris Co., Inc.
ORNAMENTAL cabbage
W. J. Unwin, Ltd.
ORNAMENTAL corn
Nichols Garden Nursery
ORNAMENTAL cotton (see Cotton,
ornamental)
ORNAMENTAL eggplant (see
Eggplant, ornamental)
ORNAMENTAL gourds
Nichols Garden Nursery
Otis S. Twilley Seed Co.
W. J. Unwin, Ltd.
ORNAMENTAL grasses
Stokes Seeds, Inc.
W. J. Unwin, Ltd.
ORNAMENTAL kale
W. J. Unwin, Ltd.
ORNAMENTAL pepper (see
Pepper, ornamental)
ORNAMENTAL trees
Girard Nurseries
Lawson's Nursery
J. E. Miller Nurseries, Inc.
ORNAMENTAL tree seed
Stokes Seeds, Inc.
ORNITHOGALUM
Geo. W. Park Seed Co., Inc.
ORTHOCARPUS
Clyde Robin Seed Co., Inc.
OSTRYA
F. W. Schumacher Co.
OXALLIS
W. Atlee Burpee Co.
J. W. Jung Seed Co.
L. L. Olds Seed Company
Geo. W. Park Seed Co., Inc.
R. H. Shumway Seedsman
OXYDENDRUM
F. W. Schumacher Co.
OXYPETALUM
DeGiorgi Company, Inc.
Geo. W. Park Seed Co., Inc.

OYSTER plant
  DeGiorgi Company, Inc.
  W. Attlee Burpee Co.
PACHYSANDRA
  Henry Field Seed & Nursery Co.
  Inter-State Nurseries
PACKAGE bees and queens
  Diamond International Corp.
  The Walter T. Kelley Company
  Sunstream
PAEONIA
  Clyde Robin Seed Co., Inc.
  F. W. Schumacher Co.
PAEONY
  Geo. W. Park Seed Co., Inc.
PAINT
  Diamond International Corp.
PAINTED daisy (see Daisy,
  painted)
PAINTED tongue
  DeGiorgi Company, Inc.
  Joseph Harris Co., Inc.
  Stokes Seeds, Inc.
PALIURUS
  Clyde Robin Seed Co., Inc.
PALMS
  Geo. W. Park Seed Co., Inc.
  Stokes Seeds, Inc.
PAMPAS grass
  Henry Field Seed & Nursery Co.
  Jackson & Perkins Co.
  Lakeland Nurseries Sales
  Geo. W. Park Seed Co., Inc.
PANICUM
  DeGiorgi Company, Inc.
PANSY
  W. Atlee Burpee Co.
  D. V. Burrell Seed Growers Co.
  DeGiorgi Company, Inc.
  Henry Field Seed & Nursery Co.
  Gurney Seed & Nursery Co.
  Joseph Harris Co., Inc.
  Jackson & Perkins Co.
  J. W. Jung Seed Co.
  Thomas B. Kyle, Jr. – Spring
    Hill Nurseries Co.
  Lakeland Nurseries Sales
  Earl May Seed & Nursery Co.

L. L. Olds Seed Company
Seedway, Inc.
Stokes Seeds, Inc.
Otis S. Twilley Seed Co.
W. J. Unwin, Ltd.
PANSY, heartease
  Geo. W. Park Seed Co., Inc.
PAPAVER
  DeGiorgi Company, Inc.
  Clyde Robin Seed Co., Inc.
PARADICHLOROBENZENE (PDB)
  Diamond International Corp.
PARKINSONIA
  Clyde Robin Seed Co., Inc.
  F. W. Schumacher Co.
PARSLEY
  Burgess Seed and Plant Co.
  W. Atlee Burpee Co.
  D. V. Burrell Seed Growers Co.
  DeGiorgi Company, Inc.
  Farmer Seed & Nursery Com-
    pany
  Henry Field Seed & Nursery Co.
  Gurney Seed & Nursery Co.
  Joseph Harris Co., Inc.
  Jackson & Perkins Co.
  Johnny's Selected Seeds
  J. W. Jung Seed Co.
  Earl May Seed & Nursery Co.
  Nichols Garden Nursery
  L. L. Olds Seed Company
  Seedway, Inc.
  R. H. Shumway Seedsman
  Stokes Seeds, Inc.
  Otis S. Twilley Seed Co.
  W. J. Unwin, Ltd.
PARSNIP
  Burgess Seed and Plant Co.
  W. Atlee Burpee Co.
  D. V. Burrell Seed Growers Co.
  DeGiorgi Company, Inc.
  Farmer Seed & Nursery Com-
    pany
  Henry Field Seed & Nursery Co.
  Gurney Seed & Nursery Co.
  Joseph Harris Co., Inc.
  Jackson & Perkins Co.
  Johnny's Selected Seeds

J. W. Jung Seed Co.
Earl May Seed & Nursery Co.
L. L. Olds Seed Company
R. H. Shumway Seedsman
Stokes Seeds, Inc.
Otis S. Twilley Seed Co.
W. J. Unwin, Ltd.

PARTHENOCISSUS
F. W. Schumacher Co.

PASSIFLORA
Geo. W. Park Seed Co., Inc.
F. W. Schumacher Co.

PASSION flower
DeGiorgi Company, Inc.
Wilson Brothers Floral Co., Inc.

PASTE tomato (see Tomato, paste)

PASTURE mixture
R. H. Shumway Seedsman

PATIENCE plants
Wilson Brothers Floral Co., Inc.

PAULOWNIA
F. W. Schumacher Co.

PAW paw
Burgess Seed and Plant Co.
Henry Field Seed & Nursery Co.
Gurney Seed & Nursery Co.
Lakeland Nurseries Sales
Waynesboro Nurseries, Inc.

PEACH bells
W. Atlee Burpee Co.

PEACHTARINE tree
Lakeland Nurseries Sales

PEACH trees
Armstrong Nurseries, Inc.
Burgess Seed and Plant Co.
Ferndale Gardens
Henry Field Seed & Nursery Co.
Gurney Seed & Nursery Co.
Inter-State Nurseries
J. W. Jung Seed Co.
Thomas B. Kyle, Jr. — Spring
    Hill Nurseries Co.
Lakeland Nurseries Sales
Henry Leuthardt Nurseries, Inc.
Earl May Seed & Nursery Co.
New York State Fruit Testing
    Cooperative Association
L. L. Olds Seed Company

R. H. Shumway Seedsman
Stark Bro's Nurseries
Waynesboro Nurseries, Inc.

PEA, everlasting
W. J. Unwin, Ltd.

PEANUTS
Burgess Seed and Plant Co.
W. Atlee Burpee Co.
DeGiorgi Company, Inc.
Farmer Seed & Nursery Com-
    pany
Ferndale Gardens
Henry Field Seed & Nursery Co.
Gurney Seed & Nursery Co.
J. W. Jung Seed Co.
Thomas B. Kyle, Jr. — Spring
    Hill Nurseries Co.
Lakeland Nurseries Sales
Earl May Seed & Nursery Co.
L. L. Olds Seed Company
R. H. Shumway Seedsman
Stokes Seeds, Inc.

PEAR trees
Armstrong Nurseries, Inc.
Burgess Seed and Plant Co.
Farmer Seed & Nursery Com-
    pany
Ferndale Gardens
Henry Field Seed & Nursery Co.
Inter-State Nurseries
J. W. Jung Seed Co.
Thomas B. Kyle, Jr. — Spring
    Hill Nurseries Co.
Lakeland Nurseries Sales
Lawson's Nursery
Henry Leuthardt Nurseries, Inc.
Earl May Seed & Nursery Co.
New York State Fruit Testing
    Cooperative Association
L. L. Olds Seed Company
R. H. Shumway Seedsman
Stark Bro's Nurseries
Waynesboro Nurseries, Inc.

PEAS
Burgess Seed and Plant Co.

W. Atlee Burpee Co.
D. V. Burrell Seed Growers Co.
DeGiorgi Company, Inc.
Farmer Seed & Nursery Company
Henry Field Seed & Nursery Co.
Gurney Seed & Nursery Co.
Joseph Harris Co., Inc.
Jackson & Perkins Co.
J. W. Jung Seed Co.
Earl May Seed & Nursery Co.
Nichols Garden Nursery
L. L. Olds Seed Company
Seedway, Inc.
R. H. Shumway Seedsman
Stokes Seeds, Inc.
Otis S. Twilley Seed Co.
W. J. Unwin, Ltd.
PEAT moss
Earl May Seed & Nursery Co.
PEAT pots
DeGiorgi Company, Inc.
Farmer Seed & Nursery Company
Gurney Seed & Nursery Co.
Earl May Seed & Nursery Co.
L. L. Olds Seed Company
R. H. Shumway Seedsman
PECAN trees
Burgess Seed and Plant Co.
Gurney Seed & Nursery Co.
Inter-State Nurseries
Lakeland Nurseries Sales
Stark Bro's Nurseries
PEDICULARIS
Clyde Robin Seed Co., Inc.
PELARGONIUM
W. Atlee Burpee Co.
Geo. W. Park Seed Co., Inc.
PELTOPHORUM
Clyde Robin Seed Co., Inc.
PENNISETUM
DeGiorgi Company, Inc.
PENSTEMON
Henry Field Seed & Nursery Co.
Gurney Seed & Nursery Co.
L. L. Olds Seed Company
Clyde Robin Seed Co., Inc.
W. J. Unwin, Ltd.

PENN-Sylvan planting stock
Carino Nurseries
PENTAPETES
Geo. W. Park Seed Co., Inc.
PENTAS
Geo. W. Park Seed Co., Inc.
PENTSTEMON
W. Atlee Burpee Co.
DeGiorgi Company, Inc.
Geo. W. Park Seed Co., Inc.
PEONIES
Alexander's Blueberry Nurseries
W. Atlee Burpee Co.
Farmer Seed & Nursery Company
Henry Field Seed & Nursery Co.
Gurney Seed & Nursery Co.
Inter-State Nurseries
J. W. Jung Seed Co.
L. L. Olds Seed Company
R. H. Shumway Seedsman
Stark Bro's Nurseries
Waynesboro Nurseries, Inc.
PEPEROMIA
Geo. W. Park Seed Co., Inc.
R. H. Shumway Seedsman
PEPPERMINT
Burgess Seed and Plant Co.
PEPPER, ornamental
W. Atlee Burpee Co.
Joseph Harris Co., Inc.
Geo. W. Park Seed Co., Inc.
PEPPER plants
Evans Plant Company
R. H. Shumway Seedsman
PEPPERS
Burgess Seed and Plant Co.
W. Atlee Burpee Co.
D. V. Burrell Seed Growers Co.
DeGiorgi Company, Inc.
Farmer Seed & Nursery Company
Henry Field Seed & Nursery Co.
Gurney Seed & Nursery Co.
Joseph Harris Co., Inc.
Jackson & Perkins Co.
Johnny's Selected Seeds
J. W. Jung Seed Co.

PERENNIAL flowers
  L. L. Olds Seed Company
PERENNIAL plants
  R. H. Shumway Seedsman
  Earl May Seed & Nursery Co.
  Nichols Garden Nursery
  L. L. Olds Seed Company
  Seedway, Inc.
  R. H. Shumway Seedsman
  Stokes Seeds, Inc.
  Otis S. Twilley Seed Co.
PERENNIAL rye grass (see Rye grass, perennial)
PERENNIALS
  Burgess Seed and Plant Co.
  Farmer Seed & Nursery Company
  Henry Field Seed & Nursery Co.
  Inter-State Nurseries
  Thomas B. Kyle, Jr. — Spring Hill Nurseries Co.
  Musser Forests, Inc.
PERENNIAL seeds
  Gurney Seed & Nursery Co.
PERENNIAL sweet pea
  W. Atlee Burpee Co.
PERIDERIDIA
  Clyde Robin Seed Co., Inc.
PERILLA
  DeGiorgi Company, Inc.
  Geo. W. Park Seed Co., Inc.
PERIWINKLE
  W. Atlee Burpee Co.
  D. V. Burrell Seed Growers Co.
  Joseph Harris Co., Inc.
  L. L. Olds Seed Company
  W. J. Unwin, Ltd.
PERIWINKLE, vinca
  Geo. W. Park Seed Co., Inc.
PERSIAN carpet
  Wilson Brothers Floral Co., Inc.
PERSIMMON trees
  Armstrong Nurseries, Inc.
  Burgess Seed and Plant Co.
  Henry Field Seed & Nursery Co.
  Gurney Seed & Nursery Co.
  Thomas B. Kyle, Jr. — Spring Hill Nurseries Co.

  Lakeland Nurseries Sales
  R. H. Shumway Seedsman
  Waynesboro Nurseries, Inc.
PERUVIAN lily
  W. J. Unwin, Ltd.
PETUNIA
  W. Atlee Burpee Co.
  D. V. Burrell Seed Growers Co.
  DeGiorgi Company, Inc.
  Henry Field Seed & Nursery Co.
  Gurney Seed & Nursery Co.
  Joseph Harris Co., Inc.
  Jackson & Perkins Co.
  J. W. Jung Seed Co.
  Earl May Seed & Nursery Co.
  L. L. Olds Seed Company
  Geo. W. Park Seed Co., Inc.
  Seedway, Inc.
  Stokes Seeds, Inc.
  Otis S. Twilley Seed Co.
  W. J. Unwin, Ltd.
  Wilson Brothers Floral Co., Inc.
PETUNIA plants
  Farmer Seed & Nursery Company
PHACELIA
  Clyde Robin Seed Co., Inc.
  Stokes Seeds, Inc.
  W. J. Unwin, Ltd.
PHACELLA
  DeGiorgi Company, Inc.
PHELLODENDRON
  F. W. Schumacher Co.
PHENOL
  Diamond International Corp.
PHILADELPHUS
  L. L. Olds Seed Company
  Clyde Robin Seed Co., Inc.
PHILODENDRON
  Gurney Seed & Nursery Co.
  Geo. W. Park Seed Co., Inc.
  R. H. Shumway Seedsman
  Stokes Seeds, Inc.
  W. J. Unwin, Ltd.
  Wilson Brothers Floral Co., Inc.
PHLOX
  W. Atlee Burpee Co.
  D. V. Burrell Seed Growers Co.

DeGiorgi Company, Inc.
Henry Field Seed & Nursery Co.
Gurney Seed & Nursery Co.
Inter-State Nurseries
Jackson & Perkins Co.
J. W. Jung Seed Co.
Thomas B. Kyle, Jr. — Spring
  Hill Nurseries Co.
Lakeland Nurseries Sales
L. L. Olds Seed Company
Geo. W. Park Seed Co., Inc.
Seedway, Inc.
Stokes Seeds, Inc.
Otis S. Twilley Seed Co.
W. J. Unwin, Ltd.
PHLOX, annual
  Joseph Harris Co., Inc.
PHLOX plants
  Farmer Seed & Nursery Com-
    pany
  R. H. Shumway Seedsman
PHOENIX
  F. W. Schumacher Co.
PHOLISTOMA
  Clyde Robin Seed Co., Inc.
PHYGELIUS
  DeGiorgi Company, Inc.
  Geo. W. Park Seed Co., Inc.
PHYLLODOCE
  Clyde Robin Seed Co., Inc.
PHYSALIS
  DeGiorgi Company, Inc.
  Geo. W. Park Seed Co., Inc.
  Stokes Seeds, Inc.
  W. J. Unwin, Ltd.
PHYSOCARPUS
  Clyde Robin Seed Co., Inc.
PHYSOTEGIA
  DeGiorgi Company, Inc.
  Geo. W. Park Seed Co., Inc.
PICEA
  Clyde Robin Seed Co., Inc.
  F. W. Schumacher Co.
PIERIS
  F. W. Schumacher Co.
PIGGY-back plant
  Wilson Brothers Floral Co., Inc.
PILEA
  Geo. W. Park Seed Co., Inc.

PIMENTO
  Gurney Seed & Nursery Co.
PIN cushion flower
  W. Atlee Burpee Co.
  Joseph Harris Co., Inc.
PINE
  Carino Nurseries
  Girard Nurseries
  Silver Falls Nursery
  Western Maine Forest Nursery
PINEAPPLE lily
  Henry Field Seed & Nursery Co.
  Geo. W. Park Seed Co., Inc.
PINEAPPLE plant
  Lakeland Nurseries Sales
PINK almond
  Henry Field Seed & Nursery Co.
PINK, garden
  W. J. Unwin, Ltd.
PINKS
  W. Atlee Burpee Co.
  DeGiorgi Company, Inc.
  Henry Field Seed & Nursery Co.
  Gurney Seed & Nursery Co.
  Joseph Harris Co., Inc.
  J. W. Jung Seed Co.
  Thomas B. Kyle, Jr. — Spring
    Hill Nurseries Co.
  Geo. W. Park Seed Co., Inc.
  Seedway, Inc.
  Stokes Seeds, Inc.
PIN oak tree
  Henry Field Seed & Nursery Co.
PINUS
  Clyde Robin Seed Co., Inc.
  F. W. Schumacher Co.
PITCHER plant
  Geo. W. Park Seed Co., Inc.
PITTOSPORUM
  Clyde Robin Seed Co., Inc.
  F. W. Schumacher Co.
PLANTAIN lily
  Inter-State Nurseries
PLANT supports
  W. Atlee Burpee Co.
PLASTIC base foundation
  Diamond International Corp.
PLASTIC bottom boards & covers
  The Walter T. Kelley Company
PLASTIC coating
  Diamond International Corp.
PLATANUS
  Clyde Robin Seed Co., Inc.
  F. W. Schumacher Co.

PLATE o' gold
  Thomas B. Kyle, Jr. – Spring
    Hill Nurseries Co.
PLATYCODON
  DeGiorgi Company, Inc.
  Inter-State Nurseries
  J. W. Jung Seed Co.
  Geo. W. Park Seed Co., Inc.
PLATYSTEMON
  Clyde Robin Seed Co., Inc.
PLUMBAGO
  DeGiorgi Company, Inc.
  Henry Field Seed & Nursery Co.
  Inter-State Nurseries
  Geo. W. Park Seed Co., Inc.
  F. W. Schumacher Co.
PLUM bush
  Lakeland Nurseries Sales
PLUM/prune tree
  Lakeland Nurseries Sales
PLUM trees
  Armstrong Nurseries, Inc.
  Burgess Seed and Plant Co.
  Farmer Seed & Nursery Company
  Ferndale Gardens
  Henry Field Seed & Nursery Co.
  Gurney Seed & Nursery Co.
  Inter-State Nurseries
  J. W. Jung Seed Co.
  Thomas B. Kyle, Jr. – Spring
    Hill Nurseries Co.
  Lakeland Nurseries Sales
  Henry Leuthardt Nurseries, Inc.
  New York State Fruit Testing
    Cooperative Association
  L. L. Olds Seed Company
  Stark Bro's Nurseries
  Waynesboro Nurseries, Inc.
PODALYRICA
  Clyde Robin Seed Co., Inc.
PODOCARPUS
  Clyde Robin Seed Co., Inc.
  F. W. Schumacher Co.
POINCIANA
  Geo. W. Park Seed Co., Inc.
  F. W. Schumacher Co.
POINCLANA
  DeGiorgi Company, Inc.
POINSETTIA
  Geo. W. Park Seed Co., Inc.
POLEMONIUM
  DeGiorgi Company, Inc.
  Geo. W. Park Seed Co., Inc.
POLKA dot plant
  Geo. W. Park Seed Co., Inc.

POLLEN substitutes
  Diamond International Corp.
POLLEN trap
  Diamond International Corp.
  The Walter T. Kelley Company
POLYANTHA rose (see Rose,
  polyantha)
POLYANTHUS
  W. Atlee Burpee Co.
  DeGiorgi Company, Inc.
  Joseph Harris Co., Inc.
  W. J. Unwin, Ltd.
POLYGONUM
  DeGiorgi Company, Inc.
  Inter-State Nurseries
  Geo. W. Park Seed Co.
  Stokes Seeds, Inc.
POLYGONUM cuspidatum
  Henry Field Seed & Nursery Co.
POLYSTICHUM
  Clyde Robin Seed Co., Inc.
POMEGRANATE tree
  Armstrong Nurseries, Inc.
PONY tail palm
  Lakeland Nurseries Sales
POOR man's orchid
  Joseph Harris Co., Inc.
POPCORN
  Burgess Seed and Plant Co.
  W. Atlee Burpee Co.
  D. V. Burrell Seed Growers Co.
  DeGiorgi Company, Inc.
  Farmer Seed & Nursery Company
  Henry Field Seed & Nursery Co.
  Gurney Seed & Nursery Co.
  Joseph Harris Co., Inc.
  Johnny's Selected Seeds
  J. W. Jung Seed Co.
  Earl May Seed & Nursery Co.
  L. L. Olds Seed Company
  R. H. Shumway Seedsman
  Stokes Seeds, Inc.
POPLAR trees
  Henry Field Seed & Nursery Co.
  Gurney Seed & Nursery Co.
  Inter-State Nurseries
  J. W. Jung Seed Co.
  Thomas B. Kyle, Jr. – Spring
    Hill Nurseries Co.
POPPY
  W. Atlee Burpee Co.
  D. V. Burrell Seed Growers Co.
  DeGiorgi Company, Inc.
  Henry Field Seed & Nursery Co.
  Gurney Seed & Nursery Co.
  J. W. Jung Seed Co.

Thomas B. Kyle, Jr. — Spring
Hill Nurseries Co.
Earl May Seed & Nursery Co.
L. L. Olds Seed Company
Geo. W. Park Seed Co., Inc.
Seedway, Inc.
Stokes Seeds, Inc.
W. J. Unwin, Ltd.
POPPY, iceland
W. Atlee Burpee Co.
Joseph Harris Co., Inc.
POPPY, oriental
W. Atlee Burpee Co.
Joseph Harris Co., Inc.
POPPY, shirley
W. Atlee Burpee Co.
Joseph Harris Co., Inc.
PORTULACA
W. Atlee Burpee Co.
D. V. Burrell Seed Growers Co.
DeGiorgi Company, Inc.
Henry Field Seed & Nursery Co.
Gurney Seed & Nursery Co.
Joseph Harris Co., Inc.
Jackson & Perkins Co.
J. W. Jung Seed Co.
L. L. Olds Seed Company
Geo. W. Park Seed Co., Inc.
Seedway, Inc.
Stokes Seeds, Inc.
Otis S. Twilley Seed Co.
W. J. Unwin, Ltd.
POTATOES
Farmer Seed & Nursery Co
Henry Field Seed & Nursery Co.
Gurney Seed & Nursery Co.
J. W. Jung Seed Co.
Earl May Seed & Nursery Co.
L. L. Olds Seed Company
POTENTILLA
Henry Field Seed & Nursery Co.
Inter-State Nurseries
J. W. Jung Seed Co.
Thomas B. Kyle, Jr. — Spring
Hill Nurseries Co.
Geo. W. Park Seed Co., Inc.
Clyde Robin Seed Co., Inc.
POT marigold
DeGiorgi Company, Inc.
Joseph Harris Co., Inc.
W. J. Unwin, Ltd.
POTS, hanging basket
W. Atlee Burpee Co.
POULTRY incubators
Leahy Manufacturing Co.
POWER composter
Garden Way Mfg. Co.

POWER plant
Clear Creek Farms, Inc.
POWER sprayers
Amerind-MacKissic, Inc.
POWER uncapping machine
Diamond International Corp.
PRAYER plant
Lakeland Nurseries Sales
PRAYING mantis
Bio-Control Co.
Ferndale Gardens
Lakeland Nurseries Sales
PRIMROSE
W. Atlee Burpee Co.
Gurney Seed & Nursery Co.
Joseph Harris Co., Inc.
Inter-State Nurseries
J. W. Jung Seed Co.
Thomas B. Kyle, Jr. — Spring
Hill Nurseries Co.
Lakeland Nurseries Sales
Geo. W. Park Seed Co., Inc.
Seedway, Inc.
Stokes Seeds, Inc.
W. J. Unwin, Ltd.
PRIMROSE, missouri
Henry Field Seed & Nursery Co.
J. W. Jung Seed Co.
PRIMULA
W. Atlee Burpee Co.
DeGiorgi Company, Inc.
Jackson & Perkins Co.
L. L. Olds Seed Company
Geo. W. Park Seed Co., Inc.
Clyde Robin Seed Co., Inc.
Stokes Seeds, Inc.
W. J. Unwin, Ltd.
PRIVET
Henry Field Seed & Nursery Co.
Gurney Seed & Nursery Co.
Inter-State Nurseries
J. W. Jung Seed Co.
Lakeland Nurseries Sales
L. L. Olds Seed Company
PRUNE trees
Armstrong Nurseries, Inc.
Stark Bro's Nurseries
PRUNUS
L. L. Olds Seed Company
Clyde Robin Seed Co., Inc.
F. W. Schumacher Co.
PSEUDOLARIX
F. W. Schumacher Co.
PSEUDOPANAX
Geo. W. Park Seed Co., Inc.
PSEUDOTSUGA
Clyde Robin Seed Co., Inc.

F. W. Schumacher Co.

PTERIS
   Stokes Seeds, Inc.

PUDICIA mimosa (see Mimosa, pudicia)

PUERARIA
   Clyde Robin Seed Co., Inc.
   F. W. Schumacher Co.

PUMP control tank
   Diamond International Corp.

PUMPKINS
   Burgess Seed and Plant Co.
   W. Atlee Burpee Co.
   D. V. Burrell Seed Growers Co.
   DeGiorgi Company, Inc.
   Farmer Seed & Nursery Co
   Henry Field Seed & Nursery Co.
   Gurney Seed & Nursery Co.
   Joseph Harris Co., Inc.
   Jackson & Perkins Co.
   J. W. Jung Seed Co.
   Earl May Seed & Nursery Co.
   Nichols Garden Nursery
   L. L. Olds Seed Company
   Seedway, Inc.
   R. H. Shumway Seedsman
   Stokes Seeds, Inc.
   Otis S. Twilley Seed Co.
   W. J. Unwin, Ltd.

PUMPS, honey
   Diamond International Corp.
   The Walter T. Kelley Company

PUNICA
   Geo. W. Park Seed Co., Inc.

PUNICA granatum
   W. J. Unwin, Ltd.

PURPLE leaf bush
   Henry Field Seed & Nursery Co.

PURPLE leaf plum
   Henry Field Seed & Nursery Co.

PURPLE plum trees
   Gurney Seed & Nursery Co.

PURPLE winter creeper
   Lakeland Nurseries Sales

PURSHIA
   Clyde Robin Seed Co., Inc.

PURSLANE
   W. J. Unwin, Ltd.

PUSSY willow
   Burgess Seed and Plant Co.
   Henry Field Seed & Nursery Co.
   Gurney Seed & Nursery Co.
   J. W. Jung Seed Co.

PYRANCANTHA
   Thomas B. Kyle, Jr. — Spring Hill Nurseries Co.
   F. W. Schumacher Co.
   Silver Falls Nursery

PYRACANTHA, kazan
   Henry Field Seed & Nursery Co.

PYRETHRUM
   W. Atlee Burpee Co.
   DeGiorgi Company, Inc.
   Ferndale Gardens
   Henry Field Seed & Nursery Co.
   Gurney Seed & Nursery Co.
   Joseph Harris Co., Inc.
   Inter-State Nurseries
   J. W. Jung Seed Co.
   L. L. Olds Seed Company
   Geo. W. Park Seed Co., Inc.
   Stokes Seeds, Inc.
   W. J. Unwin, Ltd.

PYRETHRUM daisy (see Daisy, pyrethrum)

PYRUS
   F. W. Schumacher Co.

QUAKING grass
   W. Atlee Burpee Co.

QUEEN anne's lace
   DeGiorgi Company, Inc.
   Geo. W. Park Seed Co., Inc.

QUEEN bees
   Diamond International Corp.
   The Walter T. Kelley Company

QUEEN cage (see Cage, queen)

QUEEN and drone traps
   Diamond International Corp.

QUEEN excluders
   Diamond International Corp.

QUEEN marking cage
   Diamond International Corp.

QUEEN rearing tools
   Diamond International Corp.

QUERCUS
   F. W. Schumacher Co.

QUINCE, flowering
   Henry Field Seed & Nursery Co.
   J. W. Jung Seed Co.
   Silver Falls Nursery

QUINCE, oriental
   L. L. Olds Seed Company

QUINCE trees
   Gurney Seed & Nursery Co.
   Inter-State Nurseries
   Henry Leuthardt Nurseries, Inc.
   Stark Bro's Nurseries

RADISHES
   Burgess Seed and Plant Co.

W. Atlee Burpee Co.
D. V. Burrell Seed Growers Co.
DeGiorgi Company, Inc.
Farmer Seed & Nursery Co
Henry Field Seed & Nursery Co.
Gurney Seed & Nursery Co.
Joseph Harris Co., Inc.
Jackson & Perkins Co.
Johnny's Selected Seeds
J. W. Jung Seed Co.
Earl May Seed & Nursery Co.
Nichols Garden Nursery
L. L. Olds Seed Company
Seedway, Inc.
R. H Shumway Seedsman
Spring Hill Farm
Stokes Seeds, Inc.
Otis S. Twilley Seed Co.
W. J. Unwin, Ltd.
RADISH, japanese
Kitayawa Seed Company
RADIEHETTA
DeGiorgi Company, Inc.
RAILLARDELLA
Clyde Robin Seed Co., Inc.
RAILLARDIA
Clyde Robin Seed Co., Inc.
RAINBOW flowers
J. W. Jung Seed Co.
RAINBOW indian corn
J. W. Jung Seed Co.
RAINBOW rock cress
Stokes Seeds, Inc.
RAIN tree
Thomas B. Kyle, Jr. — Spring
Hill Nurseries Co.
RAMONDA
Geo. W. Park Seed Co., Inc.
RANNUCULUS
W. Atlee Burpee Co.
DeGiorgi Company, Inc.
Henry Field Seed & Nursery Co.
Inter-State Nurseries
J. W. Jung Seed Co.
Earl May Seed & Nursery Co.
Geo. W. Park Seed Co., Inc.
R. H. Shumway Seedsman
RAPE
R. H. Shumway Seedsman
RASPBERRY plants
Alexander's Blueberry Nurseries
Brittingham Plant Farms
Burgess Seed and Plant Co.
W. Atlee Burpee Co.
Farmer Seed & Nursery Co
Henry Field Seed & Nursery Co.
Gurney Seed & Nursery Co.

Inter-State Nurseries
J. W. Jung Seed Co.
Thomas B. Kyle, Jr. — Spring
Hill Nurseries Co.
Lakeland Nurseries Sales
Henry Leuthardt Nurseries, Inc.
L. L. Olds Seed Company
R. H. Shumway Seedsman
Stark Bro's Nurseries
Waynesboro Nurseries, Inc.
RECHSTEINER
Geo. W. Park Seed Co., Inc.
REED canary grass
R. H. Shumway Seedsman
REDBUD
Henry Field Seed & Nursery Co.
Inter-State Nurseries
Thomas B. Kyle, Jr. — Spring
Hill Nurseries Co.
RED german garlic
Quality Seed Garlic
RED hot poker
W. Atlee Burpee Co.
DeGiorgi Company, Inc.
Thomas B. Kyle, Jr. — Spring
Hill Nurseries Co.
L. L. Olds Seed Company
W. J. Unwin, Ltd.
RED hybrid earthworm
Clear Creek Farms, Inc.
RED leaf plum
J. W. Jung Seed Co.
RED oak tree
Henry Field Seed & Nursery Co.
RED twig dogwood (see Dogwood,
red twig)
REDWOOD burl
Lakeland Nurseries Sales
REDWOOD trees
Gurney Seed & Nursery Co.
REDWORMS
Bud Kinney Worm Farm
REED, giant
Lakeland Nurseries Sales
REGAL larkspur (see Larkspur,
regal)
REGAL lilies
Gurney Seed & Nursery Co.
RESEDA
DeGiorgi Company, Inc.
RESURRECTION plant
Gurney Seed & Nursery Co.
RHAMNUS
Clyde Robin Seed Co., Inc.
F. W. Schumacher Co.
RHODANTE
224 DeGiorgi Company, Inc.

RHODANTHE
  Geo. W. Park Seed Co., Inc.
  W. J. Unwin, Ltd.
RHODODENDRON hybrids
  F. W. Schumacher Co.
RHODODENDRONS
  W. Atlee Burpee Co.
  Farmer Seed & Nursery Co
  Henry Field Seed & Nursery Co.
  Girard Nurseries
  Gurney Seed & Nursery Co.
  Thomas B. Kyle, Jr. — Spring
    Hill Nurseries Co.
  Geo. W. Park Seed Co., Inc.
  Clyde Robin Seed Co., Inc.
  F. W. Schumacher Co.
RHODOTYPOS
  Clyde Robin Seed Co., Inc.
  F. W. Schumacher Co.
RHOICISSUS
  Geo. W. Park Seed Co., Inc.
RHUBARB
  Burgess Seed and Plant Co.
  W. Atlee Burpee Co.
  DeGiorgi Company, Inc.
  Farmer Seed & Nursery Co
  Ferndale Gardens
  Henry Field Seed & Nursery Co.
  Gurney Seed & Nursery Co.
  Inter-State Nurseries
  Jackson & Perkins Co.
  J. W. Jung Seed Co.
  Thomas B. Kyle, Jr. — Spring
    Hill Nurseries Co.
  Lakeland Nurseries Sales
  Earl May Seed & Nursery Co.
  L. L. Olds Seed Company
  Seedway, Inc.
  R. H. Shumway Seedsman
  Stark Bro's Nurseries
  W. J. Unwin, Ltd.
  Waynesboro Nurseries
RHUS
  Clyde Robin Seed Co., Inc.
  F. W. Schumacher Co.
RIBES
  Clyde Robin Seed Co., Inc.
RIBBON grass
  Henry Field Seed & Nursery Co.
RICE
  Johnny's Selected Seeds
RICINUS
  DeGiorgi Company, Inc.
  Joseph Harris Co., Inc.
  L. L. Olds Seed Company
  Geo. W. Park Seed Co., Inc.
  Stokes Seeds, Inc.

W. J. Unwin, Ltd.
RIDING and walking mowers
  FMC Corporation
ROBINIA
  F. W. Schumacher Co.
ROCK cistus
  W. J. Unwin, Ltd.
ROCK cress
  W. Atlee Burpee Co.
  DeGiorgi Company, Inc.
  Joseph Harris Co., Inc.
  Stokes Seeds, Inc.
ROCKET salad (see Salad, rocket)
ROCK garden mix
  Stokes Seeds, Inc.
ROCK garden plants
  Gurney Seed & Nursery Co.
ROMAINE
  W. Atlee Burpee Co.
  Joseph Harris Co., Inc.
ROMNEYA
  Geo. W. Park Seed Co., Inc.
ROOTONE
  Earl May Seed & Nursery Co.
ROPE
  Diamond International Corp.
ROSA
  Geo. W. Park Seed Co., Inc.
  Clyde Robin Seed Co., Inc.
  F. W. Schumacher Co.
ROSA multiflora
  Henry Field Seed & Nursery Co.
  Inter-State Nurseries
ROSEMARY
  Burgess Seed and Plant Co.
  W. Atlee Burpee Co.
  DeGiorgi Company, Inc.
  Gurney Seed & Nursery Co.
  L. L. Olds Seed Company
  W. J. Unwin, Ltd.
ROSE moss
  DeGiorgi Company, Inc.
  Henry Field Seed & Nursery Co.
ROSE, multiflora
  Gurney Seed & Nursery Co.
  L. L. Olds Seed Company
ROSE of sharon
  Thomas B. Kyle, Jr. — Spring
    Hill Nurseries Co.
ROSE, polyantha
  W. J. Unwin, Ltd.
ROSES
  Armstrong Nurseries, Inc.
  Boatman Nursery & Seed Co.
  Burgess Seed and Plant Co.
  W. Atlee Burpee Co.
  Farmer Seed & Nursery Co

225

Ferndale Gardens
Henry Field Seed & Nursery Co.
Gurney Seed & Nursery Co.
Inter-State Nurseries
Jackson & Perkins Co.
J. W. Jung Seed Co.
Thomas B. Kyle, Jr. — Spring
  Hill Nurseries Co.
Lakeland Nurseries Sales
Earl May Seed & Nursery Co.
L. L. Olds Seed Company
R. H. Shumway Seedsman
Van Bourgondien Brothers
Waynesboro Nurseries, Inc.
Wilson Brothers Floral Co., Inc.
ROSE tree of china
  Henry Field Seed & Nursery Co.
ROTARY mowers
  Atlas Tool & Mfg. Co.
  FMC Corporation
ROTARY tillers
  Atlas Tool & Mfg. Co.
  Garden Way Mfg. Co.
ROYAL red bugler
  Geo. W. Park Seed Co., Inc.
RUBBER stamp
  Diamond International Corp.
RUDBECKIA
  W. Atlee Burpee Co.
  DeGiorgi Company, Inc.
  Joseph Harris Co., Inc.
  Jackson & Perkins Co.
  L. L. Olds Seed Company
  Geo. W. Park Seed Co., Inc.
  Clyde Robin Seed Co., Inc.
  Stokes Seeds, Inc.
  W. J. Unwin, Ltd.
RUDBECKIA daisy (see Daisy,
  rudbeckia)
RUE
  W. J. Unwin, Ltd.
RUMEX
  Clyde Robin Seed Co., Inc.
RUSSIAN olive (see Olive,
  russian)
RUTABAGA
  Burgess Seed and Plant Co.
  W. Atlee Burpee Co.
  D. V. Burrell Seed Growers Co.
  DeGiorgi Company, Inc.
  Farmer Seed & Nursery Co
  Henry Field Seed & Nursery Co.
  Gurney Seed & Nursery Co.
  Joseph Harris Co., Inc.
  Johnny's Selected Seeds
  J. W. Jung Seed Co.

Earl May Seed & Nursery Co.
L. L. Olds Seed Company
Seedway, Inc.
R. H. Shumway Seedsman
Stokes Seeds, Inc.
RUTA blue mound
  Henry Field Seed & Nursery Co.
  Inter-State Nurseries
RYE grass
  DeGiorgi Company, Inc.
  L. L. Olds Seed Company
RYE grass, domestic
  Joseph Harris Co., Inc.
RYE grass, perennial
  Joseph Harris Co., Inc.
SAGE
  Burgess Seed and Plant Co.
  W. Atlee Burpee Co.
  DeGiorgi Company, Inc.
  Farmer Seed & Nursery Co.
  Henry Field Seed & Nursery Co.
  Gurney Seed & Nursery Co.
  Ben Haines Company
  Joseph Harris Co., Inc.
  J. W. Jung Seed Co.
  Earl May Seed & Nursery Co.
  L. L. Olds Seed Company
  W. J. Unwin, Ltd.
SAGINA
  Geo. W. Park Seed Co., Inc.
SAINTPAULIA
  W. Atlee Burpee Co.
  Geo. W. Park Seed Co., Inc.
  Stokes Seeds, Inc.
  W. J. Unwin, Ltd.
SALAD garden
  W. Atlee Burpee Co.
SALAD, rocket
  DeGiorgi Company, Inc.
SALIX
  Inter-State Nurseries
SALPIGLOSSIS
  W. Atlee Burpee Co.
  DeGiorgi Company, Inc.
  Gurney Seed & Nursery Co.
  Joseph Harris Co., Inc.
  L. L. Olds Seed Company
  Geo. W. Park Seed Co., Inc.
  Stokes Seeds, Inc.
  W. J. Unwin, Ltd.
SALSIFY
  Burgess Seed and Plant Co.
  W. Atlee Burpee Co.
  D. V. Burrell Seed Growers Co.
  DeGiorgi Company, Inc.
  Farmer Seed & Nursery Co
  Henry Field Seed & Nursery Co.

Gurney Seed & Nursery Co.
J. W. Jung Seed Co.
Earl May Seed & Nursery Co.
Nichols Garden Nursery
L. L. Olds Seed Company
Seedway, Inc.
R. H. Shumway Seedsman
Stokes Seeds, Inc.
W. J. Unwin, Ltd.
SALVIA
W. Atlee Burpee Co.
DeGiorgi Company, Inc.
Henry Field Seed & Nursery Co.
Gurney Seed & Nursery Co.
Joseph Harris Co., Inc.
Inter-State Nurseries
Jackson & Perkins Co.
J. W. Jung Seed Co.
Earl May Seed & Nursery Co.
L. L. Olds Seed Company
Geo. W. Park Seed Co., Inc.
Clyde Robin Seed Co., Inc.
Seedway, Inc.
Stokes Seeds, Inc.
Otis S. Twilley Seed Co.
W. J. Unwin, Ltd.
SALVIA, horminum
W. J. Unwin, Ltd.
SAMANEA
Clyde Robin Seed Co., Inc.
SAMBUCUS
Clyde Robin Seed Co., Inc.
SAMPLE jars and cartons
Diamond International Corp.
SANGUINARIA
Geo. W. Park Seed Co., Inc.
Clyde Robin Seed Co., Inc.
SANGUISORBA
Clyde Robin Seed Co., Inc.
SAND cherries
Gurney Seed & Nursery Co.
SANTOLINA
DeGiorgi Company, Inc.
Geo. W. Park Seed Co., Inc.
Stokes Seeds, Inc.
SANVITALIA
Joseph Harris Co., Inc.
Geo. W. Park Seed Co., Inc.
Stokes Seeds, Inc.
SANVITALLA
DeGiorgi Company, Inc.
SAPIUM
F. W. Schumacher Co.
SAPONARIA
L. L. Olds Seed Company
Geo. W. Park Seed Co., Inc.

Clyde Robin Seed Co., Inc.
SARVISTREE
Thomas B. Kyle, Jr. — Spring
Hill Nurseries Co.
SATIN flower
W. Atlee Burpee Co.
J. W. Jung Seed Co.
SAUCE tomato (see Tomato,
sauce)
SAVORY
DeGiorgi Company, Inc.
W. J. Unwin, Ltd.
SAVORY cabbage (see Cabbage,
savory)
SAVORY, summer
Burgess Seed and Plant Co.
W. Atlee Burpee Co.
Gurney Seed & Nursery Co.
Joseph Harris Co., Inc.
L. L. Olds Seed Company
SAVOY
W. J. Unwin, Ltd.
SAXIFRAGA
DeGiorgi Company, Inc.
Geo. W. Park Seed Co., Inc.
W. J. Unwin, Ltd.
SCABIOSA
W. Atlee Burpee Co.
Joseph Harris Co., Inc.
Jackson & Perkins Co.
J. W. Jung Seed Co.
L. L. Olds Seed Company
Geo. W. Park Seed Co., Inc.
Seedway, Inc.
Stokes Seeds, Inc.
SCABIOUS
W. J. Unwin, Ltd.
SCARLET beauty tree
Lakeland Nurseries Sales
SCARLET runner
DeGiorgi Company, Inc.
SCARLET runner bean
J. W. Jung Seed Co.
Stokes Seeds, Inc.
SCARLET sage
W. Atlee Burpee Co.
Joseph Harris Co., Inc.
Geo. W. Park Seed Co., Inc.
SCHEFFLERA
Geo. W. Park Seed Co., Inc.
Stokes Seeds, Inc.
SCHEFFLERA, digitata
W. J. Unwin, Ltd.
SCHINUS
F. W. Schumacher Co.
SCHIZANTHUS
W. Atlee Burpee Co.

227

DeGiorgi Company, Inc.
Joseph Harris Co., Inc.
L. L. Olds Seed Company
Geo. W. Park Seed Co., Inc.
Stokes Seeds, Inc.
W. J. Unwin, Ltd.
SCHOTIA
Clyde Robin Seed Co., Inc.
SCIADOPITYS
Clyde Robin Seed Co., Inc.
F. W. Schumacher Co.
SCILLA
J. W. Jung Seed Co.
SCORZONERA
DeGiorgi Company, Inc.
Johnny's Selected Seeds
W. J. Unwin, Ltd.
SCUTELLARIA
Clyde Robin Seed Co., Inc.
SCYTHES
DeGiorgi Company, Inc.
SEA lavender
W. Atlee Burpee Co.
DeGiorgi Company, Inc.
Gurney Seed & Nursery Co.
SEA pink
DeGiorgi Company, Inc.
SEA holly
DeGiorgi Company, Inc.
W. J. Unwin, Ltd.
SEA kale
W. J. Unwin, Ltd.
SEA kale beet
W. J. Unwin, Ltd.
SECTION holders
Diamond International Corp.
SECTION honey boxes
Diamond International Corp.
SECTION press
Diamond International Corp.
SECTION scraping knife
Diamond International Corp.
SECTION spreader
Diamond International Corp.
SEDUM
DeGiorgi Company, Inc.
Henry Field Seed & Nursery Co.
Gurney Seed & Nursery Co.
Inter-State Nurseries
J. W. Jung Seed Co.
Thomas B. Kyle, Jr. — Spring
  Hill Nurseries Co.
Geo. W. Park Seed Co., Inc.
Stokes Seeds, Inc.
W. J. Unwin, Ltd.
SEED corn

J. W. Jung Seed Co.
SEEDER
Countryside General Store
SEEDLING trees
Earl May Seed & Nursery Co.
SEED sprouter
Dresdenn, Inc.
SEED tapes
W. Atlee Burpee Co.
SEMPERVIVUM
DeGiorgi Company, Inc.
Geo. W. Park Seed Co., Inc.
SENECIO
DeGiorgi Company, Inc.
Clyde Robin Seed Co., Inc.
SENSITIVE plant
W. Atlee Burpee Co.
DeGiorgi Company, Inc.
Henry Field Seed & Nursery Co.
Geo. W. Park Seed Co., Inc.
Stokes Seeds, Inc.
W. J. Unwin, Ltd.
SEPARATORS
Diamond International Corp.
SEQUOIAS
F. W. Schumacher Co.
Silver Falls Nursery
SERVICEBERRY
Henry Field Seed & Nursery Co.
SESAME
DeGiorgi Company, Inc.
SEVIN
Joseph Harris Co., Inc.
SHADE trees (see Trees, shade)
SHALLOTS
Ferndale Gardens
Gurney Seed & Nursery Co.
J. W. Jung Seed Co.
Lakeland Nurseries Sales
W. J. Unwin, Ltd.
SHAMROCK
W. Atlee Burpee Co.
DeGiorgi Company, Inc.
Henry Field Seed & Nursery Co.
Gurney Seed & Nursery Co.
Geo. W. Park Seed Co., Inc.
Stokes Seeds, Inc.
SHASTA daisy (see also Daisy, shasta)
D. V. Burrell Seed Growers Co.
J. W. Jung Seed Co.
Geo. W. Park Seed Co., Inc.
Stokes Seeds, Inc.
SHASTA delay
DeGiorgi Company, Inc.
SHELL flower
Henry Field Seed & Nursery Co.
Gurney Seed & Nursery Co.

Joseph Harris Co., Inc.
W. J. Unwin, Ltd.

SHEPHERDIA
Clyde Robin Seed Co., Inc.
F. W. Schumacher Co.

SHIRLEY poppy (see Poppy, shirley)

SHREDDER-baggers
Atlas Tool & Mfg. Co.

SHREDDER/mulcher
Various Designs

SHRIMP plant
Wilson Brothers Floral Co., Inc.

SHRUBS
Farmer Seed & Nursery Company
Henry Field Seed & Nursery Co.
Gurney Seed & Nursery Co.
Inter-State Nurseries
Earl May. Seed & Nursery Co.
L. L. Olds Seed Company
Geo. W. Park Seed Co., Inc.

SHRUBS, evergreen
Gurney Seed & Nursery Co.

SHRUBS, flowering
Boatman Nursery & Seed Co.
W. Atlee Burpee Co.
Carino Nurseries
Girard Nurseries
Earl May Seed & Nursery Co.
Waynesboro Nurseries, Inc.

SIBERIAN wallflower (see Wallflower, siberian)

SICKLES
DeGiorgi Company, Inc.

SIDALCEA
Geo. W. Park Seed Co., Inc.
Clyde Robin Seed Co., Inc.

SILENE
DeGiorgi Company, Inc.
Geo. W. Park Seed Co., Inc.
Clyde Robin Seed Co., Inc.

SILVER dollars
Joseph Harris Co., Inc.

SILVER king
Gurney Seed & Nursery Co.

SILVER lace vine
Henry Field Seed & Nursery Co.
Gurney Seed & Nursery Co.
Inter-State Nurseries

SIMILAX
DeGiorgi Company, Inc.

SINNINGIA
Geo. W. Park Seed Co.

SISYRINCHIUM
Clyde Robin Seed Co., Inc.

SMALL fruits & berries
J. E. Miller Nurseries, Inc.
Van Bourgondien Brothers

SMILACINA
Clyde Robin Seed Co., Inc.

SMILAX
Geo. W. Park Seed Co., Inc.
Stokes Seeds, Inc.

SMOKE bush
Henry Field Seed & Nursery Co.

SMOKE tree
Inter-State Nurseries
Thomas B. Kyle, Jr. — Spring
Hill Nurseries Co.

SMOKERS, bee
Diamond International Corp.
The Walter T. Kelley Company

SNAPDRAGON
W. Atlee Burpee Co.
D. V. Burrell Seed Growers Co.
Henry Field Seed & Nursery Co.
Gurney Seed & Nursery Co.
Joseph Harris Co., Inc.
Jackson & Perkins Co.
J. W. Jung Seed Co.
Earl May Seed & Nursery Co.
L. L. Olds Seed Company
Geo. W. Park Seed Co., Inc.
Seedway, Inc.
Stokes Seeds, Inc.
Otis S. Twilley Seed Co.
W. J. Unwin, Ltd.

SNAPDRAGON, hardy
DeGiorgi Company, Inc.

SNAPDRAGON, climbing
DeGiorgi Company, Inc.

SNOWBALLS
Henry Field Seed & Nursery Co.
Gurney Seed & Nursery Co.
Inter-State Nurseries
Thomas B. Kyle, Jr. — Spring
Hill Nurseries Co.
L. L. Olds Seed Company

SNOWBERRY
L. L. Olds Seed Company

SNOWDROPS
J. W. Jung Seed Co.

SNOW in summer
W. Atlee Burpee Co.
DeGiorgi Company, Inc.
Stokes Seeds, Inc.

SNOW on the mountain
W. Atlee Burpee Co.
Joseph Harris Co., Inc.
J. W. Jung Seed Co.
Thomas B. Kyle, Jr. — Spring
Hill Nurseries Co.

L. L. Olds Seed Company

SNOW throwers
FMC Corporation

SOIL test kits
Joseph Harris Co., Inc.
Earl May Seed & Nursery Co.
Mother's General Store
L. L. Olds Seed Company
Sudbury Laboratory, Inc.

SOLANUM
DeGiorgi Company, Inc.
Joseph Harris Co., Inc.
L. L. Olds Seed Company
Geo. W. Park Seed Co., Inc.
W. J. Unwin, Ltd.

SOLIDAGO
Clyde Robin Seed Co., Inc.
W. J. Unwin, Ltd.

SOPHORA
Clyde Robin Seed Co., Inc.
F. W. Schumacher Co.

SORBUS
Clyde Robin Seed Co., Inc.
F. W. Schumacher Co.

SORREL
DeGiorgi Company, Inc.
W. J. Unwin, Ltd.

SOY bean
DeGiorgi Company, Inc.
Gurney Seed & Nursery Co.

SOY beans, edible
W. Atlee Burpee Co.

SPACERS, frame
Diamond International Corp.
The Walter T. Kelley Company

SPARACHETTI
DeGiorgi Company, Inc.

SPARMANNIA
W. J. Unwin, Ltd.

SPARTIUM
Clyde Robin Seed Co., Inc.
F. W. Schumacher Co.

SPATHODEA
Clyde Robin Co., Inc.

SPEARMINT
Burgess Seed and Plant Co.

SPECIAL mixtures
DeGiorgi Company, Inc.

SPERGULA
DeGiorgi Company, Inc.

SPHAERALCEA
Clyde Robin Seed Co., Inc.

SPHAGNUM moss
Farmer Seed & Nursery Com-
Joseph Harris Co., Inc.
L. L. Olds Seed Company

R. H. Shumway Seedsman

SPHAGNUM peat moss
Annapolis Valley Peat Moss Co.,
Ltd.

SPIDER flower
Geo. W. Park Seed Co., Inc.
Stokes Seeds, Inc.

SPIDER plant
W. Atlee Burpee Co.
Joseph Harris Co., Inc.
J. W. Jung Seed Co.
W. J. Unwin, Ltd.

SPINACH
Burgess Seed and Plant Co.
W. Atlee Burpee Co.
D. V. Burrell Seed Growers Co.
DeGiorgi Company, Inc.
Farmer Seed & Nursery Com-
Henry Field Seed & Nursery Co.
Gurney Seed & Nursery Co.
Joseph Harris Co., Inc.
Jackson & Perkins Co.
Johnny's Selected Seeds
J. W. Jung Seed Co.
Earl May Seed & Nursery Co.
Nichols Garden Nursery
L. L. Olds Seed Company
Seedway, Inc.
R. H. Shumway Seedsman
Spring Hill Farm
Stokes Seeds, Inc.
Otis S. Twilley Seed Co.
W. J. Unwin, Ltd.

SPINACH beet
Joseph Harris Co., Inc.

SPIRAL cage
Diamond International Corp.

SPIRAEA
J. W. Jung Seed Co.
Clyde Robin Seed Co., Inc.

SPIREA
Henry Field Seed & Nursery Co.
Gurney Seed & Nursery Co.
Inter-State Nurseries
Thomas B. Kyle, Jr. — Spring
Hill Nurseries Co.
R. H. Shumway Seedsman

SPOROBOLUS
Clyde Robin Seed Co., Inc.

SPRAYERS
Earl May Seed & Nursery Co.
L. L. Olds Seed Company

SPRAYERS and dusters
W. Atlee Burpee Co.

SPRINGS, super
Diamond International Corp.
The Walter T. Kelley Company

SPRUCE
  Carino Nurseries
  DeGiorgi Company, Inc.
  Girard Nurseries
  Silver Falls Nursery
  Western Maine Forest Nursery
SQUASH
  Burgess Seed and Plant Co.
  W. Atlee Burpee Co.
  D. V. Burrell Seed Growers Co.
  DeGiorgi Company, Inc.
  Farmer Seed & Nursery Company
  Henry Field Seed & Nursery Co.
  Gurney Seed & Nursery Co.
  Joseph Harris Co., Inc.
  Jackson & Perkins Co.
  Johnny's Selected Seeds
  J. W. Jung Seed Co.
  Earl May Seed & Nursery Co.
  Nichols Garden Nursery
  L. L. Olds Seed Company
  Seedway, Inc.
  R. H. Shumway Seedsman
  Spring Hill Farm
  Stokes Seeds, Inc.
  Otis S. Twilley Seed Co.
STACHYS
  DeGiorgi Company, Inc.
STACKABLE cold frames
  Various Designs
STANDARD fruit trees (see Trees, standard fruit)
STAPLES
  Diamond International Corp.
STAR of bethlehem
  DeGiorgi Company, Inc.
STAR of the veldt
  W. J. Unwin, Ltd.
STATICE
  W. Atlee Burpee Co.
  DeGiorgi Company, Inc.
  Gurney Seed & Nursery Co.
  Joseph Harris Co., Inc.
  L. L. Olds Seed Company
  Geo. W. Park Seed Co., Inc.
  Seedway, Inc.
  Stokes Seeds, Inc.
  W. J. Unwin, Ltd.
STEAM generator
  Diamond International Corp.
  The Walter T. Kelley Company
STEAM hose (see Hose, steam)
STEAM uncapping knives
  Diamond International Corp.
STEPHANOTIS

Geo. W. Park Seed Co.
STEWARTIA
  F. W. Schumacher Co.
STING kill
  Diamond International Corp.
STIPA
  DeGiorgi Company, Inc.
STOCKS
  W. Atlee Burpee Co.
  D. V. Burrell Seed Growers Co.
  DeGiorgi Company, Inc.
  Gurney Seed & Nursery Co.
  Joseph Harris Co., Inc.
  Jackson & Perkins Co.
  J. W. Jung Seed Co.
  L. L. Olds Seed Company
  Stokes Seeds, Inc.
  W. J. Unwin, Ltd.
STOCKS, gilliflower
  Geo. W. Park Seed Co., Inc.
STOCK, night-scented
  W. Atlee Burpee Co.
  W. J. Unwin, Ltd.
STOCK, virginian
  DeGiorgi Company, Inc.
  Stokes Seeds, Inc.
  W. J. Unwin, Ltd.
STOKESIA
  DeGiorgi Company, Inc.
  Inter-State Nurseries
  Thomas B. Kyle, Jr. — Spring Hill Nurseries Co.
  Geo. W. Park Seed Co., Inc.
  Stokes Seeds, Inc.
STOLLER frame spacer
  Diamond International Corp.
STONECROP
  W. J. Unwin, Ltd.
STRAINER cloth
  Diamond International Corp.
STRAWBERRY paradise tree
  Ferndale Gardens
  Lakeland Nurseries Sales
STRAWBERRY plants
  Armstrong Nurseries, Inc.
  Brittingham Plant Farms
  Burgess Seed and Plant Co.
  W. Atlee Burpee Co.
  DeGiorgi Company, Inc.
  Farmer Seed & Nursery Company
  Ferndale Gardens
  Henry Field Seed & Nursery Co.
  Dean Foster Nurseries
  Gurney Seed & Nursery Co.
  Inter-State Nurseries

231

J. W. Jung Seed Co.
Thomas B. Kyle, Jr. — Spring
Hill Nurseries Co.
Earl May Seed & Nursery Co.
J. E. Miller Nurseries, Inc.
New York State Fruit Testing
Cooperative Association
Geo. W. Park Seed Co., Inc.
Shasta Canyon Nursery
R. H. Shumway Seedsman
Stark Bro's Nurseries
Stokes Seeds, Inc.
W. J. Unwin, Ltd.
Waynesboro Nurseries, Inc.
STRAWBERRY seed
W. Atlee Burpee Co.
STRAWFLOWER
W. Atlee Burpee Co.
DeGiorgi Company, Inc.
Henry Field Seed & Nursery Co.
Gurney Seed & Nursery Co.
Joseph Harris Co., Inc.
Jackson & Perkins Co.
L. L. Olds Seed Company
Geo. W. Park Seed Co., Inc.
Seedway, Inc.
Stokes Seeds, Inc.
Otis S. Twilley Seed Co.
STRELITZIA
Geo. W. Park Seed Co., Inc.
Clyde Robin Seed Co., Inc.
STREPTOCARPUS
Geo. W. Park Seed Co., Inc.
W. J. Unwin, Ltd.
STRING of hearts
Wilson Brothers Floral Co., Inc.
STRING of pearls
Wilson Brothers Floral Co., Inc.
STYRAX
F. W. Schumacher Co.
SUCCULENTS
Ben Haines Company
Geo. W. Park Seed Co., Inc.
SUGAR beets
Farmer Seed & Nursery Com-
L. L. Olds Seed Company
R. H. Shumway Seedsman
SUGAR cane
R. H. Shumway Seedsman
SUGAR peas
Kitayawa Seed Company
W. J. Unwin, Ltd.
SUGAR sorghum
R. H. Shumway Seedsman
SULFATHIOZOLE
Diamond International Corp.

SULTANA
Gurney Seed & Nursery Co.
Geo. W. Park Seed Co., Inc.
Wilson Brothers Floral Co., Inc.
SULTAN'S balsam
W. Atlee Burpee Co.
SUMAC
Gurney Seed & Nursery Co.
Thomas B. Kyle, Jr. — Spring
Hill Nurseries Co.
SUMMER cypress
Joseph Harris Co., Inc.
SUMMER poinsettia
W. Atlee Burpee Co.
J. W. Jung Seed Co.
SUMMER savory (see Savory,
summer)
SUMMER shade cloths
Redwood Domes
SUNFLOWER
W. Atlee Burpee Co.
D. V. Burrell Seed Growers Co.
DeGiorgi Company, Inc.
Henry Field Seed & Nursery Co.
Gurney Seed & Nursery Co.
Joseph Harris Co., Inc.
Jackson & Perkins Co.
J. W. Jung Seed Co.
Earl May Seed & Nursery Co.
L. L. Olds Seed Company
Geo. W. Park Seed Co., Inc.
Seedway, Inc.
R. H. Shumway Seedsman
Stokes Seeds, Inc.
W. J. Unwin, Ltd.
SUNFLOWER seed
Fred's Plant Farm
Johnny's Selected Seeds
Rabbit Hop Nursery
SUN plant
DeGiorgi Company, Inc.
SUNSHINE shrub
Henry Field Seed & Nursery Co.
SUPER elevator
The Walter T. Kelley Company
SUPER fixtures
The Walter T. Kelley Company
SUPER springs (see Springs, super)
SUPERS
Diamond International Corp.
The Walter T. Kelley Company
SUREWAY introducing cage (see
Introducing cage, sureway)
SURVIVAL garden
Mother's General Store
SWAN river daisy
W. Atlee Burpee Co.

SWEDE
W. J. Unwin, Ltd.
SWEET alyssum
W. Atlee Burpee Co.
DeGiorgi Company, Inc.
SWEET basil
DeGiorgi Company, Inc.
Gurney Seed & Nursery Co.
SWEET corn (see Corn, sweet)

SWEET fennel
DeGiorgi Company, Inc.
L. L. Olds Seed Company
SWEET gum
Thomas B. Kyle, Jr. — Spring
Hill Nurseries Co.
SWEET marjoram
W. Atlee Burpee Co.
Gurney Seed & Nursery Co.
Joseph Harris Co., Inc.
SWEET peas
W. Atlee Burpee Co.
D. V. Burrell Seed Growers Co.
DeGiorgi Company, Inc.
Ferndale Gardens
Henry Field Seed & Nursery Co.
Gurney Seed & Nursery Co.
Joseph Harris Co., Inc.
Inter-State Nurseries
Jackson & Perkins Co.
J. W. Jung Seed Co.
Thomas B. Kyle, Jr. — Spring
Hill Nurseries Co.
Lakeland Nurseries Sales
Earl May Seed & Nursery Co.
L. L. Olds Seed Company
Geo. W. Park Seed Co., Inc.
Seedway, Inc.
Stokes Seeds, Inc.
Otis S. Twilley Seed Co.
W. J. Unwin, Ltd.
SWEET peas, hardy
DeGiorgi Company, Inc.
SWEET potato plants
Farmer Seed & Nursery Co
Fred's Plant Farm
R. H. Shumway Seedsman
Steele Plant Co.
SWEET potatoes
Burgess Seed and Plant Co.
Henry Field Seed & Nursery Co.
Gurney Seed & Nursery Co.
Earl May Seed & Nursery Co.
L. L. Olds Seed Company
SWEET rockets
DeGiorgi Company, Inc.
SWEET shrub

Thomas B. Kyle, Jr. — Spring
Hill Nurseries Co.
SWEET sultan
W. Atlee Burpee Co.
DeGiorgi Company, Inc.
Gurney Seed & Nursery Co.
Joseph Harris Co., Inc.
W. J. Unwin, Ltd.
SWEET violet
DeGiorgi Company, Inc.
W. J. Unwin, Ltd.
SWEET william
W. Atlee Burpee Co.
D. V. Burrell Seed Growers Co.
DeGiorgi Company, Inc.
Henry Field Seed & Nursery Co.
Gurney Seed & Nursery Co.
Joseph Harris Co., Inc.
Jackson & Perkins Co.
J. W. Jung Seed Co.
L. L. Olds Seed Company
Geo. W. Park Seed Co., Inc.
Seedway, Inc.
Stokes Seeds, Inc.
Otis S. Twilley Seed Co.
W. J. Unwin, Ltd.
SWEET wivelsfield
W. Atlee Burpee Co.
DeGiorgi Company, Inc.
SWISS chard
Burgess Seed and Plant Co.
W. Atlee Burpee Co.
DeGiorgi Company, Inc.
Farmer Seed & Nursery Com-
pany
Henry Field Seed & Nursery Co.
Gurney Seed & Nursery Co.
Joseph Harris Co., Inc.
Jackson & Perkins Co.
J. W. Jung Seed Co.
Earl May Seed & Nursery Co.
L. L. Olds Seed Company
Seedway, Inc.
R. H. Shumway Seedsman
Spring Hill Farm
Stokes Seeds, Inc.
Otis S. Twilley Seed Co.
W. J. Unwin, Ltd.
SYCAMORE
Henry Field Seed & Nursery Co.
Inter-State Nurseries
Thomas B. Kyle, Jr. — Spring
Hill Nurseries Co.
SYMPHORICARPOS
Clyde Robin Seed Co., Inc.
F. W. Schumacher Co.

SYRINGA
  Clyde Robin Seed Co., Inc.
  F. W. Schumacher Co.
TABLE tomato (see Tomato, table)
TAGETES
  W. Atlee Burpee Co.
  DeGiorgi Company, Inc.
  Joseph Harris Co., Inc.
  W. J. Unwin, Ltd.
TAGETES marigold (see Marigold,
  tagetes)
TAHOKA daisy
  W. Atlee Burpee Co.
  DeGiorgi Company, Inc.
  Geo. W. Park Seed Co., Inc.
TALINUM
  Geo. W. Park Seed Co., Inc.
TAMARIX
  Henry Field Seed & Nursery Co.
  Gurney Seed & Nursery Co.
  Inter-State Nurseries
  J. W. Jung Seed Co.
  F. W. Schumacher Co.
TAMPALA
  Burgess Seed and Plant Co.
  W. Atlee Burpee Co.
TANACETUM
  Clyde Robin Seed Co., Inc.
TARRAGON
  W. J. Unwin, Ltd.
TAXODIUM
  F. W. Schumacher Co.
TAXUS
  Clyde Robin Seed Co., Inc.
  F. W. Schumacher Co.
TELLIMA
  Clyde Robin Seed Co., Inc.
TENDERGREEN
  DeGiorgi Company, Inc.
TERRAMYCIN
  Diamond International Corp.
TERRARIUMS/terrarium supplies
  Armstrong Associates
  W. Atlee Burpee Co.
  Gurney Seed & Nursery Co.
TETRANEMA
  Geo. W. Park Seed Co., Inc.
TEUCRIUM
  Geo. W. Park Seed Co., Inc.
THALASPI
  Clyde Robin Seed Co., Inc.
THALICRUM
  DeGiorgi Company, Inc.
THALICTRUM
  Geo. W. Park Seed Co., Inc.
  Clyde Robin Seed Co., Inc.

THEA tea
  Geo. W. Park Seed Co., Inc.
THERMOPSIS
  DeGiorgi Company, Inc.
  Henry Field Seed & Nursery Co.
  Geo. W. Park Seed Co., Inc.
THESPESIA
  Clyde Robin Seed Co., Inc.
THEVETIA
  F. W. Schumacher Co.
THISTLE
  Geo. W. Park Seed Co., Inc.
THRIFT
  Geo. W. Park Seed Co., Inc.
  Stokes Seeds, Inc.
THUJA
  Clyde Robin Seed Co., Inc.
  F. W. Schumacher Co.
THUNBERGIA
  W. Atlee Burpee Co.
  DeGiorgi Company, Inc.
  Joseph Harris Co., Inc.
  L. L. Olds Seed Company
  Geo. W. Park Seed Co., Inc.
  Stokes Seeds, Inc.
THYME
  Burgess Seed and Plant Co.
  W. Atlee Burpee Co.
  DeGiorgi Company, Inc.
  Henry Field Seed & Nursery Co.
  Gurney Seed & Nursery Co.
  Joseph Harris Co., Inc.
  L. L. Olds Seed Company
  Geo. W. Park Seed Co., Inc.
  W. J. Unwin, Ltd.
THYMUS
  DeGiorgi Company, Inc.
  Geo. W. Park Seed Co., Inc.
TIBETAN poppy
  W. J. Unwin, Ltd.
TIGER flower
  W. Atlee Burpee Co.
TIGRIDIA
  W. Atlee Burpee Co.
  Geo. W. Park Seed Co., Inc.
TILIA
  F. W. Schumacher Co.
TIMOTHY
  R. H. Shumway Seedsman
TINS, flat
  Diamond International Corp.
TITHONIA
  W. Atlee Burpee Co.
  D. V. Burrell Seed Growers Co.
  DeGiorgi Company, Inc.
  Henry Field Seed & Nursery Co.

234

Joseph Harris Co., Inc.
J. W. Jung Seed Co.
L. L. Olds Seed Company
Clyde Robin Seed Co., Inc.
Stokes Seeds, Inc.
TITHONIA speciosa
W. J. Unwin, Ltd.
TOADFLAX linaria (see Linaria,
toadflax)
TOBACCO
Henry Field Seed & Nursery Co.
Fred's Plant Farm
Earl May Seed & Nursery Co.
L. L. Olds Seed Company
R. H. Shumway Seedsman
Stokes Seeds, Inc.
W. J. Unwin, Ltd.
TOBACCO, flowering
Joseph Harris Co., Inc.
Geo. W. Park Seed Co., Inc.
TOBACCO plant
Gurney Seed & Nursery Co.
W. J. Unwin, Ltd.
TOBACCO seed
Fred's Plant Farm
TOFIELDIA
Clyde Robin Seed Co., Inc.
TOMATO
W. J. Unwin, Ltd.
TOMATO, paste
Burgess Seed and Plant Co.
W. Atlee Burpee Co.
DeGiorgi Company, Inc.
Gurney Seed & Nursery Co.
Joseph Harris Co., Inc.
J. W. Jung Seed Co.
Nichols Garden Nursery
L. L. Olds Seed Company
R. H. Shumway Seedsman
Stokes Seeds, Inc.
TOMATO, plants
Evans Plant Company
Farmer Seed & Nursery Com-
R. H. Shumway Seedsman
TOMATO, sauce
D. V. Burrell Seed Growers Co.
DeGiorgi Company, Inc.
Farmer Seed & Nursery Com-
Earl May Seed & Nursery Co.
Otis S. Twilley Seed Co.
TOMATO, small
Earl May Seed & Nursery Co.
TOMATO, table
Big Tomato Gardens
Burgess Seed and Plant Co.
W. Atlee Burpee Co.

D. V. Burrell Seed Growers Co.
DeGiorgi Company, Inc.
Farmer Seed & Nursery Com-
Henry Field Seed & Nursery Co.
Gurney Seed & Nursery Co.
Joseph Harris Co., Inc.
Jackson & Perkins Co.
Johnny's Selected Seeds
J. W. Jung Seed Co.
Earl May Seed & Nursery Co.
Nichols Garden Nursery
L. L. Olds Seed Company
Seedway, Inc.
R. H. Shumway Seedsman
Spring Hill Farm
Stokes Seeds, Inc.
Otis S. Twilley Seed Co.
TOMATO, yellow
Big Tomato Gardens
Burgess Seed and Plant Co.
W. Atlee Burpee Co.
D. V. Burrell Seed Growers Co.
DeGiorgi Company, Inc.
Henry Field Seed & Nursery Co.
Gurney Seed & Nursery Co.
Joseph Harris Co., Inc.
J. W. Jung Seed Co.
Earl May Seed & Nursery Co.
Nichols Garden Nursery
L. L. Olds Seed Company
Seedway, Inc.
R. H. Shumway Seedsman
Stokes Seeds, Inc.
Otis S. Twilley Seed Co.
TOOLS, hive
Diamond International Corp.
The Walter T. Kelley Company
TORCH lily
DeGiorgi Company, Inc.
TORENIA
W. Atlee Burpee Co.
DeGiorgi Company, Inc.
L. L. Olds Seed Company
Geo. W. Park Seed Co., Inc.
Stokes Seeds, Inc.
TORENIA fournieri
W. J. Unwin, Ltd.
TORREYA
Clyde Robin Seed Co., Inc.
TOUCH-me-not
Geo. W. Park Seed Co., Inc.
TOWN and country carts
Vermont-Ware
TRACHYCARPUS
Clyde Robin Seed Co., Inc.
F. W. Schumacher Co.

Geo. W. Park Seed Co., Inc.
TRANSFERRING needles (see
Needles, transferring)
TRANSVAAL daisy
W. Atlee Burpee Co.
Lakeland Nurseries Sales
Geo. W. Park Seed Co., Inc.
TREE hydrangea
Henry Field Seed & Nursery Co.
TREE lilac
Farmer Seed & Nursery Com-
TREE peonies
Thomas B. Kyle, Jr. – Spring
Hill Nurseries Co.
Van Bourgondien Brothers
TREE roses
Inter-State Nurseries
Lakeland Nurseries Sales
TREES, dwarf fruit
W. Atlee Burpee Co.
TREES, flowering
Boatman Nursery & Seed Co.
W. Atlee Burpee Co.
Carino Nurseries
Henry Field Seed & Nursery Co.
Earl May Seed & Nursery Co.
Stark Bro's Nurseries
Waynesboro Nurseries, Inc.
TREES, nut
Boatman Nursery & Seed Co.
W. Atlee Burpee Co.
Carino Nurseries
Henry Field Seed & Nursery Co.
Gurney Seed & Nursery Co.
Thomas B. Kyle, Jr. – Spring
Hill Nurseries Co.
J. E. Miller Nurseries, Inc.
R. H. Shumway Seedsman
Waynesboro Nurseries, Inc.
TREES, shade
Boatman Nursery & Seed Co.
W. Atlee Burpee Co.
Carino Nurseries
Farmer Seed & Nursery Com-
Girard Nurseries
Gurney Seed & Nursery Co.
Inter-State Nurseries
J. E. Miller Nurseries, Inc.
R. H. Shumway Seedsman
Stark Bro's Nurseries
Waynesboro Nurseries, Inc.
TREES, standard fruit
W. Atlee Burpee Co.
J. E. Miller Nurseries, Inc.
TREE tomatoes
Lakeland Nurseries Sales

TRICHOGRAMMA (egg parasite)
California Green Lacewings
TRICHOSTEMA
Clyde Robin Seed Co., Inc.
TRILLIUM
Geo. W. Park Seed Co., Inc.
Clyde Robin Seed Co., Inc.
TRINITY flower
Thomas B. Kyle, Jr. – Spring
Hill Nurseries Co.
TRITOMA
W. Atlee Burpee Co.
Henry Field Seed & Nursery Co.
Inter-State Nurseries
J. W. Jung Seed Co.
Geo. W. Park Seed Co., Inc.
Stokes Seeds, Inc.
W. J. Unwin, Ltd.
TROLLIUS
DeGiorgi Company, Inc.
Geo. W. Park Seed Co., Inc.
W. J. Unwin, Ltd.
TROPAEOLUM
W. J. Unwin, Ltd.
TROPICAL plants
World Gardens
TROPICAL plum
Burgess Seed and Plant Co.
TROPICAL seeds
World Gardens
TRUMPET flower
Geo. W. Park Seed Co., Inc.
TRUMPET vine
W. Atlee Burpee Co.
DeGiorgi Company, Inc.
Henry Field Seed & Nursery Co.
Gurney Seed & Nursery Co.
J. W. Jung Seed Co.
TSUGA
Clyde Robin Seed Co., Inc.
F. W. Schumacher Co.
TUBEROSE
W. Atlee Burpee Co.
Henry Field Seed & Nursery Co.
Gurney Seed & Nursery Co.
Inter-State Nurseries
J. W. Jung Seed Co.
Thomas B. Kyle, Jr. – Spring
Hill Nurseries Co.
Earl May Seed & Nursery Co.
L. L. Olds Seed Company
Geo. W. Park Seed Co., Inc.
R. H. Shumway Seedsman
TUFTED pansy
Joseph Harris Co., Inc.
TULIP poppy
J. W. Jung Seed Co.

TULIPS
  Farmer Seed & Nursery Com-
  J. W. Jung Seed Co.
  L. L. Olds Seed Company
TUNICA
  DeGiorgi Company, Inc.
TURNIP broccoli
  DeGiorgi Company, Inc.
TURNIP celery
  J. W. Jung Seed Co.
TURNIPS
  Burgess Seed and Plant Co.
  W. Atlee Burpee Co.
  D. V. Burrell Seed Growers Co.
  DeGiorgi Company, Inc.
  Farmer Seed & Nursery Com-
  Henry Field Seed & Nursery Co.
  Gurney Seed & Nursery Co.
  Joseph Harris Co., Inc.
  Jackson & Perkins Co.
  Johnny's Selected Seeds
  J. W. Jung Seed Co.
  Earl May Seed & Nursery Co.
  Nichols Garden Nursery
  L. L. Olds Seed Company
  Seedway, Inc.
  R. H. Shumway Seedsman
  Stokes Seeds, Inc.
  Otis S. Twilley Seed Co.
  W. J. Unwin, Ltd.
ULEX
  Clyde Robin Seed Co., Inc.
  F. W. Schumacher Co.
ULMUS
  Clyde Robin Seed Co., Inc.
  F. W. Schumacher Co.
UMBELLULARIA
  Clyde Robin Seed Co., Inc.
UMBRELLA plant
  DeGiorgi Company, Inc.
UNCAPPING equipment
  Diamond International Corp.
UNCAPPING knives (see Knives, uncapping)
UNCAPPING machine
  The Walter T. Kelley Company
UNIOLA
  DeGiorgi Company, Inc.
URSINIA
  Stokes Seeds, Inc.
UTILITY and garden tractors
  FMC Corporation
VACCINUM
  F. W. Schumacher Co.
VALERIANA
  DeGiorgi Company, Inc.

Geo. W. Park Seed Co., Inc.
Clyde Robin Seed Co., Inc.
VEGETABLE marrow
  W. J. Unwin, Ltd.
VEGETABLES
  Boatman Nursery & Seed Co.
  Geo. W. Park Seed Co., Inc.
  Van Bourgondien Brothers
VEGETABLE seed collections
  W. J. Unwin, Ltd.
VEGETABLE seeds
  Jardin du Gourmet
VEGETABLE spaghetti
  Burgess Seed and Plant Co.
  W. J. Unwin, Ltd.
VEGETABLES, giant
  Gurney Seed & Nursery Co.
VEGETABLES, winter
  W. Atlee Burpee Co.
VEILS, bee
  Diamond International Corp.
  The Walter T. Kelley Company
VELVET flower
  W. Atlee Burpee Co.
  J. W. Jung Seed Co.
VELVET plant
  R. H. Shumway Seedsman
VENEGASIA
  Clyde Robin Seed Co., Inc.
VENIDIUM
  Geo. W. Park Seed Co., Inc.
VENUS fly trap
  Geo. W. Park Seed Co., Inc.
VERATRUM
  Clyde Robin Seed Co., Inc.
VERBASCUM
  DeGiorgi Company, Inc.
  Geo. W. Park Seed Co., Inc.
  Clyde Robin Seed Co., Inc.
  W. J. Unwin, Ltd.
VERBENA
  W. Atlee Burpee Co.
  D. V. Burrell Seed Growers Co.
  DeGiorgi Company, Inc.
  Henry Field Seed & Nursery Co.
  Gurney Seed & Nursery Co.
  Joseph Harris Co., Inc.
  Jackson & Perkins Co.
  J. W. Jung Seed Co.
  Thomas B. Kyle, Jr. — Spring
    Hill Nurseries Co.
  Earl May Seed & Nursery Co.
  L. L. Olds Seed Company
  Geo. W. Park Seed Co., Inc.
  Otis S. Twilley Seed Co.
  W. J. Unwin, Ltd.

VERBESINA
  Geo. W. Park Seed Co., Inc.
VERONICA
  DeGiorgi Company, Inc.
  Inter-State Nurseries
  Thomas B. Kyle, Jr. — Spring
    Hill Nurseries Co.
  Geo. W. Park Seed Co., Inc.
  Stokes Seeds, Inc.
VERNONIA
  Clyde Robin Seed Co., Inc.
VETCH
  L. L. Olds Seed Company
VIBURNUM
  Inter-State Nurseries
  L. L. Olds Seed Company
  Clyde Robin Seed Co., Inc.
  F. W. Schumacher Co.
VIBURNUM carlesi
  DeGiorgi Company, Inc.
VIBURNUM, fragrant
  Henry Field Seed & Nursery Co.
VIDA
  Clyde Robin Seed Co., Inc.
VINCA
  W. Atlee Burpee Co.
  DeGiorgi Company, Inc.
  Gurney Seed & Nursery Co.
  L. L. Olds Seed Company
  W. J. Unwin, Ltd.
VINCA minor
  Henry Field Seed & Nursery Co.
  Inter-State Nurseries
  J. W. Jung Seed Co.
VINCA periwinkle (see Periwinkle,
  vinca)
VINCA rosea
  Joseph Harris Co., Inc.
  Jackson & Perkins Co.
  J. W. Jung Seed Co.
  Stokes Seed Co.
VINE okra (see Okra, vine)
VINE peach
  Burgess Seed and Plant Co.
VINES
  W. Atlee Burpee Co.
  Farmer Seed & Nursery Com-
  Gurney Seed & Nursery Co.
  Inter-State Nurseries
  Thomas B. Kyle, Jr. — Spring
    Hill Nurseries Co.
  Earl May Seed & Nursery Co.
  L. L. Olds Seed Company
  Geo. W. Park Seed Co., Inc.
  R. H. Shumway Seedsman
  Waynesboro Nurseries, Inc.

VIOLA
  W. Atlee Burpee Co.
  DeGiorgi Company, Inc.
  Joseph Harris Co., Inc.
  Jackson & Perkins Co.
  L. L. Olds Seed Company
  Geo. W. Park Seed Co., Inc.
  Clyde Robin Seed Co., Inc.
  Stokes Seeds, Inc.
  W. J. Unwin, Ltd.
VIOLET
  DeGiorgi Company, Inc.
  Ferndale Gardens
  Henry Field Seed & Nursery Co.
  Gurney Seed & Nursery Co.
  Inter-State Nurseries
  Thomas B. Kyle, Jr. — Spring
    Hill Nurseries Co.
  Stokes Seeds, Inc.
  W. J. Unwin, Ltd.
VIOLET plants
  W. Atlee Burpee Co.
  R. H. Shumway Seedsman
VIRGILIA
  Clyde Robin Seed Co., Inc.
VIRGINIAN stock (see Stock,
  virginian)
VISCARIA
  DeGiorgi Company, Inc.
  W. J. Unwin, Ltd.
VISCARIS
  DeGiorgi Company, Inc.
VITEX
  F. W. Schumacher Co.
VITIS
  Clyde Robin Seed Co., Inc.
  F. W. Schumacher Co.
VOO doo lily
  Henry Field Seed & Nursery Co.
WAHLENBERGIA
  Geo. W. Park Seed Co., Inc.
WALDMEISTER
  DeGiorgi Company, Inc.
WALK in cooler
  Various Designs
WALLFLOWER
  W. Atlee Burpee Co.
  DeGiorgi Company, Inc.
  L. L. Olds Seed Company
  Geo. W. Park Seed Co., Inc.
  Stokes Seeds, Inc.
  W. J. Unwin, Ltd.
WALLFLOWER, siberian
  W. Atlee Burpee Co.
  W. J. Unwin, Ltd.
WALNUT trees

Burgess Seed and Plant Co.
Gurney Seed & Nursery Co.
Inter-State Nurseries
J. W. Jung Seed Co.
WASHINGTONIA
Clyde Robin Seed Co., Inc.
F. W. Schumacher Co.
WASP killer
Diamond International Corp.
WATERCRESS
W. Atlee Burpee Co.
DeGiorgi Company, Inc.
Joseph Harris Co., Inc.
Stokes Seeds, Inc.
WATER lilies
Gurney Seed & Nursery Co.
Geo. W. Park Seed Co., Inc.
William Tricker, Inc.
WATERMELONS
Burgess Seed and Plant Co.
W. Atlee Burpee Co.
DeGiorgi Company, Inc.
Farmer Seed & Nursery Com-
Henry Field Seed & Nursery Co.
Gurney Seed & Nursery Co.
Joseph Harris Co., Inc.
J. W. Jung Seed Co.
Lakeland Nurseries Sales
Earl May Seed & Nursery Co.
Nichols Garden Nursery
L. L. Olds Seed Company
Seedway, Inc.
R. H. Shumway Seedsman
Spring Hill Farms
Stokes Seeds, Inc.
Otis S. Twilley Seed Co.
WAX and wood cell cups
Diamond International Corp.
WAX extractors (see Extractors,
wax)
WAX melters
Diamond International Corp.
WAX mould pans
The Walter T. Kelley Company
WAX press
The Walter T. Kelley Company
WAX separator
The Walter T. Kelley Company
WAX tube fastener
Diamond International Corp.
The Walter T. Kelley Company
WAX vine
Wilson Brothers Floral Co., Inc.
WAX working
The Walter T. Kelley Company
WEED killers

Earl May Seed & Nursery Co.
WEEPING willows
Lakeland Nurseries Sales
WEIGELA
Henry Field Seed & Nursery Co.
Gurney Seed & Nursery Co.
Inter-State Nurseries
J. W. Jung Seed Co.
Thomas B. Kyle, Jr. — Spring
Hill Nurseries Co.
L. L. Olds Seed Company
F. W. Schumacher Co.
WHITE clover (see Clover, white)
WILDFLOWERS
Ferndale Gardens
Lakeland Nurseries Sales
Geo. W. Park Seed Co., Inc.
WILLOW, fantail
Henry Field Seed & Nursery Co.
WILLOW trees
Henry Field Seed & Nursery Co.
J. W. Jung Seed Co.
WILLOWS
Gurney Seed & Nursery Co.
Inter-State Nurseries
Thomas B. Kyle, Jr. — Spring
Hill Nurseries Co.
WINE grapes
Gurney Seed & Nursery Co.
"WIN" garden
Lakeland Nurseries Sales
WINTER cauliflower
W. J. Unwin, Ltd.
WIRE
The Walter T. Kelley Company
WIRE embedder (see Embedder,
wire)
WIRE, frame
Diamond International Corp.
WIRING device
The Walter T. Kelley Company
WIRING embedder
Diamond International Corp.
WISHBONE flower
W. Atlee Burpee Co.
WISTERIA
W. Atlee Burpee Co.
DeGiorgi Company, Inc.
Henry Field Seed & Nursery Co.
J. W. Jung Seed Co.
Geo. W. Park Seed Co., Inc.
Clyde Robin Seed Co., Inc.
F. W. Schumacher Co.
WITCHHAZEL
Thomas B. Kyle, Jr. — Spring
Hill Nurseries Co.

WITLOOF chicory
  Joseph Harris Co., Inc.
WOODLAND plants
  W. Atlee Burpee Co.
WOODSIA
  Clyde Robin Seed Co., Inc.
WORMWOOD
  DeGiorgi Company, Inc.
WOOD rose
  DeGiorgi Company, Inc.
  Geo. W. Park Seed Co., Inc.
WRAPS, comb honey
  Diamond International Corp.
WYETHIA
  Clyde Robin Seed Co., Inc.
XERANTHEMUM
  W. Atlee Burpee Co.
  DeGiorgi Company, Inc.
  Geo. W. Park Seed Co., Inc.
  W. J. Unwin, Ltd.
XEROPHYLLUM
  Clyde Robin Seed Co., Inc.
XYLOCOCCUS
  Clyde Robin Seed Co., Inc.
YARROW
  Henry Field Seed & Nursery Co.
YEAST
  Diamond International Corp.
YELLOW jasmine (see Jasmine,
  yellow)
YELLOW tomato (see Tomato,
  yellow)
YEWS
  Girard Nurseries
  Gurney Seed & Nursery Co.
  J. W. Jung Seed Co.
  Western Maine Forest Nursery
YOUNG berries
  R. H. Shumway Seedsman
YUCCA
  W. Atlee Burpee Co.
  DeGiorgi Company, Inc.
  Henry Field Seed & Nursery Co.
  Gurney Seed & Nursery Co.
  Ben Haines Company
  J. W. Jung Seed Co.

Thomas B. Kyle, Jr. — Spring
  Hill Nurseries Co.
Geo. W. Park Seed Co., Inc.
F. W. Schumacher Co.
ZAUSCHNERIA
  Clyde Robin Seed Co., Inc.
ZEA japonica
  W. J. Unwin, Ltd.
ZEBRA plant
  Wilson Brothers Floral Co., Inc.
ZELKOVA
  Clyde Robin Seed Co., Inc.
  F. W. Schumacher Co.
ZEPHYRANTHES
  Geo. W. Park Seed Co., Inc.
  Clyde Robin Seed Co., Inc.
ZIGADENUS
  Clyde Robin Seed Co., Inc.
ZINNIA
  W. Atlee Burpee Co.
  D. V. Burrell Seed Growers Co.
  DeGiorgi Company, Inc.
  Henry Field Seed & Nursery Co.
  Gurney Seed & Nursery Co.
  Joseph Harris Co., Inc.
  Jackson & Perkins Co.
  J. W. Jung Seed Co.
  Earl May Seed & Nursery Co.
  L. L. Olds Seed Company
  Geo. W. Park Seed Co., Inc.
  Seedway, Inc.
  Stokes Seeds, Inc.
  Otis S. Twilley Seed Co.
  W. J. Unwin, Ltd.
ZIZYPHUS
  Clyde Robin Seed Co., Inc.
ZOECON pherocon kits
  California Green Lacewings
ZOYSIA
  Henry Field Seed & Nursery Co.
  Geo. W. Park Seed Co., Inc.
ZUCCHINI
  W. Atlee Burpee Co.
  Gurney Seed & Nursery Co.
  Joseph Harris Co., Inc.

OLIVER PRESS BOOKS

JOSEPH ROSENBLOOM

Kits and Plans
Finder's Guide No. 1

Where to purchase plans and kits for practically anything you can think of. From mini-bikes to harpsichords, this guide tells who offers what and what it costs. *288 pages*

ISBN 0-914400-00-2   Price $3.95 paper

JOSEPH ROSENBLOOM

Craft Supplies Supermarket
Finder's Guide No. 2

An illustrated and indexed directory of craft supplies. Thousands of products including materials, kits, tools from over 450 companies are analyzed from their catalogs. *Index, illustrations, 224 pages*

ISBN 0-914400-01-0   Price $3.95 paper

ANNE HECK

The Complete Kitchen
Finder's Guide No. 3

A comprehensive guide to hard-to-find utensils. This book describes the companies supplying such utensils as well as offering information on their catalogs. *Illustrated, 96 pages*

ISBN 0-914400-02-9   Price $2.95 paper

GARY WADE
Homegrown Energy
Power for the Home and Homestead
Finder's Guide No. 4

A complete directory to the thousands of available products involved in the production of home grown power. Water wheels, solar cells, windmills and other exotic equipment are covered and indexed in depth.
Illustrated, 96 pages
ISBN 0-914400-03-7   Price $2.95 paper

ARMAND BITEAUX
The New Consciousness
Finder's Guide No. 5

A guide to spiritual groups: name; address, international, national, local; statement of philosophy; biographies of leaders; bibliography of publications of the group. *Index, 300 pages*
ISBN 0-914400-04-5   Price $3.95 paper

ROLAND ROBERTSON
Spices, Condiments, Teas, Coffees, and Other Delicacies
Finder's Guide No. 6

This illustrated and indexed directory answers difficult questions involved with finding and purchasing unusual ingredients, beverages and foods which are difficult to obtain locally. *Index, illustrated, 208 pages*
ISBN 0-914400-05-3   Price $3.95 paper

FRED DAVIS
Country Tools
Essential Hardware and Livery
Finder's Guide No. 7

Locates sources for otherwise difficult-to-find tools essential to country living. This indispensible guide to the country resident working his land covers everything from bell scrapers to goat harnesses to spoke shavers. *Illustrated, 160 pages*
ISBN 0-914400-06-1   Price $3.95 paper

242

PAT FALGE and ARNOLD LEGGETT
The Complete Garden
Finder's Guide No. 8

The catalogs of over 400 garden tool and seed companies which sell
by mail order organized into a comprehensive guide. From carrots to
kohlrabi, from tomato stakes to rabbit repellent, it tells who sells what
and how to get it. *Illustrated, 256 pages*
ISBN 0-914400-11-8   Price $3.95 paper

DERWOOD McCRAKEN
Mother Nature's Recipe Book
Mother Nature Series No. 1

Includes some 85 commonly found wild plants with detailed draw-
ings of each plant and recipes for preparing a main course from each.
Plant identification is emphasized as are tested, nutritional meals which
can contribute to the average household's fight against rising food costs.
Illustrated, 160 pages
ISBN 0-914400-07-X   Price $3.95 paper

DEZIRINA GOUZIL
Mother Nature's Herbs and Teas
Mother Nature Series No. 2

A guide to approximately 110 easily found herbs and other plants
that are used in the preparation of seasonings and beverages. This intro-
duction for the layman includes detailed illustrations of each plant and
a description of its habitat. *Illustrated, 224 pages*
ISBN 0-914400-08-8   Price $3.95 paper

WILL BEARFOOT
Mother Nature's Dyes and Fibers
Mother Nature Series No. 3

A book of plants and trees utilized in the preparation of dyes and
weaving materials by North American Indians. The author has drawn
his research from interviews with Indians still using the original methods.
Step-by-step procedures are outlined and accompanied by detailed illustrations of the plants and trees used. *Illustrated, 192 pages*
ISBN 0-914400-10-X   Price $3.95 paper

DR. JUDY WILSON
Mother Nature's Homestead First Aid
Mother Nature Series No. 4

This book is a rural emergency first aid tool, emphasizing self-help
procedures for everything from sprains to major injuries. It is indispensible for those who live in remote areas with little access to professional
medical help. Special attention is given to the preparation of the sick
or injured for transportation to medical facilities. *Illustrated, 192 pages*
ISBN 0-914400-09-6   Price $3.95 paper

MICHAEL BARLEYCORN
Moonshiner's Manual

A do-it-yourself detailed guide to making your own whiskey. Laws
of the fifty states and the Federal government are included along with
chapters on history, recipes, safety and chemistry—all written in an easy
to understand, delightfully entertaining manner. *Illustrated, 281 pages*
ISBN 0-914400-12-6   Price $3.95 paper